BACK TO METHUSELAH

Back to Methuselah. A Metabiological Penta-teuch. By Bernard Shaw

BRENTANO'S - New York
MCMXXIX

CONTENTS

The Infidel Half Century vii
  The Dawn of Darwinism vii
  The Advent of the Neo-Darwinians . . ix
  Political Inadequacy of the Human Animal x
  Cowardice of the Irreligious . . . x
  Is there any Hope in Education? . . xii
  Homeopathic Education xiii
  The Diabolical Efficiency of Technical Education xv
  Flimsiness of Civilization xvii
  Creative Evolution xvii
  Voluntary Longevity xviii
  The Early Evolutionists xx
  The Advent of the Neo-Lamarckians . . xxiii
  How Acquirements are Inherited . . xxiv
  The Miracle of Condensed Recapitulation . xxvi
  Heredity an Old Story xxxi
  Discovery Anticipated by Divination . . xxxii
  Corrected Dates for the Discovery of Evolution xxxiv
  Defying the Lightning: a Frustrated Experiment xxxvi
  In Quest of the First Cause . . . xxxviii
  Paley's Watch xl
  The Irresistible Cry of Order, Order! . . xli
  The Moment and the Man . . . xliii
  The Brink of the Bottomless Pit . . . xlvi
  Why Darwin Converted the Crowd . . xlviii
  How We Rushed Down a Steep Place . . li
  Darwinism not Finally Refutable . . liv

v

Three Blind Mice lv
The Greatest of These is Self-Control . lix
A Sample of Lamarcko-Shavian Invective. lx
The Humanitarians and the Problem of Evil. lxii
How One Touch of Darwin Makes the Whole
    World Kin lxiv
Why Darwin Pleased the Socialists . . lxv
Darwin and Karl Marx lxviii
Why Darwin Pleased the Profiteers also . lxix
The Poetry and Purity of Materialism . lxxi
The Viceroys of the King of Kings . . lxxiii
Political Opportunism in Excelsis . . lxxv
The Betrayal of Western Civilization. . lxxvii
Circumstancial Selection in Finance . lxxix
The Homeopathic Reaction against Darwinism lxxx
Religion and Romance lxxxiii
The Danger of Reaction lxxxv
A Touchstone for Dogma lxxxvi
What to do with the Legends . . . lxxxviii
A Lesson from Science to the Churches . lxxxix
The Religious Art of the Twentieth Century xc
The Artist-Prophets xcii
Evolution in the Theatre xciv
My Own Part in the Matter xcviii

PREFACE

THE INFIDEL HALF CENTURY

The Dawn of Darwinism

ONE day early in the eighteen hundred and sixties, I, being then a small boy, was with my nurse, buying something in the shop of a petty newsagent, bookseller, and stationer in Camden Street, Dublin, when there entered an elderly man, weighty and solemn, who advanced to the counter, and said pompously, "Have you the works of the celebrated Buffoon?"

My own works were at that time unwritten, or it is possible that the shop assistant might have misunderstood me so far as to produce a copy of Man and Superman. As it was, she knew quite well what he wanted; for this was before the Education Act of 1870 had produced shop assistants who know how to read and know nothing else. The celebrated Buffoon was not a humorist, but the famous naturalist Buffon. Every literate child at that time knew Buffon's Natural History as well as Esop's Fables. And no living child had heard the name that has since obliterated Buffon's in the popular consciousness: the name of Darwin.

Ten years elapsed. The celebrated Buffoon was forgotten; I had doubled my years and my length; and I had discarded the religion of my forefathers. One day the richest and consequently most dogmatic of my uncles came into a restaurant where I was dining, and found himself, much against his will, in conversation with the most questionable of his nephews. By way of making myself agreeable, I spoke of modern thought and Darwin. He said, "Oh, thats the fellow who wants to make out that we all have tails like monkeys." I tried to explain that what Darwin had insisted on in this connection was that some monkeys have no tails. But my uncle was as impervious to what Darwin really said as any Neo-Darwinian nowadays. He died impenitent, and did not mention me in his will.

Twenty years elapsed. If my uncle had been alive, he would have known all about Darwin, and known it all wrong. In spite of the efforts of Grant Allen to set him right, he would have accepted Darwin as the discoverer of the Evolution, or Heredity, and of modification of species by Selection. For the pre-Darwinian age had come to be regarded as a Dark Age in which men still believed that the book of Genesis was a standard scientific treatise, and that the only additions to it were Galileo's demonstration of Leonardo da Vinci's simple remark that the earth is a moon of the sun, Newton's theory of gravitation, Sir Humphry Davy's invention of the safety-lamp, the discovery of electricity, the application of steam to industrial purposes, and the penny post. It was just the same in other subjects. Thus Nietzsche, by the two or three who had come across his writings, was supposed to have been the first man to whom it occurred that mere morality and legality and urbanity lead nowhere, as if Bunyan had never written Badman. Schopenhauer was credited with inventing the distinction between the Covenant of Grace and the Covenant of Works which troubled Cromwell on his deathbed. People talked as if there had been no dramatic or descriptive music before Wagner; no impressionist painting before Whistler; whilst as to myself, I was finding that the surest way to produce an effect of daring innovation and originality was to revive the ancient attraction of long rhetorical speeches; to stick closely to the methods of Molière; and to lift characters bodily out of the pages of Charles Dickens.

The Advent of the Neo-Darwinians

This particular sort of ignorance does not always or often matter. But in Darwin's case it did matter. If Darwin had really led the world at one bound from the book of Genesis to Heredity, to Modification of Species by Selection, and to Evolution, he would have been a Philosopher and a prophet as well as an eminent professional naturalist, with geology as a hobby. The delusion that he had actually achieved this feat did no harm at first, because if people's views are sound, about evolution or anything else, it does not make two straws difference whether they call the revealer of their views Tom or Dick. But later on such apparently negligible errors have awkward consequences. Darwin was given an imposing reputation as not only an Evolutionist, but as *the* Evolutionist, with the immense majority who never read his books. The few who never read any others were led by them to concentrate exclusively on Circumstantial Selection as the explanation of all the transformations and adaptations which were the evidence for Evolution. And they presently found themselves so cut off by this specialization from the majority who knew Darwin only by his spurious reputation, that they were obliged to distinguish themselves, not as Darwinians, but as Neo-Darwinians.

Before ten more years had elapsed, the Neo-Darwinians were practically running current Science. It was 1906; I was fifty; I had published my own view of evolution in a play called Man and Superman; and I found that most people were unable to understand how

I could be an Evolutionist and not a Neo-Darwinian, or
why I habitually derided Neo-Darwinism as a ghastly
idiocy, and would fall on its professors slaughterously in
public discussions.   It was in the hope of making me
clear the matter up that the Fabian Society, which was
then organizing a series of lectures on Prophets of the
Nineteenth Century, asked me to deliver a lecture on the
prophet Darwin.   I did so; and scraps of that lecture,
which was never published, variegate these pages.

Political Inadequacy of the Human Animal

Ten more years elapsed.   Neo-Darwinism in politics
had produced a European catastrophe of a magnitude
so appalling, and a scope so unpredictable, that as I
write these lines in 1920, it is still far from certain
whether our civilization will survive it.   The circumstances of this catastrophe, the boyish cinema-fed
romanticism which made it possible to impose it on the
people as a crusade, and especially the ignorance and
errors of the victors of Western Europe when its violent
phase had passed and the time for reconstruction
arrived, confirmed a doubt which had grown steadily in
my mind during my forty years' public work as a
Socialist: namely, whether the human animal, as he
exists at present, is capable of solving the social
problems raised by his own aggregation, or, as he calls
it, his civilization.

Cowardice of the Irreligious

Another observation I had made was that good-
natured unambitious men are cowards when they have no
religion.   They are dominated and exploited not only
by greedy and often half-witted and half-alive weaklings who will do anything for cigars, champagne, motor

cars, and the more childish and selfish uses of money, but by able and sound administrators who can do nothing else with them than dominate and exploit them. Government and exploitation become synonymous under such circumstances; and the world is finally ruled by the childish, the brigands, and the blackguards. Those who refuse to stand in with them are persecuted and occasionally executed when they give any trouble to the exploiters. They fall into poverty when they lack lucrative specific talents. At the present moment one half of Europe, having knocked the other half down, is trying to kick it to death, and may succeed: a procedure which is, logically, sound Neo-Darwinism. And the good-natured majority are looking on in helpless horror, or allowing themselves to be persuaded by the newspapers of their exploiters that the kicking is not only a sound commercial investment, but an act of divine justice of which they are the ardent instruments.

But if Man is really incapable of organizing a big civilization, and cannot organize even a village or a tribe any too well, what is the use of giving him a religion? A religion may make him hunger and thirst for righteousness; but will it endow him with the practical capacity to satisfy that appetite? Good intentions do not carry with them a grain of political science, which is a very complicated one. The most devoted and indefatigable, the most able and disinterested students of this science in England, as far as I know, are my friends Sidney and Beatrice Webb. It has taken them forty years of preliminary work, in the course of which they have published several treatises comparable to Adam Smith's Wealth of Nations, to formulate a political construction adequate to existing needs. If this is the measure of what can be done in a lifetime by extraordinary ability, keen natural aptitude, exceptional opportunities, and freedom from the preoccupations of bread-winning, what are we to expect from the parliament man to whom political science is as remote and distasteful as the differential calculus, and to whom such an elementary but vital point as the law of economic rent is a *pons asinorum* never to be approached, much less crossed? Or from the common voter who is mostly so hard at work all day earning a living that he cannot keep awake for five minutes over a book?

Is There Any Hope in Education?

The usual answer is that we must educate our masters: that is, ourselves. We must teach citizenship and political science at school. But must we? There is no must about it, the hard fact being that we must *not* teach political science or citizenship at school. The schoolmaster who attempted it would soon find himself penniless in the streets without pupils, if not in the dock pleading to a pompously worded indictment for sedition against the exploiters. Our schools teach the morality of feudalism corrupted by commercialism, and hold up the military conqueror, the robber baron, and the profiteer, as models of the illustrious and the successful. In vain do the prophets who see through this imposture preach and teach a better gospel: the individuals whom they convert are doomed to pass away in a few years; and the new generations are dragged back in the schools to the morality of the fifteenth century, and think them-selves Liberal when they are defending the ideas of Henry VII, and gentlemanly when they are opposing to them the ideas of Richard III. Thus the educated man is a greater nuisance than the uneducated one: indeed it is the inefficiency and sham of the educational side of our schools (to which, except under compulsion, children would not be sent by their parents at all if they did not act as prisons in which the immature are kept from worrying the mature) that save us from being dashed on the rocks of false doctrine instead of drifting down the midstream of mere ignorance. There is no way out through the schoolmaster.

Homeopathic Education

In truth, mankind cannot be saved from without, by schoolmasters or any other sort of masters: it can only be lamed and enslaved by them. It is said that if you wash a cat it will never again wash itself. This may or may not be true: what is certain is that if you teach a man anything he will never learn it; and if you cure him of a disease he will be unable to cure himself the next time it attacks him. Therefore, if you want to see a cat clean, you throw a bucket of mud over it, when it will immediately take extraordinary pains to lick the mud off, and finally be cleaner than it was before. In the same way doctors who are up-to-date (say .00005 per cent of all the registered practitioners, and 20 per cent of the unregistered ones), when they want to rid you of a disease or a symptom, inoculate you with that disease or give you a drug that produces that symptom, in order to provoke you to resist it as the mud provokes the cat to wash itself.

Now an acute person will at once ask why, if this be so, our false education does not provoke our scholars to find out the truth. The answer is partly that it does. Voltaire was a pupil of the Jesuits; Samuel Butler was the pupil of a hopelessly conventional and erroneous country parson. But then Voltaire was Voltaire, and Butler was Butler: that is, their minds were so abnormally strong that they could throw off the doses of poison that paralyse ordinary minds. When the doctors

inoculate you and the homeopathists dose you, they give
you an infinitesimally attenuated dose. If they gave you
the virus at full strength it would overcome your resistance and produce its direct effect. The doses of false
doctrine given at public schools and universities are so
big that they overwhelm the resistance that a tiny dose
would provoke. The normal student is corrupted beyond
redemption, and will drive the genius who resists out of
the country if he can. Byron and Shelley had to fly to
Italy, whilst Castlereagh and Eldon ruled the roost at
home. Rousseau was hunted from frontier to frontier;
Karl Marx starved in exile in a Soho lodging; Ruskin's
articles were refused by the magazines (he was too rich
to be otherwise persecuted); whilst mindless forgotten
nonentities governed the land; sent men to the prison or
the gallows for blasphemy and sedition (meaning the
truth about Church and State); and sedulously stored
up the social disease and corruption which explode from
time to time in gigantic boils that have to be lanced by
a million bayonets. This is the result of allopathic education. Homeopathic education has not yet been
officially tried, and would obviously be a delicate matter
if it were. A body of schoolmasters inciting their pupils
to infinitesimal peccadilloes with the object of provoking
them to exclaim, "Get thee behind me, Satan," or telling
them white lies about history for the sake of being contradicted, insulted, and refuted, would certainly do less
harm than our present educational allopaths do; but
then nobody will advocate homeopathic education. Allo-
pathy has produced the poisonous illusion that it
enlightens instead of darkening. The suggestion may,
however, explain why, whilst most people's minds suc-
cumb to inculcation and environment, a few react vigorously: honest and decent people coming from thievish
slums, and sceptics and realists from country parsonages.

The Diabolical Efficiency of Technical Education

But meanwhile—and here comes the horror of it—our technical instruction is honest and efficient. The public schoolboy who is carefully blinded, duped, and corrupted as to the nature of a society based on profiteering, and is taught to honor parisitic idleness and luxury, learns to shoot and ride and keep fit with all the assistance and guidance that can be procured for him by the most anxiously sincere desire that he may do these things well, and if possible superlatively well. In the army he learns to fly; to drop bombs; to use machine-guns to the utmost of his capacity. The discovery of high explosives is rewarded and dignified: instruction in the manufacture of the weapons, battleships, submarines, and land batteries by which they are applied destructively, is quite genuine: the instructors know their business, and really mean the learners to succeed. The result is that powers of destruction that could hardly without uneasiness be entrusted to infinite wisdom and infinite benevolence are placed in the hands of romantic schoolboy patriots who, however generous by nature, are by education ignoramuses, dupes, snobs, and sportsmen to whom fighting is a religion and killing an accomplishment; whilst political power, useless under such circumstances except to militarist imperialists in chronic terror of invasion and subjugation, pompous tufthunting fools, commercial adventurers to whom the organization by the nation of its own industrial services would mean checkmate, financial parasites on the money market, and merely stupid conservators of everything that exists merely because they are used to it, is obtained by heredity, by simple purchase, by keeping newspapers and pretending that they are organs of public opinion,

by the wiles of seductive women, and by prostituting
ambitious talent to the service of the profiteers, who call
the tune because, having secured all the spare plunder,
they alone can afford to pay the piper. Neither the
rulers nor the ruled understand high politics. They do
not even know that there is such a branch of knowledge
as political science; but between them they can coerce
and enslave with the deadliest efficiency, even to the
wiping out of civilization, because their education as
slayers has been honestly and thoroughly carried out.
Essentially the rulers are all defectives; and there is
nothing worse than government by defectives who wield
irresistible powers of physical coercion. The commonplace sound people submit, and compel the rest to submit, because they have been taught to do so as an article
of religion and a point of honor. Those in whom
natural enlightenment has reacted against artificial
education submit because they are compelled; but they
would resist, and finally resist effectively, if they were
not cowards. And they are cowards because they have
neither an officially accredited and established religion
nor a generally recognized point of honor, and are all at
sixes and sevens with their various private speculations,
sending their children perforce to the schools where they
will be corrupted for want of any other schools. The
rulers are equally intimidated by the immense extension
and cheapening of the means of slaughter and destruction. The British Government is more afraid of Ireland
now that submarines, bombs, and poison gas are cheap
and easily made than it was of the German Empire
before the war; consequently the old British caution
which maintaineed a balance of power through command
of the sea is intensified into a terror that sees security in
nothing short of absolute military mastery of the entire
globe: that is, in an impossibility that will yet seem pos-

sible in detail to soldiers and to parochial and insular
patriotic civilians.

Flimsiness of Civilization

This situation has occurred so often before, always
with the same result of a collapse of civilization (Professor Flinders Petrie has let out the secret of previous
collapses), that the rich are instinctively crying "Let
us eat and drink; for tomorrow we die," and the poor,
"How long, O Lord, how long?" But the pitiless reply
still is that God helps those who help themselves. This
does not mean that if Man cannot find the remedy no
remedy will be found. The power that produced Man
when the monkey was not up to the mark, can produce a
higher creature than Man if Man does not come up to
the mark. What it means is that if Man is to be saved,
Man must save himself. There seems no compelling
reason why he should be saved. He is by no means an
ideal creature. At his present best many of his ways
are so unpleasant that they are unmentionable in polite
society, and so painful that he is compelled to pretend
that pain is often a good. Nature holds no brief for
the human experiment: it must stand or fall by its
results. If Man will not serve, Nature will try another
experiment.

What hope is there then of human improvement?
According to the Neo-Darwinists, to the Mechanists, no
hope whatever, because improvement can come only
through some senseless accident which must, on the
statistical average of accidents, be presently wiped out
by some other equally senseless accident.

Creative Evolution

But this dismal creed does not discourage those who
believe that the impulse that produces evolution is

creative. They have observed the simple fact that the will to do anything can and does, at a certain pitch of intensity set up by conviction of its necessity, create and organize new tissue to do it with. To them therefore mankind is by no means played out yet. If the weight lifter, under the trivial stimulus of an athletic competition, can "put up a muscle," it seems reasonable to believe that an equally earnest and convinced philosopher could "put up a brain." Both are directions of vitality to a certain end. Evolution shows us this direction of vitality doing all sorts of things: providing the centipede with a hundred legs, and ridding the fish of any legs at all; building lungs and arms for the land and gills and fins for the sea; enabling the mammal to gestate its young inside its body, and the fowl to incubate hers outside it; offering us, we may say, our choice of any sort of bodily contrivance to maintain our activity and increase our resources.

Voluntary Longevity

Among other matters apparently changeable at will is the duration of individual life. Weismann, a very clever and suggestive biologist who was unhappily reduced to idiocy by Neo-Darwinism, pointed out that death is not an eternal condition of life, but an expedient introduced to provide for continual renewal without overcrowding. Now Circumstantial Selection does not account for natural death: it accounts only for the survival of species in which the individuals have sense enough to decay and die on purpose. But the individuals do not seem to have calculated very reasonably: nobody can explain why a parrot should live ten times as long as a dog, and a turtle be almost immortal. In the case of man, the operation has overshot its mark: men do not live long enough: they are, for all the purposes of high civilization, mere children when they die; and our Prime Ministers, though rated as mature, divide their time between the golf course and the Treasury Bench in parliament. Presumably, however, the same power that made this mistake can remedy it. If on opportunist grounds Man now fixes the term of his life at three score and ten years, he can equally fix it at three hundred, or three thousand, or even at the genuine Circumstantial Selection limit, which would be until a sooner-or-later-inevitable fatal accident makes an end of the individual. All that is necessary to make him extend his present span is that tremendous catastrophes such as the late war shall convince him of the necessity of at least outliving his taste for golf and cigars if the race is to be saved. This is not fantastic speculation: it is deductive biology, if there is such a science as biology. Here, then, is a stone what we have left unturned, and that may be worth turning. To make the suggestion more entertaining than it would be to most people in the form of a biological treatise, I have written Back to Methuselah as a contribution to the modern Bible.

Many people, however, can read treatises and cannot read Bibles. Darwin could not read Shakespear. Some who can read both, like to learn the history of their ideas. Some are so entangled in the current confusion of Creative Evolution with Circumstantial Selection by their historical ignorance that they are puzzled by any distinction between the two. For all their sakes I must give here a little history of the conflict between the view of Evolution taken by the Darwinians (though not altogether by Darwin himself) and called Natural Selection, and that which is emerging, under the title of Creative Evolution, as the genuinely scientific religion for which all wise men are now anxiously looking.

The Early Evolutionists

The idea of Evolution, or Transformation as it is now sometimes called, was not first conceived by Charles Darwin, or by Alfred Russel Wallace, who observed the operation of Circumstantial Selection simultaneously with Charles. The celebrated Buffoon was a better Evolutionist than either of them; and two thousand years before Buffon was born, the Greek philosopher Empedocles opined that all forms of life are transformations of four elements, Fire, Air, Earth, and Water, effected by the two innate forces of attraction and repulsion, or love and hate. As lately as 1860 I myself was taught as a child that everything was made out of these four elements. Both the Empedocleans and the Evolutionists were opposed to those who believed in the separate creation of all forms of life as described in the book of Genesis. This "conflict between religion and science," as the phrase went then, did not perplex my infant mind in the least: I knew perfectly well, without knowing that I knew it, that the validity of a story is not the same as the occurrence of a fact. But as I grew up I found that I had to choose between Evolution and Genesis. If you believed that dogs and cats and snakes and birds and beetles and oysters and whales and men and women were all separately designed and made and named in Eden garden at the beginning of things, and have since survived simply by reproducing their kind, then you were not an Evolutionist. If you believed, on the contrary, that all the different species are modifications, variations, and elaborations of one primal stock, or even of a few primal stocks, then you were an Evolutionist. But you were not necessarily a Darwinian; for you might have been a modern Evolutionist twenty years before Charles Darwin was born, and a whole lifetime before he published his Origin of Species. For that matter, when Aristotle grouped animals with backbones as blood relations, he began the sort of classification which, when extended by Darwin to monkeys and men, so shocked my uncle.

Genesis had held the field until the time (1707–1778) of Linnæus the famous botanist. In the meantime the microscope had been invented. It revealed a new world of hitherto invisible creatures called Infusorians, as common water was found to be an infusion of them. In the eighteenth century naturalists were very keen on the Infusorian Amœbas, and were much struck by the way in which the members of this old family behaved and developed. But it was still possible for Linnæus to begin a treatise by saying "There are just so many species as there were forms created in the beginning," though there were hundreds of commonplace Scotch gardeners, pigeon fanciers, and stock breeders then living who knew better. Linnæus himself knew better before he died. In the last edition of his System of Nature, he began to wonder whether the transmutation of species by variation might not be possible. Then came the great poet who jumped over the facts to the conclusion. Goethe said that all the shapes of creation were cousins; that there must be some common stock from which all the species had sprung; that it was the environment of air that had produced the eagle, of water the seal, and of earth the mole. He could not say how this happened; but he divined that it did happen. Erasmus Darwin, the grandfather of Charles, carried the environment theory much further, pointing out instance after instance of modifications made in species apparently to adapt it to circumstances and environment: for instance, that the brilliant colours of the leopard, which make it so conspicuous in Regent's Park, conceal it in a tropical jungle. Finally he wrote, as his declaration of faith, "The world has been evolved, not created: it has arisen

little by little from a small beginning, and has increased
through the activity of the elemental forces embodied in
itself, and so has rather grown than come into being at
an almighty word.   What a sublime idea of the infinite
might of the great Architect, the Cause of all causes,
the Father of all fathers, the Ens Entium!   For if we
would compare the Infinite, it would surely require a
greater Infinite to cause the causes of effects than to
produce the effects themselves."   In this, published in
the year 1794, you have nineteenth-century Evolution
precisely defined.   And Erasmus Darwin was by no
means its only apostle.   It was in the air then.   A German biologist named Treviranus, whose book was published in 1802, wrote, "In every living being there exists
a capacity for endless diversity of form.   Each possesses
the power of adapting its organization to the variations
of the external world; and it is this power, called into
activity by cosmic changes, which has enabled the simple
zoophytes of the primitive world to climb to higher and
higher stages of organization, and has brought endless
variety into nature."   There you have your evolution of
Man from the amœba all complete whilst Nelson was still
alive on the seas.   And in 1809, before the battle of
Waterloo, a French soldier named Lamarck, who had
beaten his musket into a microscope and turned
zooloist, declared that species were an illusion produced
by the shortness of our individual lives, and that they
were constantly changing and melting into one another
and into new forms as surely as the hand of a clock is
continually moving, though it moves so slowly that it
looks stationary to us.   We have since come to think
that its industry is less continuous: that the clock stops
for a long time, and then is suddenly "put on" by a
mysterious finger.   But never mind that just at
present.

The Advent of the Neo-Lamarckians

I call your special attention to Lamarck, because later on there were Neo-Lamarckians as well as Neo-Darwinians. I was a Neo-Lamarckian. Lamarck passed on from the conception of Evolution as a general law to Charles Darwin's department of it, which was the method of Evolution. Lamarck, whilst making many ingenious suggestions as to the reaction of external causes on life and habit, such as changes of climate, food supply, geological upheavals and so forth, really held as his fundamental proposition that living organisms changed because they wanted to. As he stated it, the great factor in Evolution is use and disuse. If you have no eyes, and want to see, and keep trying to see, you will finally get eyes. If, like a mole or subterranean fish, you have eyes and dont want to see, you will lose your eyes. If you like eating the tender tops of trees enough to make you concentrate all your energies on the stretching of your neck, you will finally get a long neck, like the giraffe. This seems absurd to inconsiderate people at the first blush; but it is within the personal experience of all of us that it is just by this process that a child tumbling about the floor becomes a boy walking erect; and that a man sprawling on the road with a bruised chin, or supine on the ice with a bashed occiput, becomes a bicyclist and a skater. The process is not continuous, as it would be if mere practice had anything to do with it; for though you may improve at each bicycling lesson *during* the lesson, when you begin your next lesson you do not begin at the point at which you left off: you relapse apparently to the beginning. Finally, you succeed quite suddenly, and do not relapse again. More miraculous still, you at once exercise the new power unconsciously. Although you are adapting

your front wheel to your balance so elaborately and
actively that the accidental locking of your handle bars
for a second will throw you off; though five minutes
before you could not do it at all, yet now you do it as
unconsciously as you grow your finger nails. You have
a new faculty, and must have created some new bodily
tissue as its organ. And you have done it solely by
willing. For here there can be no question of Circumstantial Selection, or the survival of the fittest. The
man who is learning how to ride a bicycle has no advantage over the non-cyclist in the struggle for existence:
quite the contrary. He has acquired a new habit, an
automatic unconscious habit, solely because he wanted
to, and kept trying until it was added into him.

How Acquirements are Inherited

But when your son tries to skate or bicycle in his turn,
he does not pick up the accomplishment where you left
it, any more than he is born six feet high with a beard
and a tall hat. The set-back that occurred between your
lessons occurs again. The race learns exactly as the
individual learns. Your son relapses, not to the very
beginning, but to a point which no mortal method of
measurement can distinguish from the beginning. Now
this is odd; for certain other habits of yours, equally
acquired (to the Evolutionist, of course, all habits are
acquired), equally unconscious, equally automatic, are
transmitted without any perceptible relapse. For instance, the very first act of your son when he enters the
world as a separate individual is to yell with indignation: that yell which Shakespear thought the most tragic
and piteous of all sounds. In the act of yelling he
begins to breathe: another habit, and not even a necessary one, as the object of breathing can be achieved in

other ways, as by deep sea fishes. He circulates his blood by pumping it with his heart. He demands a meal, and proceeds at once to perform the most elaborate chemical operations on the food he swallows. He manufactures teeth; discards them; and replaces them with fresh ones. Compared to these habitual feats, walking, standing upright, and bicycling are the merest trifles; yet it is only by going through the wanting, trying process that he can stand, walk, or cycle, whereas in the other and far more difficult and complex habits he not only does not consciously want nor consciously try, but actually consciously objects very strongly. Take that early habit of cutting the teeth; would he do that if he could help it? Take that later habit of decaying and eliminating himself by death—equally as acquired habit, remember—how he abhors it! Yet the habit has become so rooted, so automatic, that he must do it in spite of himself, even to his own destruction.

We have here a routine which, given time enough for it to operate, will finally produce the most elaborate forms of organized life on Lamarckian lines without the intervention of Circumstantial Selection at all. If you can turn a pedestrian into a cyclist, and a cyclist into a pianist or violinist, without the intervention of Circumstantial Selection, you can turn an amœba into a man, or a man into a superman, without it. All of which is rank heresy to the Neo-Darwinian, who imagines that if you stop Circumstantial Selection, you not only stop development but inaugurate a rapid and disastrous degeneration.

Let us fix the Lamarckian evolutionary process well in our minds. You are alive; and you want to be more alive. You want an extension of consciousness and of power. You want, consequently, additional organs, or additional uses of your existing organs: that is, addi-

tional habits. You get them because you want them
badly enough to keep trying for them until they come.
Nobody knows how: nobody knows why: all we know is
that the thing actually takes place. We relapse miserably from effort to effort until the old organ is modified or the new one created, when suddenly the impossible
becomes possible and the habit is formed. The moment
we form it we want to get rid of the consciousness of it
so as to economize our consciousness for fresh conquests
of life; as all consciousness means preoccupation and
obstruction. If we had to think about breathing or
digesting or circulating our blood we should have no
attention to spare for anything else, as we find to our
cost when anything goes wrong with these operations.
We want to be unconscious of them just as we wanted to
acquire them; and we finally win what we want. But we
win unconsciousness of our habits at the cost of losing
our control of them; and we also build one habit and its
corresponding functional modification of our organs on
another, and so become dependent on our old habits.
Consequently we have to persist in them even when they
hurt us. We cannot stop breathing to avoid an attack
of asthma, or to escape drowning. We can lose a habit
and discard an organ when we no longer need them, just
as we acquired them; but this process is slow and broken
by relapses; and relics of the organ and the habit long
survive its utility. And if other and still indispensable
habits and modifications have been built on the ones we
wish to discard, we must provide a new foundation for
them before we demolish the old one. This is also a slow
process and a very curious one.

The Miracle of Condensed Recapitulation

The relapses between the efforts to acquire a habit are
important because, as we have seen, they recur not only

from effort to effort in the case of the individual, but
from generation to generation in the case of the race.
This relapsing from generation to generation is an in-
variable characteristic of the evolutionary process. For
instance, Raphael, though descended from eight unin-
terrupted generations of painters, had to learn to paint
apparently as if no Sanzio had ever handled a brush
before. But he had also to learn to breathe, and digest,
and circulate his blood. Although his father and mother
were fully grown adults when he was conceived, he was
not conceived or even born fully grown; he had to go
back and begin as a speck of protoplasm, and to struggle through an embryonic lifetime, during part of which
he was indistinguishable from an embryonic dog, and
had neither a skull nor a backbone. When he at last
acquired these articles, he was for some time doubtful
whether he was a bird or a fish. He had to compress
untold centuries of development into nine months before
he was human enough to break loose as an independent
being. And even then he was still so incomplete that his
parents might well have exclaimed "Good Heavens! have
you learnt nothing from our experience that you come
into the world in this ridiculously elementary state?
Why cant you talk and walk and paint and behave
decently?" To that question Baby Raphael had no
answer. All he could have said was that this is how
evolution or transformation happens. The time may
come when the same force that compressed the development of millions of years into nine months may pack
many more millions into even a shorter space; so that
Raphaels may be born painters as they are now born
breathers and blood circulators. But they will still
begin as specks of protoplasm, and acquire the faculty
of painting in their mother's womb at quite a late stage
of their embryonic life. They must recapitulate the

history of mankind in their own persons, however briefly they may condense it.

Nothing was so astonishing and significant in the discoveries of the embryologists, nor anything so absurdly little appreciated, as this recapitulation, as it is now called: this power of hurrying up into months a process which was once so long and tedious that the mere contemplation of it is unendurable by men whose span of life is three-score-and-ten. It widened human possibilities to the extent of enabling us to hope that the most prolonged and difficult operations of our minds may yet become instantaneous, or, as we call it, instinctive. It also directed our attention to examples of this packing up of centuries into seconds which were staring us in the face in all directions. As I write these lines the newspapers are occupied by the exploits of a child of eight, who has just defeated twenty adult chess players in twenty games played simultaneously, and has been able afterwards to reconstruct all the twenty games without any apparent effort of memory. Most people, including myself, play chess (when they play it at all) from hand to mouth, and can hardly recall the last move but one, or foresee the next but two. Also, when I have to make an arithmetical caluclation, I have to do it step by step with pencil and paper, slowly, reluctantly, and with so little confidence in the result that I dare not act on it without "proving" the sum by a further calculation involving more ciphering. But there are men who can neither read, write, nor cipher, to whom the answer to such sums as I can do is instantly obvious without any conscious calculation at all; and the result is infallible. Yet some of these natural arithmeticians have but a small vocabulary; are at a loss when they have to find words for any but the simplest everyday occasions; and cannot for the life of them describe mechanical operations which they perform daily in the course of their trade; whereas to me the whole vocabulary of English literature, from Shakespear to the latest edition of the Encyclopædia Britannica, is so completely and instantaneously at my call that I have never had to consult even a thesaurus except once or twice when for some reason I wanted a third or fourth synonym. Again, though I have tried and failed to draw recognizable portraits of persons I have seen every day for years, Mr. Bernard Partridge, having seen a man once, will, without more strain than is involved in eating a sandwich, draw him to the life. The keyboard of a piano is a device I have never been able to master; yet Mr. Cyril Scott uses it exactly as I use my own fingers; and to Sir Edward Elgar an orchestral score is as instantaneously intelligible at sight as a page of Shakespear is to me. One man cannot, after trying for years, finger the flute fluently. Another will take up a flute with a newly invented arrangement of keys on it, and play it at once with hardly a mistake. We find people to whom writing is so difficult that they prefer to sign their name with a mark, and beside them men who master systems of shorthand and improvise new systems of their own as easily as they learnt the alphabet. These contrasts are to be seen on all hands, and have nothing to do with variations in general intelligence, nor even in the specialized intelligence proper to the faculty in question: for example, no composer or dramatic poet has ever pretended to be able to perform all the parts he writes for the singers, actors, and players who are his executants. One might as well expect Napoleon to be a fencer, or the Astronomer Royal to know how many beans make five any better than his bookkeeper. Even exceptional command of language does not imply the possession of ideas to express: Mezzofanti, the master of fifty-eight

languages, had less to say in them than Shakespear
with his little Latin and less Greek; and public life is
the paradise of voluble windbags.

All these examples, which might be multiplied by millions, are cases in which a long, laborious, conscious,
detailed process of acquirement has been condensed into
an instinctive and unconscious inborn one. Factors
which formerly had to be considered one by one in succession are integrated into what seems a single simple
factor. Chains of hardly soluble problems have coalesced
in one problem which solves itself the moment it is raised.
What is more, they have been pushed back (or forward,
if you like) from post-natal to pre-natal ones. The
child in the womb may take some time over them; but it
is a miraculously shortened time.

The time phenomena involved are curious, and suggest
that we are either wrong about our history or else that
we enormously exaggerate the periods required for the
pre-natal acquirement of habits. In the nineteenth century we talked very glibly about geological periods, and
flung millions of coins about in the most lordly manner
in our reaction against Archbishop Ussher's chronology.
We had a craze for big figures, and positively liked to
believe that the progress made by the child in the womb
in a month was represented in prehistoric time by ages
and ages. We insisted that Evolution advanced more
slowly than any snail ever crawled, and that Nature does
not proceed by leaps and bounds. This was all very well
as long as we were dealing with such acquired habits as
breathing or digestion. It was possible to believe that
dozens of epochs had gone to the slow building up of
these habits. But when we have to consider the case
of a man born not only as an accomplished metabolist,
but with such an aptitude for shorthand and keyboard
manipulation that he is a stenographer or pianist at

least five sixths ready-made as soon as he can control his
hands intelligently, we are forced to suspect either that
keyboards and shorthand are older inventions than we
suppose, or else that acquirements can be assimilated
and stored as congenial qualifications in a shorter time
than we think; so that, as between Lyell and Archbishop
Ussher, the laugh may not be with Lyell quite so up-
roariously as it seemed fifty years ago.

Heredity an Old Story

It is evident that the evolutionary process is a hereditary one, or, to put it less drily, that human life is continuous and immortal. The Evolutionists took heredity
for granted. So did everybody. The human mind has
been soaked in heredity as long back as we can trace
its thought. Hereditary peers, hereditary monarchs,
hereditary castes and trades and classes were the best
known of social institutions, and in some cases of public
nuisances. Pedigree men counted pedigree dogs and
pedigree horses among their most cherished possessions.
Far from being unconscious of heredity, or sceptical,
men were insanely credulous about it: they not only
believed in the transmission of qualities and habits from
generation to generation, but expected the son to begin
mentally where the father left off.

This belief in heredity led naturally to the practice of
Intentional Selection. Good blood and breeding were
eagerly sought after in human marriage. In dealing
with plants and animals, selection with a view to the
production of new varieties and the improvement and
modification of species had been practised ever since men
began to cultivate them. My pre-Darwinian uncle knew
as well as Darwin that the race-horse and the dray-
horse are not separate creations from the Garden of

Eden, but adaptations by deliberate human selection of the medieval war-horse to modern racing and industrial haulage. He knew that there are nearly two hundred different sorts of dogs, all capable of breeding with one another and of producing cross varieties unknown to Adam. He knew that the same thing is true of pigeons. He knew that gardeners had spent their lives trying to breed black tulips and green carnations and unheard-of orchids, and had actually produced flowers just as strange to Eve. His quarrel with the Evolutionists was not a quarrel with the evidence for Evolution: he had accepted enough of it to prove Evolution ten times over before he ever heard of it. What he repudiated was cousinship with the ape, and the implied suspicion of a rudimentary tail, because it was offensive to his sense of his own dignity, and because he thought that apes were ridiculous, and tails diabolical when associated with the erect posture. Also he believed that Evolution was a heresy which involved the destruction of Christianity, of which, as a member of the Irish Church (the pseudo-Protestant one), he conceived himself a pillar. But this was only his ignorance; for a man may deny his descent from an ape and be eligible as a churchwarden without being any the less a convinced Evolutionist.

Discovery Anticipated by Divination

What is more, the religious folk can claim to be among the pioneers of Evolutionism. Weismann, Neo-Darwinist though he was, devoted a long passage in his History of Evolution to the Nature Philosophy of Lorenz Oken, published in 1809. Oken defined natural science as "the science of the everlasting transmutations of the Holy Ghost in the world." His religion had started him on the right track, and not only led him to think out a whole scheme of Evolution in abstract terms, but guided his aim in a significantly good scientific shot which brought him within the scope of Weismann. He not only defined the original substance from which all forms of life have developed as protoplasm, or, as he called it, primitive slime (*Urschleim*), but actually declared that this slime took the form of vesicles out of which the universe was built. Here was the modern cell morphology guessed by a religious thinker long before the microscope and the scalpel forced it on the vision of mere laboratory workers who could not think and had no religion. The laboratory workers worked very hard indeed to find out what would happen to a dog if they tied up its bile ducts, or to a monkey if half its brains were burnt out by a man with no brains at all, much as a child will pull off a fly's legs to see what will happen to the fly. Lorenz Oken *thought* very hard to find out what was happening to the Holy Ghost, and thereby made a contribution of extraordinary importance to our understanding of creatures having nothing wrong with their bile ducts or brains. The man who was scientific enough to see that the Holy Ghost is the most interesting of all the hard facts of life got easily in front of the blockheads who could only sin against it. Hence my uncle was turning his back on very respectable company when he derided Evolution, and would probably have recanted and apologized at once had anybody pointed out to him what a solecism he was committing.

The metaphysical side of Evolution was thus no novelty when Darwin arrived. Had Oken never lived, there would still have been millions of persons trained from their childhood to believe that we are continually urged upwards by a force called the Will of God. In 1819 Schopenhauer published his treatise on The World as Will, which is the metaphysical complement to Lamarck's natural history, as it demonstrates that the driving force behind Evolution is a will-to-live, and to live, as Christ said long before, more abundantly. And the earlier philosophers, from Plato to Leibnitz, had kept the human mind open for the thought of the universe as one idea behind all its physically apprehensible transformations.

Corrected Dates for the Discovery of Evolution

All this, remember, is the state of things in the pre-Darwin period, which so many of us still think of as a pre-evolutionary period. Evolutionism was the rage before Queen Victoria came to the throne. To fix this chronology, let me repeat the story told by Weismann of the July revolution in Paris in 1830, when the French got rid of Charles the Tenth. Goethe was then still living; and a French friend of his called on him and found him wildly excited: "What do you think of the great event?" said Goethe. "The volcano is in eruption; and all is in flames. There can no longer be discussion with closed doors." The Frenchman replied that no doubt it was a terrible business; but what could they expect with such a ministry and such a king? "Stuff!" said Goethe: "I am not thinking of these people at all, but of the open rupture in the French Academy between Cuvier and St. Hilaire. It is of the utmost importance to science." The rupture Goethe meant was about Evolution, Cuvier contending that there were four species, and St. Hilaire that there was only one.

From 1830, when Darwin was an apparently unpromising lad of seventeen, until 1859, when he turned the world upside down by his Origin of Species, there was a slump in Evolutionism. The first generation of its enthusiasts was ageing and dying out; and their successors were being taught from the Book of Genesis, just as Edward VI was (and Edward VII too, for that matter). Nobody who knew the theory was adding anything to it. This slump not only heightened the impression of entire novelty when Darwin brought the subject to the front again: it probably prevented him from realizing how much had been done before, even by his own grandfather, to whom he was accused of being unjust. Besides, he was not really carrying on the family business. He was an entirely original worker; and he was on a new tack, as we shall see presently. And he would not in any case have thought much, as a practical naturalist, of the more or less mystical intellectual speculations of the Deists of 1790–1830. Scientific workers were very tired of Deism just then. They had given up the riddle of the Great First Cause as insoluble, and were calling themselves, accordingly, Agnostics. They had turned from the inscrutable question of Why things existed, to the spade work of discovering What was really occurring in the world and How it really occurred.

With all his attention bent in this new direction, Darwin soon noticed that a good deal was occurring in an entirely unmystical and even unmeaning way of which the older speculative Deist-Evolutionists had taken little or no account. Nowadays, when we are turning in weary disgust and disillusion from Neo-Darwinism and Mechanism to Vitalism and Creative Evolution, it is difficult to imagine how this new departure of Darwin's could possibly have appealed to his contemporaries as exciting, agreeable, above all as hopeful. Let me therefore try to bring back something of the atmosphere of that time by describing a scene, very characteristic of its superstitions, in which I took what was then considered an unspeakably shocking part.

Defying the Lightning: a Frustrated Experiment

One evening in 1878 or thereabouts, I, being then in my earliest twenties, was at a bachelor party of young men of the professional class in the house of a doctor in the Kensingtonian quarter of London. They fell to talking about religious revivals; and an anecdote was related of a man who, having incautiously scoffed at the mission of Messrs Moody and Sankey, a then famous firm of American evangelists, was subsequently carried home on a shutter, slain by divine vengeance as a blasphemer. A timid minority, without quite venturing to question the truth of the incident—for they naturally did not care to run the risk of going home on shutters themselves—nevertheless shewed a certain disposition to cavil at those who exulted in it; and something approaching to an argument began. At last it was alleged by the most evangelical of the disputants that Charles Bradlaugh, the most formidable atheist on the Secularist platform, had taken out his watch publicly and challenged the Almighty to strike him dead in five minutes if he really existed and disapproved of atheism. The leader of the cavillers, with great heat, repudiated this as a gross calumny, declaring that Bradlaugh had repeatedly and indignantly contradicted it, and implying that the atheist champion was far too pious a man to commit such a blasphemy. This exquisite confusion of ideas roused my sense of comedy. It was clear to me that the challenge attributed to Charles Bradlaugh was a scientific experiment of a quite simple, straightforward, and proper kind to ascertain whether the expression of atheistic opinions really did involve any personal risk. It was certainly the method taught in the Bible, Elijah having confuted the prophets of Baal in precisely that

way, with every circumstance of bitter mockery of their
god when he failed to send down fire from heaven. Accordingly I said that if the question at issue were
whether the penalty of questioning the theology of
Messrs Moody and Sankey was to be struck dead on the
spot by an incensed deity, nothing could effect a more
convincing settlement of it than the very obvious experiment attributed to Mr Bradlaugh, and that consequently
if he had not tried it, he ought to have tried it. The
omission, I added, was one which could easily be reme-
died there and then, as I happened to share Mr. Bradlaugh's views as to the absurdity of the belief in these
violent interferences with the order of nature by a short-
tempered and thin-skinned supernatural deity. Therefore—and at that point I took out my watch.

The effect was electrical. Neither sceptics nor devo-
tees were prepared to abide the result of the experiment.
In vain did I urge the pious to trust in the accuracy of
their deity's aim with a thunderbolt, and the justice of
his discrimination between the innocent and the guilty.
In vain did I appeal to the sceptics to accept the logical
outcome of their scepticism: it soon appeared that when
thunderbolts were in question there were no sceptics.
Our host, seeing that his guests would vanish precipi-
tately if the impious challenge were uttered, leaving him
alone with a solitary infidel under sentence of extermina-
tion in five minutes, interposed and forbade the experiment, pleading at the same time for a change of subject.
I of course complied, but could not refrain from remarking that though the dreadful words had not been uttered,
yet, as the thought had been formulated in my mind, it
was very doubtful whether the consequences could be
averted by sealing my lips. However, the rest appeared
to feel that the game would be played according to the
rules, and it mattered very little what I thought so long

as I said nothing. Only the leader of the evangelical
party, I thought, was a little preoccupied until five minutes had elapsed and the weather was still calm.

In Quest of the First Cause

Another reminiscence. In those days we thought in
terms of time and space, of cause and effect, as we still
do; but we do not now demand from a religion that it
shall explain the universe completely in terms of cause
and effect, and present the world to us as a manufac-
tured article and as the private property of its Manu-
facturer. We did then. We were invited to pity the
delusion of certain heathens who held that the world is
supported by an elephant who is supported by a tortoise.
Mahomet decided that the mountains are great weights
to keep the world from being blown away into space.
But we refuted these orientals by asking triumphantly
what the tortoise stands on? Freethinkers asked which
came first: the owl or the egg. Nobody thought of saying that the ultimate problem of existence, being clearly
insoluble and even unthinkable on causation lines, could
not be a causation problem. To pious people this would
have been flat atheism, because they assumed that God
must be a Cause, and sometimes called him The Great
First Cause, or, in still choicer language, The Primal
Cause. To the Rationalists it would have been a renun-
ciation of reason. Here and there a man would confess
that he stood as with a dim lantern in a dense fog, and
could see but a little way in any direction into infinity.
But he did not really believe that infinity was infinite or
that the eternal was also sempiternal: he assumed that all
things, known and unknown, were caused.

Hence it was that I found myself one day towards
the end of the eighteen-seventies in a cell in the old

Brompton Oratory arguing with a Jesuit father who had been called by one of his flock to attempt my conversion to Roman Catholicism. The universe exists, said the father: somebody must have made it. If that somebody exists, said I, somebody must have made him. I grant you that for the sake of argument, said the Jesuit. I grant you a maker of God. I grant you a maker of the maker of God. I grant you as long a line of makers as you please; but an infinity of makers is unthinkable and extravagant: it is no harder to believe in number one than in number fifty thousand or fifty million; so why not accept number one and stop there, since no attempt to get behind him will remove your logical difficulty? By your leave, said I, it is as easy for me to believe that the universe made itself as that a maker of the universe made himself; in fact much easier; for the universe visibly exists and makes itself as it goes along, whereas a maker for it is a hypothesis. Of course we could get no further on these lines. He rose and said that we were like two men working a saw, he pushing it forward and I pushing it back, and cutting nothing; but when we had dropped the subject and were walking through the refectory, he returned to it for a moment to say that he should go mad if he lost his belief. I, glorying in the robust callousness of youth and the comedic spirit, felt quite comfortable and said so; though I was touched, too, by his evident sincerity.

These two anecdotes are superficially trivial and even comic; but there is an abyss of horror beneath them. They reveal a condition so utterly irreligious that religion means nothing but belief in a nursery bogey, and its inadequacy is demonstrated by a toy logical dilemma, neither the bogey nor the dilemma having anything to do with religion, or being serious enough to impose on or confuse any properly educated child over the age of six. One hardly knows which is the more appalling: the abjectness of the credulity or the flippancy of the scepticism. The result was inevitable. All who were strong-minded enough not to be terrified by the bogey were left stranded in empty contemptuous negation, and argued, when they argued at all, as I argued with the Jesuit. But their position was not intellectually comfortable. A member of parliament expressed their discomfort when, objecting to the admission of Charles Bradlaugh into parliament, he said "Hang it all, a man should believe in something or somebody." It was easy to throw the bogey into the dust-bin; but none the less the world, our corner of the universe, did not look like a pure accident: it presented evidences of design in every direction. There was mind and purpose behind it. As the anti-Bradlaugh member would have put it, there must be somebody behind the something: no atheist could get over that.

Paley's Watch

Paley had put the argument in an apparently unanswerable form. If you found a watch, full of mechanism exquisitely adapted to produce a series of operations all leading to the fulfilment of one central purpose of measuring for mankind the march of the day and night, could you believe that it was not the work of a cunning artificer who had designed and contrived it all to that end? And here was a far more wonderful thing than a watch, a man with all his organs wonderfully contrived, cords and levers, girders and kingposts, circulating systems of pipes and valves, dialysing membranes, chemical retorts, carburettors, ventilators, inlets and outlets, telephone transmitters in his ears, light recorders and lenses in his eyes: was it conceivable that this was the work of chance? that no artificer had wrought here, that there was no purpose in this, no design, no guiding intelligence? The thing was incredible. In vain did Helmholtz declare that "the eye has every possible defect that can be found in an optical instrument, and even some peculiar to itself," and that "if an optician tried to sell me an instrument which had all these defects I should think myself quite justified in blaming his carelessness in the strongest terms, and sending him back his instrument." To discredit the optician's skill was not to get rid of the optician. The eye might not be so cleverly made as Paley thought: but it was made somehow, by somebody.

And then my argument with the Jesuit began all over again. It was easy enough to say that every man makes his own eyes: indeed the embryologists had actually caught him doing it. But what about the very evident purpose that prompted him to do it? Why did he want to see, if not to extend his consciousness and his knowledge and his power? That purpose was at work everywhere, and must be something bigger than the individual eye-making man. Only the stupidest muckrakers could fail to see this, and even to know it as part of their own consciousness. Yet to admit it seemed to involve letting the bogey come back, so inextricably had we managed to mix up belief in the bogey's existence with belief in the existence of design in the universe.

The Irresistible Cry of Order, Order!

Our scornful young scientific and philosophic lions of today must not blame the Church of England for this confusion of thought. In 1562 the Church, in convocation in London "for the avoiding of diversities of opinions and for the establishment of consent touching true

religion," proclaimed in their first utterance, and as an
Article of Religion, that God is "without body, parts, or
passions," or, as we say, an *Élan Vital* or Life Force.
Unfortunately neither parents, parsons, nor pedagogues
could be induced to adopt that article. St. John might
say that "God is spirit" as pointedly as he pleased; our
Sovereign Lady Elizabeth might ratify the Article
again and again; serious divines might feel as deeply
as they could that a God with body, parts, and passions
could be nothing but an anthropomorphic idol; no matter: people at large could not conceive a God who was
not anthropomorphic: they stood by the Old Testament
legends of a God whose parts had been seen by one of
the patriarchs, and finally set up as against the Church,
a God who, far from being without body, parts, or passions, was composed of nothing else, and of very evil
passions too. They imposed this idol in practice on the
Church itself, in spite of the First Article, and thereby
homeopathically produced the atheist, whose denial of
God was simply a denial of the idol and a demonstration
against an unbearable and most unchristian idolatry.
The idol was, as Shelley had been expelled from Oxford
for pointing out, an almighty fiend, with a pretty character and unlimited power, spiteful, cruel, jealous, vin-
dictive, and physically violent. The most villainous
schoolmasters, the most tyrannical parents, fell far short
in their attempts to imitate it. But it was not its social
vices that brought it low. What made it scientifically
intolerable was that it was ready at a moment's notice to
upset the whole order of the universe on the most trum-
pery provocation, whether by stopping the sun in the
valley of Ajalon or sending an atheist home dead on a
shutter (the shutter was indispensable because it marked
the utter unpreparedness of the atheist, who, unable to
save himself by a deathbed repentance, was subsequently

roasted through all eternity in blazing brimstone). It was this disorderliness, this refusal to obey its own laws of nature, that created a scientific need for its destruction. Science could stand a cruel and unjust god; for nature was full of suffering and injustice. But a disorderly god was impossible. In the Middle Ages a compromise had been made by which two different orders of truth, religious and scientific, had been recognized, in order that a school man might say that two and two make four without being burnt for heresy. But the nineteenth century, steeped in a meddling, presumptuous, reading-and-writing, socially and politically powerful ignorance inconceivable by Thomas Aquinas or even Roger Bacon, was incapable of so convenient an arrangement; and science was strangled by bigoted ignoramuses claiming infallibility for their interpretation of the Bible, which was regarded, not as a literature nor even as a book, but partly as an oracle which answered and settled all questions, and partly as a talisman to be carried by soldiers in their breast pockets or placed under the pillows of persons who were afraid of ghosts. The tract shops exhibited in their windows bullet-dinted testaments, mothers' gifts to their soldier sons whose lives had been saved by it; for the muzzle-loaders of those days could not drive a projectile through so many pages.

The Moment and the Man

This superstition of a continual capricious disorder in nature, of a lawgiver who was also a lawbreaker, made atheists in all directions among clever and lightminded people. But atheism did not account for Paley's watch. Atheism accounted for nothing; and it was the business of science to account for everything that was plainly accountable. Science had no use for mere negation:

what was desired by it above all things just then was a demonstration that the evidences of design could be explained without resort to the hypothesis of a personal designer. If only some genius, whilst admitting Paley's facts, could knock the brains out of Paley by the discovery of a method whereby watches could happen without watchmakers, that genius was assured of such a welcome from the thought of his day as no natural philosopher had ever enjoyed before.

The time being thus ripe, the genius appeared; and his name was Charles Darwin. And now, what did Darwin really discover?

Here, I am afraid, I shall require once more the assistance of the giraffe, or, as he was called in the days of the celebrated Buffoon, the camelopard (by children, cammyleopard). I do not remember how this animal imposed himself illustratively on the Evolution controversy; but there was no getting away from him then; and I am old-fashioned enough to be unable to get away from him now. How did he come by his long neck? Lamarck would have said, by wanting to get at the tender leaves high up on the tree, and trying until he succeeded in wishing the necessary length of neck into existence. Another answer was also possible: namely, that some prehistoric stock-breeder, wishing to produce a natural curiosity, selected the longest-necked animals he could find, and bred from them until at last an animal with an abnormally long neck was evolved by intentional selection, just as the race-horse or the fantail pigeon has been evolved. Both these explanations, you will observe, involve consciousness, will, design, purpose, either on the part of the animal itself or on the part of a superior intelligence controlling its destiny. Darwin pointed out—and this and no more was Darwin's famous discovery—that a third explanation, involving neither will nor purpose nor design either in the animal or anyone else, was on the cards. If your neck is too short to reach your food, you die. That may be the simple explanation of the fact that all the surviving animals that feed on foliage have necks or trunks long enough to reach it. So bang goes your belief that the necks must have been designed to reach the food. But Lamarck did not believe that the necks were so designed in the beginning: he believed that the long necks were evolved by wanting and trying. Not necessarily, said Darwin. Consider the effect on the giraffes of the natural multiplication of their numbers, as insisted on by Malthus. Suppose the average height of the foliage-eating animals is four feet, and that they increase in numbers until a time comes when all the trees are eaten away to within four feet of the ground. Then the animals who happen to be an inch or two short of the average will die of starvation. All the animals who happen to be an inch or so above the average will be better fed and stronger than the others. They will secure the strongest and tallest mates; and their progeny will survive whilst the average ones and the sub-average ones will die out. This process, by which the species gains, say, an inch in reach, will repeat itself until the giraffe's neck is so long that he can always find food enough within his reach, at which point, of course, the selective process stops and the length of the giraffe's neck stops with it. Otherwise, he would grow until he could browse off the trees in the moon. And this, mark you, without the intervention of any stock-breeder, human or divine, and without will, purpose, design, or even consciousness beyond the blind will to satisfy hunger. It is true that this blind will, being in effect a will to live, gives away the whole case; but still, as compared to the open-eyed intelligent wanting and trying of Lamarck, the Darwinian process may be described as a chapter of accidents. As such, it seems simple, because you do not at first realize all that it involves. But when its whole significance dawns on you, your heart sinks into a heap of sand within you. There is a hideous fatalism about it, a ghastly and damnable reduction of beauty and intelligence, of strength and purpose, of honor and aspiration, to such casually picturesque changes as an avalanche may make in landscape, or a railway accident in a human figure. To call this Natural Selection is a blasphemy, possible to many for whom Nature is nothing but a casual aggregation of inert and dead matter, but eternally impossible to the spirits and souls of the righteous. If it be no blasphemy, but a truth of science, then the stars of heaven, the showers and dew, the winter and summer, the fire and heat, the mountains and hills, may no longer be called to exalt the Lord with us by praise: their work is to modify all things by blindly starving and murdering everything that is not lucky enough to survive in the universal struggle for hogwash.

The Brink of the Bottomless Pit

Thus did the neck of the giraffe reach out across the whole heavens and make men believe that what they saw there was a gloaming of the gods. For if this sort of selection could turn an antelope into a giraffe, it could conceivably turn a pond full of amœbas into the French Academy. Though Lamarck's way, the way of life, will, aspiration, and achievement, remained still possible, this newly shewn way of hunger, death, stupidity, delusion, chance, and bare survival was also possible: was indeed most certainly the way in which many apparently intelligently designed transformations had actually come to pass. Had I not preluded with the apparently idle

Back to Methuselah xlvii

story of my revival of the controversial methods of
Elijah, I should be asked how it was that the explorer
who opened up this gulf of despair, far from being stoned
or crucified as the destroyer of the honor of the race and
the purpose of the world, was hailed as Deliverer, Savior,
Prophet, Redeemer, Enlightener, Rescuer, Hope Giver,
and Epoch Maker; whilst poor Lamarck was swept aside
as a crude and exploded guesser hardly worthy to be
named as his erroneous forerunner. In the light of my
anecdote, the explanation is obvious. The first thing
the gulf did was to swallow up Paley, and the Disorderly
Designer, and Shelley's Almighty Fiend, and all the rest
of the pseduo-religious rubbish that had blocked every
upward and onward path since the hopes of men had
turned to Science as their true Savior. It seemed such
a convenient grave that nobody at first noticed that it
was nothing less than the bottomless pit, now become a
very real terror. For though Darwin left a path round
it for his soul, his followers presently dug it right across
the whole width of the way. Yet for the moment, there
was nothing but wild rejoicing: a sort of scientific maf-
ficking. We had been so oppressed by the notion that
everything that happened in the world was the arbitrary
personal act of an arbitrary personal god of dangerously jealous and cruel personal character, so that even
the relief of the pains of childbed and the operating
table by chloroform was objected to as an interference
with his arrangements which he would probably resent,
that we just jumped at Darwin. When Napoleon was
asked what would happen when he died, he said that
Europe would express its intense relief with a great
"Ouf!" Well, when Darwin killed the god who objected
to chloroform, everybody who had ever thought about it
said "Ouf!" Paley was buried fathoms deep with his
watch, now fully accounted for without any divine arti-

ficer at all. We were so glad to be rid of both that we
never gave a thought to the consequences. When a
prisoner sees the door of his dungeon open, he dashes
for it without stopping to think where he shall get his
dinner outside. The moment we found that we could do
without Shelley's almighty fiend intellectually, he went
into the gulf that seemed only a dustbin with a sudden-
ness that made our own lives one of the most astonishing
periods in history. If I had told that uncle of mine that
within thirty years from the date of our conversation
I should be exposing myself to suspicions of the grossest
superstition by questioning the sufficiency of Darwin;
maintaining the reality of the Holy Ghost; and declaring that the phenomenon of the Word becoming Flesh
was occurring daily, he would have regarded me as the
most extravagant madman our family had ever produced. Yet it was so. Iu 1906 I might have vituper-
ated Jehovah more heartily than ever Shelley did without
eliciting a protest in any circle of thinkers, or shocking
any public audience accustomed to modern discussion;
but when I described Darwin as "an intelligent and in-
dustrious pigeon fancier," that blasphemous levity, as it
seemed, was received with horror and indignation. The
tide has now turned; and every puny whipster may say
what he likes about Darwin; but anyone who wants to
know what it was to be a Lamarckian during the last
quarter of the nineteenth century has only to read Mr.
Festing Jones's memoir of Samuel Butler to learn how
completely even a man of genius could isolate himself by
antagonizing Darwin on the one hand and the Church
on the other.

Why Darwin Converted the Crowd

I am well aware that in describing the effect of Darwin's discovery on naturalists and on persons capable of

serious reflection on the nature and attributes of God, I am leaving the vast mass of the British public out of account. I have pointed out elsewhere that the British nation does not consist of atheists and Plymouth Brothers; and I am not now going to pretend that it ever consisted of Darwinians and Lamarckians. The average citizen is irreligious and unscientific: you talk to him about cricket and golf, market prices and party politics, not about evolution and relativity, transubstantiation and predestination. Nothing will knock into his head the fateful distinction between Evolution as promulgated by Erasmus Darwin, and Circumstantial (socalled Natural) Selection as revealed by his grandson. Yet the doctrine of Charles reached him, though the doctrine of Erasmus had passed over his head. Why did not Erasmus Darwin popularize the word Evolution as effectively as Charles?

The reason was, I think, that Circumstantial Selection is easier to understand, more visible and concrete, than Lamarckian evolution. Evolution as a philosophy and physiology of the will is a mystical process, which can be apprehended only by a trained, apt, and comprehensive thinker. Though the phenomena of use and disuse, of wanting and trying, of the manufacture of weight lifters and wrestlers from men of ordinary strength, are familiar enough as facts, they are extremely puzzling as subjects of thought, and lead you into metaphysics the moment you try to account for them. But pigeon fanciers, dog fanciers, gardeners, stock breeders, or stud grooms, can understand Circumstantial Selection, because it is their business to produce transformation by imposing on flowers and animals a Selection From Without. All that Darwin had to say to them was that the mere chapter of accidents is always doing on a huge scale what they themselves are

doing on a very small scale. There is hardly a laborer
attached to an English country house who has not taken
a litter of kittens or puppies to the bucket, and drowned
all of them except the one he thinks the most promising.
Such a man has nothing to learn about the survival of
the fittest except that it acts in more ways than he has
yet noticed; for he knows quite well, as you will find if
you are not too proud to talk to him, that this sort of
selection occurs naturally (in Darwin's sense) too: that,
for instance, a hard winter will kill off a weakly child as
the bucket kills off a weakly puppy. Then there is the
farm laborer. Shakespear's Touchstone, a court-bred
fool, was shocked to find in the shepherd a natural
philosopher, and opined that he would be damned for
the part he took in the sexual selection of sheep. As to
the production of new species by the selection of variations, that is no news to your gardener. Now if you
are familiar with these three processes: the survival of
the fittest, sexual selection, and variation leading to
new kinds, there is nothing to puzzle you in Darwinism.

That was the secret of Darwin's popularity. He
never puzzled anybody. If very few of us have read
The Orgin of Species from end to end, it is not because
it overtaxes our mind, but because we take in the whole
case and are prepared to accept it long before we have
come to the end of the innumerable instances and illus-
trations of which the book mainly consists. Darwin
becomes tedious in the manner of a man who insists on
continuing to prove his innocence after he has been
acquitted. You assure him that there is not a stain on
his character, and beg him to leave the court; but he
will not be content with enough evidence: he will have
you listen to all the evidence that exists in the world.
Darwin's industry was enormous. His patience, his
perseverance, his conscientiousness reached the human

limit. But he never got deeper beneath or higher above his facts than an ordinary man could follow him. He was not conscious of having raised a stupendous issue, because, though it arose instantly, it was not his business. He was conscious of having discovered a process of transformation and modification which accounted for a great deal of natural history. But he did not put it forward as accounting for the whole of natural history. He included it under the heading of Evolution, though it was only pseudo-evolution at best; but he revealed it as *a* method of evolution, not as *the* method of evolution. He did not pretend that it excluded other methods, or that it was the chief method. Though he demonstrated that many transformations which had been taken as functional adaptations (the current phrase for Lamarckian evolution) either certainly were or conceivably might be due to Circumstantial Selection, he was careful not to claim that he had superseded Lamarck or disproved Functional Adaptation. In short, he was not a Darwinian, but an honest naturalist working away at his job with so little preoccupation with theological speculation that he never quarrelled with the small evangelical sect into which he was born, and remained to the end the engagingly simple and socially easygoing soul he had been in his boyhood, when his elders doubted whether he would ever be of much use in the world.

How We Rushed Down a Steep Place

Not so the rest of us intellectuals. We all began going to the devil with the utmost cheerfulness. Every one who had a mind to change, changed it. Only Samuel Butler, on whom Darwin had acted homeopathically, reacted against him furiously; ran up the Lamarckian flag to the top-gallant peak; declared with penetrating

accuracy that Darwin had "banished mind from the universe"; and even attacked Darwin's personal character,
unable to bear the fact that the author of so abhorrent
a doctrine was an amiable and upright man. Nobody
would listen to him. He was so completely submerged
by the flowing tide of Darwinism that when Darwin
wanted to clear up the misunderstanding on which Butler
was basing his personal attacks, Darwin's friends, very
foolishly and snobbishly, persuaded him that Butler was
too ill-conditioned and negligible to be answered. That
they could not recognize in Butler a man of genius mattered little: what did matter was that they could not
understand the provocation under which he was raging.
They actually regarded the banishment of mind from
the universe as a glorious enlightenment and emancipa-
tion for which he was ignorantly ungrateful. Even now,
when Butler's eminence is unchallenged, and his bi-
ographer, Mr. Festing Jones, is enjoying a vogue like
that of Boswell or Lockhart, his memoirs shew him
rather as a shocking example of the bad controversial
manners of our country parsonages than as a prophet
who tried to head us back when we were gaily dancing
to our damnation across the rainbow bridge which Darwinism had thrown over the gulf which separates life
and hope from death and despair. We were intellectually intoxicated with the idea that the world could
make itself without design, purpose, skill, or intelligence: in short, without life. We completely overlooked
the difference between the modification of species by
adaptation to their environment and the appearance of
new species: we just threw in the word "variations" or
the word "sports" (fancy a man of science talking of an
unknown factor as a sport instead of as x!) and left
them to "accumulate" and account for the difference
between a cockatoo and a hippopotamus. Such phrases

set us free to revel in demonstrating to the Vitalists and Bible worshippers that if we once admit the existence of any kind of force, however unintelligent, and stretch out the past to unlimited time for such force to operate accidentally in, that force may conceivably, by the action of Circumstantial Selection, produce a world in which every function has an organ perfectly adapted to perform it, and therefore presents every appearance of having been designed, like Paley's watch, by a conscious and intelligent artificer for the purpose. We took a perverse pleasure in arguing, without the least suspicion that we were reducing ourselves to absurdity, that all the books in the British Museum library might have been written word for word as they stand on the shelves if no human being had ever been conscious, just as the trees stand in the forest doing wonderful things without consciousness.

And the Darwinians went far beyond denying consciousness to trees. Weismann insisted that the chick breaks out of its eggshell automatically; that the butterfly, springing into the air to avoid the pounce of the lizard, "does not wish to avoid death; knows nothing about death," what has happened being simply that a flight instinct evolved by Circumstantial Selection reacts promptly to a visual impression produced by the lizard's movement. His proof is that the butterfly immediately settles again on the flower, and repeats the performance every time the lizard springs, thus shewing that it learns nothing from experience, and—Weismann concludes— is not conscious of what it does.

It should hardly have escaped so curious an observer that when the cat jumps up on the dinner table, and you put it down, it instantly jumps up again, and finally establishes its right to a place on the cloth by convincing you that if you put it down a hundred times it will jump up a hundred and one times; so that if you desire its company at dinner you can have it only on its own terms. If Weismann really thought that cats act thus without any consciousness or any purpose, immediate or ulterior, he must have known very little about cats. But a thoroughgoing Weismannite, if any such still survive from those mad days, would contend that I am not at present necessarily conscious of what I am doing; that my writing of these lines, and your reading of them, are effects of Circumstantial Selection; that I need know no more about Darwinism than a butterfly knows of a lizard's appetite; and that the proof that I actually am doing it unconsciously is that as I have spent forty years in writing in this fashion without, as far as I can see, producing any visible effect on public opinion, I must be incapable of learning from experience, and am therefore a mere automaton. And the Weismannite demonstration of this would of course be an equally unconscious effect of Circumstantial Selection.

Darwinism Not Finally Refutable

Do not too hastily say that this is inconceivable. To Circumstantial Selection all mechanical and chemical reactions are possible, provided you accept the geologists' estimates of the great age of the earth, and therefore allow time enough for the circumstances to operate. It is true that mere survival of the fittest in the struggle for existence plus sexual selection fail as hopelessly to account for Darwin's own life work as for my conquest of the bicycle; but who can prove that there are not other soulless factors, unnoticed or undiscovered, which only require imagination enough to fit them to the evolution of an automatic Jesus or Shakespear? When a man tells you that you are a product of Circumstantial

Selection solely, you cannot finally disprove it. You
can only tell him out of the depths of your inner conviction that he is a fool and a liar. But as this, though
British, is uncivil, it is wiser to offer him the counter-
assurance that you are the product of Lamarckian
evolution, formerly called Functional Adaptation and
new Creative Evolution, and challenge him to disprove
that, which he can no more do than you can disprove
Circumstantial Selection, both forces being conceivably
able to produce anything if you only give them rope
enough. You may also defy him to act for a single
hour on the assumption that he may safely cross Oxford
Street in a state of unconsciousness, trusting to his
dodging reflexes to react automatically and promptly
enough to the visual impression produced by a motor
bus, and the audible impression produced by its hooter.
But if you allow yourself to defy him to explain any
particular action of yours by Circumstantial Selection,
he should always be able to find some explanation that
will fit the case if only he is ingenious enough and goes
far enough to find it. Darwin found several such explanations in his controversies. Anybody who really
wants to believe that the universe has been produced by
Circumstantial Selection co-operating with a force as
inhuman as we conceive magnetism to be can find a
logical excuse for his belief if he tries hard enough.

Three Blind Mice

The stultification and damnation which ensued are
illustrated by a comparison of the ease and certainty
with which Butler's mind moved to humane and inspiring conclusions with the grotesque stupidities and
cruelties of the idle and silly controversy which arose
among the Darwinians as to whether acquired habits

can be transmitted from parents to offspring. Consider,
for example, how Weismann set to work on that subject.
An Evolutionist with a live mind would first have
dropped the popular expression "acquired habits," because to an Evolutionist there are no other habits and
can be no others, a man being only an amœba with
acquirements. He would then have considered carefully
the process by which he himself had acquired his habits.
He would have assumed that the habits with which he
was born must have been acquired by a similar process.
He would have known what a habit is: that is, an action
voluntarily attempted until it has become more or less
automatic and involuntary; and it would never have
occurred to him that injuries or accidents coming from
external sources against the will of the victim could possibly establish a habit: that, for instance, a family could
acquire a habit of being killed in railway accidents.

And yet Weismann began to investigate the point by
behaving like the butcher's wife in the old catch. He
got a colony of mice, and cut off their tails. Then he
waited to see whether their children would be born without tails. They were not, as Butler could have told him
beforehand. He then cut off the children's tails, and
waited to see whether the grandchildren would be born
with at least rather short tails. They were not, as I
could have told him beforehand. So with the patience
and industry on which men of science pride themselves,
he cut off the grandchildren's tails too, and waited, full
of hope, for the birth of curtailed great-grandchildren.
But their tails were quite up to the mark, as any fool
could have told him beforehand. Weismann then
gravely drew the inference that acquired habits cannot
be transmitted. And yet Weismann was not a born
imbecile. He was an exceptionally clever and studious
man, not without roots of imagination and philosophy in

him which Darwinism killed as weeds. How was it that
he did not see that he was not experimenting with habits
or characteristics at all? How had he overlooked the
glaring fact that his experiment had been tried for many
generations in China on the feet of Chinese women without producing the smallest tendency on their part to be
born with abnormally small feet? He must have known
about the bound feet even if he knew nothing of the
mutilations, the clipped ears and docked tails, practised
by dog fanciers and horse breeders on many generations
of the unfortunate animals they deal in. Such amazing
blindness and stupidity on the part of a man who was
naturally neither blind nor stupid is a telling illustration
of what Darwin unintentionally did to the minds of his
disciples by turning their attention so exclusively
towards the part played in Evolution by accident and
violence operating with entire callousness to suffering
and sentiment.

A vital conception of Evolution would have taught
Weismann that biological problems are not to be solved
by assaults on mice. The scientific form of his experiment would have been something like this. First, he
should have procured a colony of mice highly susceptible
to hypnotic suggestion. He should then have hypnotized
them into an urgent conviction that the fate of the
musque world depended on the disappearance of its tail,
just as some ancient and forgotten experimenter seems
to have convinced the cats of the Isle of Man. Having
thus made the mice desire to lose their tails with a life-
or-death intensity, he would very soon have seen a few
mice born with little or no tail. These would be recognized by the other mice as superior beings, and privileged in the division of food and in sexual selection.
Ultimately the tailed mice would be put to death as

monsters by their fellows, and the miracle of the tailless
mouse completely achieved.

The objection to this experiment is not that it seems
too funny to be taken seriously, and is not cruel enough
to overawe the mob, but simply that it is impossible
because the human experimenter cannot get at the
mouse's mind. And that is what is wrong with all the
barren cruelties of the laboratories. Darwin's followers
did not think of this. Their only idea of investigation
was to imitate "Nature" by perpetrating violent and
senseless cruelties, and watch the effect of them with a
paralyzing fatalism which forbade the smallest effort to
use their minds instead of their knives and eyes, and
established an abominable tradition that the man who
hesitates to be as cruel as Circumstantial Selection itself
is a traitor to science. For Weismann's experiment
upon the mice was a mere joke compared to the atrocities
committed by other Darwinians in their attempts to
prove that mutilations could not be transmitted. No
doubt the worst of these experiments were not really
experiments at all, but cruelties committed by cruel men
who were attracted to the laboratory by the fact that it
was a secret refuge left by law and public superstition
for the amateur of passionate torture. But there is no
reason to suspect Weismann of Sadism. Cutting off the
tails of several generations of mice is not voluptuous
enough to tempt a scientific Nero. It was a mere piece
of one-eyedness; and it was Darwin who put out Weismann's humane and sensible eye. He blinded many
another eye and paralyzed many another will also. Ever
since he set up Circumstantial Selection as the creator
and ruler of the universe, the scientific world has been
the very citadel of stupidity and cruelty. Fearful as
the tribal god of the Hebrews was, nobody ever shud-
dered as they passed even his meanest and narrowest

Little Bethel or his proudest war-consecrating cathedral
as we shudder now when we pass a physiological laboratory. If we dreaded and mistrusted the priest, we could
at least keep him out of the house; but what of the
modern Darwinist surgeon whom we dread and mistrust
ten times more, but into whose hands we must all give
ourselves from time to time? Miserably as religion had
been debased, it did at least still proclaim that our relation to one another was that of a fellowship in which we
were all equal and members one of another before the judg-
ment-seat of our common father. Darwinism proclaimed
that our true relation is that of competitors and com-
batants in a struggle for mere survival, and that every
act of pity or loyalty to the old fellowship is a vain and
mischievous attempt to lessen the severity of the
struggle and preserve inferior varieties from the efforts
of Nature to weed them out. Even in Socialist Societies
which existed solely to substitute the law of fellowship
for the law of competition, and the method of providence
and wisdom for the method of rushing violently down a
steep place into the sea, I found myself regarded as a
blasphemer and an ignorant sentimentalist because whenever the Neo-Darwinian doctrine was preached there I
made no attempt to conceal my intellectual contempt for
its blind coarseness and shallow logic, or my natural
abhorrence of its sickening inhumanity.

The Greatest of These is Self-Control

As there is no place in Darwinism for free will, or any
other sort of will, the Neo-Darwinists held that there is
no such thing as self-control. Yet self-control is just
the one quality of survival value which Circumstantial
Selection must invariably and inevitably develop in the
long run. Uncontrolled qualities may be selected for

survival and development for certain periods and under
certain circumstances. For instance, since it is the un-
governable gluttons who strive the hardest to get food
and drink, their efforts would develop their strength and
cunning in a period of such scarcity that the utmost
they could do would not enable them to over-eat themselves. But a change of circumstances involving a
plentiful supply of food would destroy them. We see
this very thing happening often enough in the case of
the healthy and vigorous poor man who becomes a mil-
lionaire by one of the accidents of our competitive commerce, and immediately proceeds to dig his grave with
his teeth. But the self-controlled man survives all such
changes of circumstance, because he adapts himself to
them, and eats neither as much as he can hold nor as
little as he can scrape along on, but as much as is good
for him. What *is* self-control? It is nothing but a
highly developed vital sense, dominating and regulating
the mere appetites. To overlook the very existence of
this supreme sense; to miss the obvious inference that it
is the quality that distinguishes the fittest to survive;
to omit, in short, the highest moral claim of Evolutionary Selection: all this, which the Neo-Darwinians did
in the name of Natural Selection, shewed the most
pitiable want of mastery of their own subject, the dullest lack of observation of the forces upon which Natural
Selection works.

A Sample of Lamarcko-Shavian Invective

The Vitalist philosophers made no such mistakes.
Nietzsche, for example, thinking out the great central
truth of the Will to Power instead of cutting off mouse-
tails, had no difficulty in concluding that the final ob-
jective of this Will was power over self, and that the

seekers after power over others and material possessions
were on a false scent.

The stultification naturally became much worse as the
first Darwinians died out. The prestige of these
pioneers, who had the older evolutionary culture to build
on, and were in fact no more Darwinian in the modern
sense than Darwin himself, ceased to dazzle us when
Huxley and Tyndall and Spencer and Darwin passed
away, and we were left with the smaller people who began
with Darwin and took in nothing else. Accordingly, I
find that in the year 1906 I indulged my temper by
hurling invectives at the Neo-Darwinians in the following terms.

"I really do not wish to be abusive; but when I think
of these poor little dullards, with their precarious hold
of just that corner of evolution that a blackbeetle can
understand—with their retinue of twopenny-halfpenny
Torquemadas wallowing in the infamies of the vivi-
sector's laboratory, and solemnly offering us as epoch-
making discoveries their demonstrations that dogs get
weaker and die if you give them no food; that intense
pain makes mice sweat; and that if you cut off a dog's
leg the three-legged dog will have a four-legged puppy,
I ask myself what spell has fallen on intelligent and
humane men that they allow themselves to be imposed
on by this rabble of dolts, blackguards, imposters,
quacks, liars, and, worst of all, credulous conscientious
fools. Better a thousand times Moses and Spurgeon [a
then famous preacher] back again. After all, you cannot understand Moses without imagination nor Spurgeon without metaphysics; but you can be a thoroughgoing Neo-Darwinian without imagination, metaphysics,
poetry, conscience, or decency. For 'Natural Selection'
has no moral significance: it deals with that part of
evolution which has no purpose, no intelligence, and

might more appropriately be called accidental selection,
or better still, Unnatural Selection, since nothing is
more unnatural than an accident. If it could be proved
that the whole universe had been produced by such
Selection, only fools and rascals could bear to live."

The Humanitarians and the Problem of Evil

Yet the humanitarians were as delighted as anybody
with Darwinism at first. They had been perplexed by
the Problem of Evil and the Cruelty of Nature. They
were Shelleyans, but not atheists. Those who believed
in God were at a terrible disadvantage with the atheist.
They could not deny the existence of natural facts so
cruel that to attribute them to the will of God is to make
God a demon. Belief in God was impossible to any
thoughtful person without belief in the Devil as well.
The painted Devil, with his horns, his barbed tail, and
his abode of burning brimstone, was an incredible bogey;
but the evil attributed to him was real enough; and the
atheists argued that the author of evil, if he exists, must
be strong enough to overcome God, else God is morally
responsible for everything he permits the Devil to do.
Neither conclusion delivered us from the horror of
attributing the cruelty of nature to the workings of an
evil will, or could reconcile it with our impulses towards
justice, mercy, and a higher life.

A complete deliverance was offered by the discovery
of Circumstantial Selection: that is to say, of a method
by which horrors having every appearance of being
elaborately planned by some intelligent contriver are
only accidents without any moral significance at all.
Suppose a watcher from the stars saw a frightful accident produced by two crowded trains at full speed
crashing into one another! How could he conceive that

a catastrophe brought about by such elaborate machinery, such ingenious preparation, such skilled direction, such vigilant industry, was quite unintentional? Would he not conclude that the signal-men were devils?

Well, Circumstantial Selection is largely a theory of collisions: that is, a theory of the innocence of much apparently designed devilry. In this way Darwin brought intense relief as well as an enlarged knowledge of facts to the humanitarians. He destroyed the omnipotence of God for them; but he also exonerated God from a hideous charge of cruelty. Granted that the comfort was shallow, and that deeper reflection was bound to shew that worse than all conceivable devil-deities is a blind, deaf, dumb, heartless, senseless mob of forces that strike as a tree does when it is blown down by the wind, or as the tree itself is struck by lightning. That did not occur to the humanitarians at the moment: people do not reflect deeply when they are in the first happiness of escape from an intolerably oppressive situation. Like Bunyan's pilgrim they could not see the wicket gate, nor the Slough of Despond, nor the castle of Giant Despair; but they saw the shining light at the end of the path, and so started gaily towards it as Evolutionists.

And they were right; for the problem of evil yields very easily to Creative Evolution. If the driving power behind Evolution is omnipotent only in the sense that there seems no limit to its final achievement; and if it must meanwhile struggle with matter and circumstance by the method of trial and error, then the world must be full of its unsuccessful experiments. Christ may meet a tiger, or a High Priest arm-in-arm with a Roman Governor, and be the unfittest to survive under the circumstances. Mozart may have a genius that prevails against Emperors and Archbishops, and a lung that

succumbs to some obscure and noxious property of foul
air. If all our calamities are either accidents or sincerely
repented mistakes, there is no malice in the Cruelty of
Nature and no Problem of Evil in the Victorian sense
at all. The theology of the women who told us that they
became atheists when they sat by the cradles of their
children and saw them strangled by the hand of God is
succeeded by the theology of Blanco Posnet, with his
"It was early days when He made the croup, I guess.
It was the best He could think of then; but when it
turned out wrong on His hands He made you and me
to fight the Croup for Him."

How One Touch of Darwin Makes the Whole World Kin

Another humanitarian interest in Darwinism was that
Darwin popularized Evolution generally, as well as
making his own special contribution to it. Now the
general conception of Evolution provides the humanitarian with a scientific basis, because it establishes the
fundamental equality of all living things. It makes the
killing of an animal murder in exactly the same sense
as the killing of a man is murder. It is sometimes necessary to kill men as it is always necessary to kill tigers;
but the old theoretic distinction between the two acts has
been obliterated by Evolution. When I was a child and
was told that our dog and our parrot, with whom I was
on intimate terms, were not creatures like myself, but
were brutal whilst I was reasonable, I not only did not
believe it, but quite consciously and intellectually formed
the opinion that the distinction was false; so that afterwards, when Darwin's views were first unfolded to me, I
promptly said that I had found out all that for myself
before I was ten years old; and I am far from sure that

my youthful arrogance was not justified; for this sense
of the kinship of all forms of life is all that is needed to
make Evolution not only a conceivable theory, but an
inspiring one. St. Anthony was ripe for the Evolution
theory when he preached to the fishes, and St. Francis
when he called the birds his little brothers. Our vanity,
and our snobbish conception of Godhead as being, like
earthly kingship, a supreme class distinction instead of
the rock on which Equality is built, had led us to insist
on God offering us special terms by placing us apart
from and above all the rest of his creatures. Evolution
took that conceit out of us; and now, though we may
kill a flea without the smallest remorse, we at all events
know that we are killing our cousin. No doubt it shocks
the flea when the creature that an almighty Celestial
Flea created expressly for the food of fleas, destroys the
jumping lord of creation with his sharp and enormous
thumbnail; but no flea will ever be so foolish as to preach
that in slaying fleas Man is applying a method of
Natural Selection which will finally evolve a flea so swift
that no man can catch him, and so hardy of constitution
that Insect Powder will have no more effect on him than
strychnine on an elephant.

Why Darwin Pleased the Socialists

The Humanitarians were not alone among the agi-
tators in their welcome to Darwin. He had the luck to
please everybody who had an axe to grind. The militarists were as enthusiastic as the Humanitarians, the
Socialists as the Capitalists. The Socialists were
specially encouraged by Darwin's insistence on the influence of environment. Perhaps the strongest moral
bulwark of Capitalism is the belief in the efficacy of
individual righteousness. Robert Owen made desperate

efforts to convince England that her criminals, her drunkards, her ignorant and stupid masses, were the victims of circumstance: that if we would only establish his new moral world we should find that the masses born into an educated and moralized community would be themselves educated and moralized. The stock reply to this is to be found in Lewes's Life of Goethe. Lewes scorned the notion that circumstances govern character. He pointed to the variety of character in the governing rich class to prove the contrary. Similarity of circumstance can hardly be carried to a more desolating dead level than in the case of the individuals who are born and bred in English country houses, and sent first to Eton or Harrow, and then to Oxford or Cambridge, to have their minds and habits formed. Such a routine would destroy individuality if anything could. Yet individuals come out from it as different as Pitt from Fox, as Lord Russell from Lord Curzon, as Mr. Winston Churchill from Lord Robert Cecil. This acceptance of the congenital character of the individual as the determining factor in his destiny had been reinforced by the Lamarckian view of Evolution. If the giraffe can develop his neck by wanting and trying, a man can develop his character in the same way. The old saying, "Where there is a will, there is a way," condenses Lamarck's theory of functional adaptation into a proverb. This felt bracingly moral to strong minds, and reassuringly pious to feeble ones. There was no more effective retort to the Socialist than to tell him to reform himself before he pretends to reform society. If you were rich, how pleasant it was to feel that you owed your riches to the superiority of your own character! The industrial revolution had turned numbers of greedy dullards into monstrously rich men. Nothing could be more humiliating and threatening to them than the

view that the falling of a shower of gold into their
pockets was as pure an accident of our industrial
system as the falling of a shower of hail on their
umbrellas. Nothing could be more flattering and forti-
fying to them than the assumption that they were rich
because they were virtuous.

Now Darwinism made a clean sweep of all such self-
righteousness. It more than justified Robert Owen by
discovering in the environment of an organism an influence on it more patent than Owen had ever claimed. It
implied that street arabs are produced by slums and not
by original sin: that prostitutes are produced by starvation wages and not by feminine concupiscence. It threw
the authority of science on the side of the Socialist who
said that he who would reform himself must first reform
society. It suggested that if we want healthy and
wealthy citizens we must have healthy and wealthy
towns; and that these can exist only in healthy and
wealthy countries. It could be led to the conclusion
that the type of character which remains indifferent to
the welfare of its neighbors as long as its own personal
appetite is satisfied is the disastrous type, and the type
which is deeply concerned about its environment the only
possible type for a permanently prosperous community.
It shewed that the surprising changes which Robert
Owen had produced in factory children by a change in
their circumstances which does not seem any too generous to us nowadays, were as nothing to the changes—
changes not only of habits but of species, not only of
species but of orders—which might conceivably be the
work of environment acting on individuals without any
character or intellectual consciousness whatever. No
wonder the Socialists received Darwin with open arms.

Darwin and Karl Marx

Besides, the Socialists had an evolutionary prophet of
their own, who had discredited Manchester as Darwin
discredited the Garden of Eden. Karl Marx had proclaimed in his Communist Manifesto of 1848 (now
enjoying Scriptural authority in Russia) that civilization is an organism evolving irresistibly by circumstantial selection; and he published the first volume of
his Das Kapital in 1867. The revolt against anthropomorphic idolatry, which was, as we have seen, the secret
of Darwin's success, had been accompanied by a revolt
against the conventional respectability which covered
not only the brigandage and piracy of the feudal barons,
but the hypocrisy, inhumanity, snobbery, and greed of
the bourgeoisie, who were utterly corrupted by an
essentially diabolical identification of success in life with
big profits. The moment Marx shewed that the relation
of the bourgeoisie to society was grossly immoral and
disastrous, and that the whited wall of starched shirt
fronts concealed and defended the most infamous of all
tyrannies and the basest of all robberies, he became an
inspired prophet in the mind of every generous soul
whom his book reached. He had said and proved what
they wanted to have proved; and they would hear
nothing against him. Now Marx was by no means
infallible: his economics, half borrowed, and half home-
made by a literary amateur, were not, when strictly followed up, even favorable to Socialism. His theory of
civilization had been promulgated already in Buckle's
History of Civilization, a book as epoch-making in the
minds of its readers as Das Kapital. There was nothing
about Socialism in the widely read first volume of Das
Kapital: every reference it made to workers and capitalists shewed that Marx had never breathed industrial

air, and had dug his case out of bluebooks in the British
Museum. Compared to Darwin, he seemed to have no
power of observation: there was not a fact in Das
Kapital that had not been taken out of a book, nor a
discussion that had not been opened by somebody else's
pamphlet. No matter: he exposed the bourgeoisie and
made an end of its moral prestige. That was enough:
like Darwin he had for the moment the World Will by
the ear. Marx had, too, what Darwin had not: im-
placability and a fine Jewish literary gift, with terrible
powers of hatred, invective, irony, and all the bitter
qualities bred, first in the oppression of a rather pam-
pered young genius (Marx was the spoilt child of a
well-to-do family) by a social system utterly uncon-
genial to him, and later on by exile and poverty. Thus
Marx and Darwin between them toppled over two closely
related idols, and became the prophets of two new creeds.

Why Darwin Pleased the Profiteers Also

But how, at this rate, did Darwin succeed with the
capitalists too? It is not easy to make the best of both
worlds when one of the worlds is preaching a Class War,
and the other vigorously practising it. The explanation
is that Darwinism was so closely related to Capitalism
that Marx regarded it as an economic product rather
than as a biological theory. Darwin got his main
postulate, the pressure of population on the available
means of subsistence, from the treatise of Malthus on
Population, just as he got his other postulate of a
practically unlimited time for that pressure to operate
from the geologist Lyell, who made an end of Archbishop Ussher's Biblical estimate of the age of the earth
as 4004 B.C. plus A.D. The treatises of the Ricardian
economists on the Law of Diminishing Return, which

was only the Manchester School's version of the giraffe and the trees, were all very fiercely discussed when Darwin was a young man. In fact the discovery in the eighteenth century by the French Physiocrats of the economic effects of Commercial Selection in soils and sites, and by Malthus of a competition for subsistence which he attributed to pressure of population on available subsistence, had already brought political science into that unbreathable atmosphere of fatalism which is the characteristic blight of Darwinism. Long before Darwin published a line, the Ricardo-Malthusian economists were preaching the fatalistic Wages Fund doctrine, and assuring the workers that Trade Unionism is a vain defiance of the inexorable laws of political economy, just as the Neo-Darwinians were presently assuring us that Temperance Legislation is a vain defiance of Natural Selection, and that the true way to deal with drunkenness is to flood the country with cheap gin and let the fittest survive. Cobdenism is, after all, nothing but the abandonment of trade to Circumstantial Selection.

It is hardly possible to exaggerate the importance of this preparation for Darwinism by a vast political and clerical propaganda of its moral atmosphere. Never in history, as far as we know, had there been such a determined, richly subsidized, politically organized attempt to persuade the human race that all progress, all prosperity, all salvation, individual and social, depend on an unrestrained conflict for food and money, on the suppression and elimination of the weak by the strong, on Free Trade, Free Contract, Free Competition, Natural Liberty, Laisser-faire: in short, on "doing the other fellow down" with impunity, all interference by a guiding government, all organization except police organization to protect legalized fraud against fisticuffs,

all attempt to introduce human purpose and design and
forethought into the industrial welter being "contrary
to the laws of political economy." Even the proletariat
sympathized, though to them Capitalist liberty meant
only wage slavery without the legal safeguards of
chattel slavery. People were tired of governments and
kings and priests and providences, and wanted to find
out how Nature would arrange matters if she were let
alone. And they found it out to their cost in the days
when Lancashire used up nine generations of wage slaves
in one generation of their masters. But their masters,
becoming richer and richer, were very well satisfied; and
Bastiat proved convincingly that Nature had arranged
Economic Harmonies which would settle social questions
far better than theocracies or aristocracies or mobo-
cracies, the real *deus ex machina* being unrestrained
plutocracy.

The Poetry and Purity of Materialism

Thus the stars in their courses fought for Darwin.
Every faction drew a moral from him; every catholic
hater of faction founded a hope on him; every blackguard felt justified by him; and every saint felt encouraged by him. The notion that any harm could
come of so splendid an enlightenment seemed as silly as
the notion that the atheists would steal all our spoons.
The physicists went further than the Darwinians.
Tyndall declared that he saw in Matter the promise
and potency of all forms of life, and with his Irish
graphic lucidity made a picture of a world of magnetic
atoms, each atom with a positive and a negative pole,
arranging itself by attraction and repulsion in orderly
crystalline structure. Such a picture is dangerously
fascinating to thinkers oppressed by the bloody dis-

orders of the living world. Craving for purer subjects
of thought, they find in the contemplation of crystals
and magnets a happiness more dramatic and less childish
than the happiness found by the mathematicians in
abstract numbers, because they see in the crystals beauty
and movement without the corrupting appetites of
fleshly vitality.   In such Materialism as that of
Lucretius and Tyndall there is a nobility which produces
poetry: John Davidson found his highest inspiration in it.
Even its pessimism as it faces the cooling of the sun and
the return of the ice caps does not degrade the pessimist:
for example, the Quincy Adamses, with their insistence
on modern democratic degradation as an inevitable
result of solar shrinkage, are not dehumanized as the
vivisectionists are.   Perhaps nobody is at heart fool
enough to believe that life is at the mercy of temperature: Dante was not troubled by the objection that
Brunetto could not have lived in the fire nor Ugolino in
the ice.

But the physicists found their intellectual vision of
the world incommunicable to those who were not born
with it.   It came to the public simply as Materialism;
and Materialism lost its peculiar purity and dignity
when it entered into the Darwinian reaction against
Bible fetichism.   Between the two of them religion was
knocked to pieces; and where there had been a god, a
cause, a faith that the universe was ordered however
inexplicable by us its order might be, and therefore a
sense of moral responsibility as part of that order, there
was now an utter void.   Chaos had come again.   The
first effect was exhilarating: we had the runaway child's
sense of freedom before it gets hungry and lonely and
frightened.   In this phase we did not desire our God
back again.   We printed the verses in which William
Blake, the most religious of our great poets, called the

anthropomorphic idol Old Nobodaddy, and gibed at him
in terms which the printer had to leave us to guess from
his blank spaces. We had heard the parson droning that
God is not mocked; and it was great fun to mock Him
to our hearts' content and not be a penny the worse. It
did not occur to us that Old Nobodaddy, instead of
being a ridiculous fiction, might be only an imposter, and
that the exposure of this Koepenik Captain of the
heavens, far from proving that there was no real captain, rather proved the contrary: that, in short, Nobodaddy could not have impersonated anybody if there
had not been Somebodaddy to impersonate. We did not
see the significance of the fact that on the last occasion
on which God had been "expelled with a pitchfork," men
so different as Voltaire and Robespierre had said, the one
that if God did not exist it would be necessary to invent
him, and the other that after an honest attempt to dis-
pense with a Supreme Being in practical politics, some
such hypothesis had been found quite indispensable, and
could not be replaced by a mere Goddess of Reason. If
these two opinions were quoted at all, they were quoted
as jokes at the expense of Nobodaddy. We were quite
sure for the moment that whatever lingering superstition might have daunted these men of the eighteenth
century, we Darwinians could do without God, and had
made a good riddance of him.

The Viceroys of the King of Kings

Now in politics it is much easier to do without God
than to do without his viceroys and vicars and lieutenants; and we begin to miss the lieutenants long before
we begin to miss their principal. Roman Catholics do
what their confessors advise without troubling God; and
Royalists are content to worship the King and ask the

policeman.   But God's trustiest lieutenants often lack
official credentials.   They may be professed atheists who
are also men of honor and high public spirit.   The old
belief that it matters dreadfully to God whether a man
thinks himself an atheist or not, and that the extent to
which it matters can be stated with exactness as one
single damn, was an error; for the divinity is in the
honor and public spirit, not in the mouthed *credo* or *non
credo*.   The consequences of this error became grave
when the fitness of a man for public trust was tested,
not by his honor and public spirit, but by asking him
whether he believed in Nobodaddy or not.   If he said
yes, he was held fit to be a Prime Minister, though, as
our ablest Churchman has said, the real implication was
that he was either a fool, a bigot, or a liar.   Darwin
destroyed this test; but when it was only thoughtlessly
dropped, there was no test at all; and the door to public
trust was open to the man who had no sense of God
because he had no sense of anything beyond his own
business interests and personal appetites and ambitions.
As a result, the people who did not feel in the least inconvenienced by being no longer governed by Nobodaddy
soon found themselves very acutely inconvenienced by
being governed by fools and commercial adventurers.
They had forgotten not only God but Goldsmith, who
had warned them that "honor sinks where commerce long
prevails."

The lieutenants of God are not always persons: some
of them are legal and parliamentary fictions.   One of
them is Public Opinion.   The pre-Darwinian statesmen
and publicists were not restrained directly by God; but
they restrained themselves by setting up an image of a
Public Opinion which would not tolerate any attempt to
tamper with British liberties.   Their favorite way of
putting it was that any Government which proposed

such and such an infringement of such and such a British liberty would be hurled from office in a week. This was not true: there was no such public opinion, no limit to what the British people would put up with in the abstract, and no hardship short of immediate and sudden starvation that it would not and did not put up with in the concrete. But this very helplessness of the people had forced their rulers to pretend that they were not helpless, and that the certainty of a sturdy and unconquerable popular resistance forbade any trifling with Magna Carta or the Petition of Rights or the authority of parliament. Now the reality behind this fiction was the divine sense that liberty is a need vital to human growth. Accordingly, though it was difficult enough to effect a political reform, yet, once parliament had passed it, its wildest opponent had no hope that the Government would cancel it, or shelve it, or be bought off from executing it. From Walpole to Campbell Bannerman there was no Prime Minister to whom such renagueing or trafficking would ever have occurred, though there were plenty who employed corruption unsparingly to procure the votes of members of parliament for their policy.

Political Opportunism in Excelsis

The moment Nobodaddy was slain by Darwin, Public Opinion, as divine deputy, lost its sanctity. Politicians no longer told themselves that the British public would never suffer this or that: they allowed themselves to know that for their own personal purposes, which are limited to their ten or twenty years on the front benches in parliament, the British Public can be humbugged and coerced into believing and suffering everything that it pays to impose on them, and that any false excuse for an unpopular step will serve if it can be kept in countenance for a fortnight: that is, until the terms of the excuse are forgotten. The people, untaught or mistaught, are so ignorant and incapable politically that this in itself would not greatly matter; for a statesman who told them the truth would not be understood, and would in effect mislead them more completely than if he dealt with them according to their blindness instead of to his own wisdom. But though there is no difference in this respect between the best demagogue and the worst, both of them having to present their cases equally in terms of melo-drama, there is all the difference in the world between the statesman who is humbugging the people into allowing him to do the will of God, in whatever disguise it may come to him, and one who is humbugging them into furthering his personal ambition and the commercial interests of the plutocrats who own the newspapers and support him on reciprocal terms. And there is almost as great a difference between the statesman who does this naively and automatically, or even does it telling himself that he is ambitious and selfish and unscrupulous, and the one who does it on principle, believing that if everyone takes the line of least material resistance the result will be the survival of the fittest in a perfectly harmonious universe. Once produce an atmosphere of fatalism on principle, and it matters little what the opinions or superstitions of the individual statesmen concerned may be. A Kaiser who is a devout reader of sermons, a Prime Minister who is an emotional singer of hymns, and a General who is a bigoted Roman Catholic may be the executants of the policy; but the policy itself will be one of unprincipled opportunism; and all the Governments will be like the tramp who walks always with the wind and ends as a pauper, or the stone that rolls down the hill and ends as an avalanche: their way is the way to destruction.

The Betrayal of Western Civilization

Within sixty years from the publication of Darwin's
Origin of Species political opportunism had brought
parliaments into contempt; created a popular demand for
direct action by the organized industries ("Syndical-
ism"); and wrecked the centre of Europe in a paroxysm
of that chronic terror of one another, that cowardice of
the irreligious, which, masked in the bravado of militarist patriotism, had ridden the Powers like a night-
mare since the Franco-Prussian war of 1870–71. The
sturdy old cosmopolitan Liberalism vanished almost unnoticed. At the present moment all the new ordinances
for the government of our Crown Colonies contain, as a
matter of course, prohibitions of all criticism, spoken
or written, of their ruling officials, which would have
scandalized George III and elicited Liberal pamphlets
from Catherine II. Statesmen are afraid of the suburbs,
of the newspapers, of the profiteers, of the diplomatists,
of the militarists, of the country houses, of the trade
unions, of everything ephemeral on earth except the
revolutions they are provoking; and they would be
afraid of these if they were not too ignorant of society
and history to appreciate the risk, and to know that a
revolution always seems hopeless and impossible the day
before it breaks out, and indeed never does break out
until it seems hopeless and impossible; for rulers who
think it possible take care to insure the risk by ruling
reasonably. This brings about a condition fatal to all
political stability: namely, that you never know where
to have the politicians. If the fear of God was in them
it might be possible to come to some general understanding as to what God disapproves of; and Europe might
pull together on that basis. But the present panic,
in which Prime Ministers drift from election to election,

either fighting or running away from everybody who
shakes a fist at them, makes a European civilization impossible.   Such peace and prosperity as we enjoyed
before the war depended on the loyalty of the Western
States to their own civilization.   That loyalty could find
practical expression only in an alliance of the highly
civilized Western Powers against the primitive tyrannies
of the East.   Britain, Germany, France, and the United
States of America could have imposed peace on the
world, and nursed modern civilization in Russia, Turkey,
and the Balkans.   Every meaner consideration should
have given way to this need for the solidarity of the
higher civilization.   What actually happened was that
France and England, through their clerks the diplomatists, made an alliance with Russia to defend themselves
against Germany; Germany made an alliance with
Turkey to defend herself against the three; and the two
unnatural and suicidal combinations fell on one another
in a war that came nearer to being a war of extermina-
tion than any wars since those of Timur the Tartar;
whilst the United States held aloof as long as they could,
and the other States either did the same or joined in the
fray through compulsion, bribery, or their judgment
as to which side their bread was buttered.   And at the
present moment, though the main fighting has ceased
through the surrender of Germany on terms which the
victors have never dreamt of observing, the extermina-
tion by blockade and famine, which was what forced
Germany to surrender, still continues, although it is
certain that if the vanquished starve the victors will
starve too, and Europe will liquidate its affairs by going,
not into bankruptcy, but into chaos.

Now all this it will be noticed, was fundamentally
nothing but an idiotic attempt on the part of each bel-
ligerent State to secure for itself the advantage of the

survival of the fittest through Circumstantial Selection.
If the Western Powers had selected their allies in the
Lamarckian manner intelligently, purposely ,and vitally,
ad majorem Dei gloriam, as what Nietzsche called good
Europeans, there would have been a League of Nations
and no war.   But because the selection relied on was
purely circumstantial opportunist selection, so that the
alliances were mere marriages of convenience, they have
turned out, not merely as badly as might have been expected, but far worse than the blackest pessimist had
ever imagined possible.

Circumstantial Selection in Finance

How it will all end we do not yet know.   When wolves
combine to kill a horse, the death of the horse only sets
them fighting one another for the choicest morsels.   Men
are no better than wolves if they have no better principles : accordingly, we find that the Armistice and the
Treaty have not extricated us from the war.   A hand-
ful of Serbian assassins flung us into it as a sporting
navvy throws a bull pup at a cat; but the Supreme
Council, with all its victorious legions and all its prestige, cannot get us out of it, though we are heartily sick
and tired of the whole business, and know now very well
that it should never have been allowed to happen.   But
we are helpless before a slate scrawled with figures of
National Debts.   As there is no money to pay them because it was all spent on the war (wars have to be paid
for on the nail) the sensible thing to do is to wipe the
slate and let the wrangling States distribute what they
can spare, on the sound communist principle of from
each according to his ability, to each according to his
need.   But no : we have no principles left, not even commercial ones ; for what sane commercialist would decree

that France must not pay for her failure to defend her
own soil; that Germany must pay for her success in
carrying the war into the enemy's country; and that as
Germany has not the money to pay, and under our commercial system can make it only by becoming once more
a commercial competitor of England and France, which
neither of them will allow, she must borrow the money
from England, or America, or even from France: an
arrangement by which the victorious creditors will pay
one another, and wait to get their money back until
Germany is either strong enough to refuse to pay or
ruined beyond the possibility of paying?   Meanwhile
Russia, reduced to a scrap of fish and a pint of cabbage
soup a day, has fallen into the hands of rulers who per-
ceive that Materialist Communism is at all events more
effective than Materialist Nihilism, and are attempting
to move in an intelligent and ordered manner, practising
a very strenuous Intentional Selection of workers as
fitter to survive than idlers; whilst the Western Powers
are drifting and colliding and running on the rocks, in
the hope that if they continue to do their worst they will
get Naturally Selected for survival without the trouble
of thinking about it.

The Homeopathic Reaction Against Darwinism

When, like the Russians our Nihilists have it urgently
borne in on them, by the brute force of rising wages that
never overtake rising prices, that they are being Naturally Selected for destruction, they will perhaps remember that "Dont Care came to a bad end," and begin to
look round for a religion.   And the whole purpose of
this book is to shew them where to look.   For, throughout all the godless welter of the infidel half-century,
Darwinism has been acting not only directly but homeo-

pathically, its poison rallying our vital forces not only
to resist it and cast it out, but to achieve a new Reformation and put a credible and healthy religion in its place.
Samuel Butler was the pioneer of the reaction as far as
the casting out was concerned; but the issue was confused by the physiologists, who were divided on the question into Mechanists and Vitalists. The Mechanists said
that life is nothing but physical and chemical action;
that they have demonstrated this in many cases of so-
called vital phenomena; and that there is no reason to
doubt that with improved methods they will presently be
able to demonstrate it in all of them. The Vitalists said
that a dead body and a live one are physically and chemically identical, and that the difference can be accounted
for only by the existence of a Vital Force. This seems
simple; but the Anti-Mechanists objected to be called Vitalists (obviously the right name for them) on two con-
tradictory grounds. First, that vitality is scientifically
inadmissible, because it cannot be isolated and experi-
mented with in the laboratory. Second, that force, being
by definition anything that can alter the speed or direction, of matter in motion (briefly, that can overcome
inertia), is essentially a mechanistic conception. Here
we had the New Vitalist only half extricated from the
Old Mechanist, objecting to be called either, and unable
to give a clear lead in the new direction. And there was
a deeper antagonism. The Old Vitalists, in postulating
a Vital Force, were setting up a comparatively mechanical conception as against the divine idea of the life
breathed into the clay nostrils of Adam, whereby he became a living soul. The New Vitalists, filled by their
laboratory researches with a sense of the miraculousness
of life that went far beyond the comparatively unin-
formed imaginations of the authors of the Book of Genesis, regarded the Old Vitalists as Mechanists who had

tried to fill up the gulf between life and death with an empty phrase denoting an imaginary physical force.

These professional faction fights are ephemeral, and need not trouble us here. The Old Vitalist, who was essentially a Materialist, has evolved into the New Vitalist, who is, as every genuine scientist must be, finally a metaphysician. And as the New Vitalist turns from the disputes of his youth to the future of his science, he will cease to boggle at the name Vitalist, or at the inevitable, ancient, popular, and quite correct use of the term Force to denote metaphysical as well as physical overcomers of inertia.

Since the discovery of Evolution as the method of the Life Force, the religion of metaphysical Vitalism has been gaining the definiteness and concreteness needed to make it assimilable by the educated critical man. But it has always been with us. The popular religions, disgraced by their Opportunist cardinals and bishops, have been kept in credit by canonized saints whose secret was their conception of themselves as the instruments and vehicles of divine power and aspiration: a conception which at moments becomes an actual experience of ecstatic possession by that power. And above and below all have been millions of humble and obscure persons, sometimes totally illiterate, sometimes unconscious of having any religion at all, sometimes believing in their simplicity that the gods and temples and priests of their district stood for their instinctive righteousness, who have kept sweet the tradition that good people follow a light that shines within and above and ahead of them, that bad people care only for themselves, and that the good are saved and blessed and the bad damned and miserable. Protestantism was a movement towards the pursuit of a light called an inner light because every man must see it with his own eyes and not take any priest's words for it or any Church's account of it. In short, there is no question of a new religion, but rather of redistilling the eternal spirit of religion and thus extricating it from the sludgy residue of temporalities and legends that are making belief impossible, though they are the stock-in-trade of all the Churches and all the Schools.

Religion and Romance

It is the adulteration of religion by the romance of miracles and paradises and torture chambers that makes it reel at the impact of every advance in science, instead of being clarified by it. If you take an English village lad, and teach him that religion means believing that the stories of Noah's Ark and the Garden of Eden are literally true on the authority of God himself, and if that boy becomes an artisan and goes into the town among the sceptical city proletariat, then, when the jibes of his mates set him thinking, and he sees that these stories cannot be literally true, and learns that no candid prelate now pretends to believe them, he does not make any fine distinctions: he declares at once that religion is a fraud, and parsons and teachers hypocrites and liars. He becomes indifferent to religion if he has little conscience, and indignantly hostile to it if he has a good deal.

The same revolt against wantonly false teaching is happening daily in the professional classes whose recreation is reading and whose intellectual sport is controversy. They banish the Bible from their houses, and sometimes put into the hands of their unfortunate children Ethical and Rationalist tracts of the deadliest dullness, compelling these wretched infants to sit out the discourses of Secularist lecturers (I have delivered some

of them myself), who bore them at a length now forbidden by custom in the established pulpit. Our minds
have reacted so violently towards provable logical theo-
rems and demonstrable mechanical or chemical facts that
we have become incapable of metaphysical truth, and
try to cast out incredible and silly lies by credible and
clever ones, calling in Satan to cast out Satan, and
getting more into his clutches than ever in the process.
Thus the world is kept sane less by the saints than by
the vast mass of the indifferent, who neither act nor
react in the matter. Butler's preaching of the gospel
of Laoddica was a piece of common sense founded on
his observation of this.

But indifference will not guide nations through civilization to the establishment of the perfect city of God.
An indifferent statesman is a contradiction in terms;
and a statesman who is indifferent on principle, a Laisser-faire or Muddle-Through doctrinaire, plays the deuce
with us in the long run. Our statesmen must get a
religion by hook or crook; and as we are committed to
Adult Suffrage it must be a religion capable of vulgari-
zation. The thought first put into words by the Mills
when they said "There is no God; but this is a family
secret," and long held unspoken by aristocratic statesmen and diplomatists, will not serve now; for the revival
of civilization after the war cannot be effected by artificial
breathing: the driving force of an undeluded popular
consent is indispensable, and will be impossible until the
statesman can appeal to the vital instincts of the people
in terms of a common religion. The success of the Hang
the Kaiser cry at the last General Election shews us very
terrifyingly how a common irreligion can be used by
myopic demagogy; and common irreligion will destroy
civilization unless it is countered by common religion.

The Danger of Reaction

And here arises the danger that when we realize this we shall do just what we did half a century ago, and what Pliable did in The Pilgrim's Progress when Christian landed him in the Slough of Despond: that is, run back in terror to our old superstitions. We jumped out of the frying-pan into the fire; and we are just as likely to jump back again, now that we feel hotter than ever. History records very little in the way of mental activity on the part of the mass of mankind except a series of stampedes from affirmative errors into negative ones and back again. It must therefore be said very precisely and clearly that the bankruptcy of Darwinism does not mean that Nobodaddy was Somebodaddy *with* "body, parts, and passions" after all; that the world was made in the year 4004 B.C.; that damnation means an eternity of blazing brimstone; that the Immaculate Conception means that sex is sinful and that Christ was parthenogenetically brought forth by a virgin descended in like manner from a line of virgins right back to Eve; that the Trinity is an anthropomorphic monster with three heads which are yet only one head; that in Rome the bread and wine on the altar become flesh and blood, and in England, in a still more mystical manner, they do and they do not; that the Bible is an infallible scientific manual, an accurate historical chronicle, and a complete guide to conduct; that we may lie and cheat and murder and then wash ourselves innocent in the blood of the lamb on Sunday at the cost of a *credo* and a penny in the plate, and so on and so forth. Civilization cannot be saved by people not only crude enough to believe these things, but irreligious enough to believe that such belief constitutes a religion. The education of children cannot safely be left in their hands. If dwindling sects like the Church of England, the Church of Rome, the Greek Church, and the rest, persist in trying to cramp the human mind within the limits of these grotesque perversions of natural truths and poetic metaphors, then they must be ruthlessly banished from the schools until they either perish in general contempt or discover the soul that is hidden in every dogma. The real Class War will be a war of intellectual classes; and its conquest will be the souls of the children.

A Touchstone for Dogma

The test of a dogma is its universality. As long as the Church of England preaches a single doctrine that the Brahman, the Buddhist, the Mussulman, the Parsee, and all the other sectarians who are British subjects cannot accept, it has no legitimate place in the counsels of the British Commonwealth, and will remain what it is at present, a corrupter of youth, a danger to the State, and an obstruction to the fellowship of the Holy Ghost. This has never been more strongly felt than at present, after a war in which the Church failed grossly in the courage of its profession, and sold its lilies for the laurels of the soldiers of the Victoria Cross. All the cocks in Christendom have been crowing shame on it ever since; and it will not be spared for the sake of the two or three faithful who were found even among the bishops. Let the Church take it on authority, even my authority (as a professional legend maker) if it cannot see the truth by its own light: no dogma can be a legend. A legend can pass an ethnical frontier as a legend, but not as a truth; whilst the only frontier to the currency of a sound dogma as such is the frontier of capacity for understanding it.

This does not mean that we should throw away legend

and parable and drama: they are the natural vehicles of
dogma; but woe to the Churches and rulers who substitute the legend for the dogma, the parable for the history, the drama for the religion! Better by far declare
the throne of God empty than set a liar and a fool on
it.   What are called wars of religion are always wars
to destroy religion by affirming the historical truth or
material substantiality of some legend, and killing those
who refuse to accept it as historical or substantial.   But
who has ever refused to accept a good legend with delight
as a legend?   The legends, the parables, the dramas, are
among the choicest treasures of mankind.   No one is
ever tired of stories of miracles.   In vain did Mahomet
repudiate the miracles ascribed to him: in vain did Christ
furiously scold those who asked him to give them an
exhibition as a conjuror: in vain did the saints declare
that God chose them not for their powers but for their
weaknesses; that the humble might be exalted, and the
proud rebuked.   People will have their miracles, their
stories, their heroes and heroines and saints and martyrs
and divinities to exercise their gifts of affection, admi-
ration, wonder, and worship, and their Judases and
devils to enable them to be angry and yet feel that they
do well to be angry.   Every one of these legends is the
common heritage of the human race; and there is only
one inexorable condition attached to their healthy enjoy-
ment, which is that no one shall believe them literally.
The reading of stories and delighting in them made
Don Quixote a gentleman: the believing them literally
made him a madman who slew lambs instead of feeding
them.   In England to-day good books of Eastern religious legends are read eagerly; and Protestants and
Atheists read Roman Catholic legends of the Saints with
pleasure.   But such fare is shirked by Indians and
Roman Catholics.   Freethinkers read the Bible: indeed

they seem to be its only readers now except the reluctant
parsons at the church lecterns, who communicate their
discomfort to the congregation by gargling the words
in their throats in an unnatural manner that is as repul-
sive as it is unintelligible. And this is because the im-
position of the legends as literal truths at once changes
them from parables into falsehoods. The feeling
against the Bible has become so strong at last that educated people not only refuse to outrage their intellectual
consciences by reading the legend of Noah's Ark, with
its funny beginning about the animals and its exquisite
end about the birds: they will not read even the chronicles
of King David, which may very well be true, and are
certainly more candid than the official biographies of
our contemporary monarchs.

What to Do With the Legends

What we should do, then, is to pool our legends and
make a delightful stock of religious folk-lore on an
honest basis for all mankind. With our minds freed
from pretence and falsehood we could enter into the
heritage of all the faiths. China would share her sages
with Spain, and Spain her saints with China. The
Ulster man who now gives his son an unmerciful thrash-
ing if the boy is so tactless as to ask how the evening
and the morning could be the first day before the sun
was created, or to betray an innocent calf-love for the
Virgin Mary, would buy him a bookful of legends of
the creation and of mothers of God from all parts of
the world, and be very glad to find his laddie as interested in such things as in marbles or Police and Rob-
bers. That would be better than beating all good feeling towards religion out of the child, and blackening
his mind by teaching him that the worshippers of the

holy virgins, whether of the Parthenon or St. Peter's, are fire-doomed heathens and idolaters. All the sweetness of religion is conveyed to the world by the hands of story-tellers and image-makers. Without their fictions the truths of religion would for the multitude be neither intelligible nor even apprehensible; and the prophets would prophesy and the teachers teach in vain. And nothing stands between the people and the fictions except the silly falsehood that the fictions are literal truths, and that there is nothing in religion but fiction.

A Lesson from Science to the Churches

Let the Churches ask themselves why there is no revolt against the dogmas of mathematics though there is one against the dogmas of religion. It is not that the mathematical dogmas are more comprehensible. The law of inverse squares is as incomprehensible to the common man as the Athanasian creed. It is not that science is free from legends, witchcraft, miracles, biographic boostings of quacks as heroes and saints, and of barren scoundrels as explorers and discoverers. On the contrary, the iconography and hagiology of Scientism are as copious as they are mostly squalid. But no student of science has yet been taught that specific gravity consists in the belief that Archimedes jumped out of his bath and ran naked through the streets of Syracuse shouting Eureka, Eureka, or that the law of inverse squares must be discarded if anyone can prove that Newton was never in an orchard in his life. When some unusually conscientious or enterprising bacteriologist reads the pamphlets of Jenner, and discovers that they might have been written by an ignorant but curious and observant nurserymaid, and could not possibly have been written by any person with

a scientifically trained mind, he does not feel that the
whole edifice of science has collapsed and crumbled, and
that there is no such thing as smallpox. It may come
to that yet; for hygiene, as it forces its way into our
schools, is being taught as falsely as religion is taught
there; but in mathematics and physics the faith is still
kept pure, and you may take the law and leave the
legends without suspicion of heresy. Accordingly, the
tower of the mathematician stands unshaken whilst the
temple of the priest rocks to its foundation.

The Religious art of the Twentieth Century

Creative Evolution is already a religion, and is indeed
now unmistakably the religion of the twentieth century,
newly arisen from the ashes of pseudo-Christianity, of
mere scepticism, and of the soulless affirmations and
blind negations of the Mechanists and Neo-Darwinians.
But it cannot become a popular religion until it has its
legends, its parables, its miracles. And when I say popular I do not mean apprehensible by villagers only. I
mean apprehensible by Cabinet Ministers as well. It is
unreasonable to look to the professional politician and
administrator for light and leading in religion. He is
neither a philosopher nor a prophet: if he were, he would
be philosophizing and prophesying, and not neglecting
both for the drudgery of practical government. Soc-
rates and Coleridge did not remain soldiers, nor could
John Stuart Mill remain the representative of Westminster in the House of Commons even when he was
willing. The Westminster electors admired Mill for
telling them that much of the difficulty of dealing with
them arose from their being inveterate liars. But they
would not vote a second time for the man who was not
afraid to break the crust of mendacity on which they

were all dancing; for it seemed to them that there was a volcanic abyss beneath, not having his philosophic conviction that the truth is the solidest standing ground in the end. Your front bench man will always be an exploiter of the popular religion or irreligion. Not being an expert, he must take it as he finds it; and before he can take it, he must have been told stories about it in his childhood and had before him all his life an elaborate iconography of it produced by writers, painters, sculptors, temple architects, and artists of all the higher sorts. Even if, as sometimes happens, he is a bit of an amateur, in metaphysics as well as a professional politician, he must still govern according to the popular iconography, and not according to his own personal interpretations if these happen to be heterodox.

It will be seen then that the revival of religion on a scientific basis does not mean the death of art, but a glorious rebirth of it. Indeed art has never been great when it was not providing an iconography for a live religion. And it has never been quite contemptible except when imitating the iconography after the religion had become a superstition. Italian painting from Giotto to Carpaccio is all religious painting; and it moves us deeply and has real greatness. Compare with it the attempts of our painters a century ago to achieve the effects of the old masters by imitation when they should have been illustrating a faith of their own. Contemplate, if you can bear it, the dull daubs of Hilton and Haydon, who knew so much more about drawing and scumbling and glazing and perspective and anatomy and "marvellous foreshortening" than Giotto, the latchet of whose shoe they were nevertheless not worthy to unloose. Compare Mozart's Magic Flute, Beethoven's Ninth Symphony, Wagner's Ring, all of them reachings-forward to the new Vitalist art, with the dreary pseudo-

sacred oratories and cantatas which were produced for
no better reason than that Handel had formerly made
splendid thunder in that way, and with the stale confectionery, mostly too would-be pious to be even cheerfully
toothsome, of Spohr and Mendelssohn, Stainer and
Parry, which spread indigestion at our musical festivals
until I publicly told Parry the bludgeoning truth about
his Job and woke him to conviction of sin.   Compare
Flaxman and Thorwaldsen and Gibson and Phidias and
Praxiteles, Stevens with Michael Angelo, Bouguereau's
Virgin with Cimabue's, or the best operatic Christs of
Scheffer and Müller with the worst Christs that the
worst painters could paint before the end of the fifteenth
century, and you must feel that until we have a great
religious movement we cannot hope for a great artistic
one.   The disillusioned Raphael could paint a mother
and child, but not a queen of Heaven as much less skilful men had done in the days of his great-grandfather;
yet he could reach forward to the twentieth century and
paint a Transfiguration of the Son of Man as they could
not.   Also, please note, he could decorate a house of
pleasure for a cardinal very beautifully with voluptuous
pictures of Cupid and Psyche; for this simple sort of
Vitalism is always with us, and, like portrait painting,
keeps the artist supplied with subject matter in the in-
tervals between the ages of faith; so that your sceptical
Rembrandts and Velasquezs are at least not compelled
to paint shop fronts for want of anything else to paint
in which they can really believe.

The Artist-Prophets

And there are always certain rare but intensely interesting anticipations.   Michael Angelo could not very well
believe in Julius II or Leo X, or in much that they be-

lieved in; but he could paint the Superman three hundred years before Nietzsche wrote Also Sprach Zarathustra and Strauss set it to music. Michael Angelo won the primacy among all modern painters and sculptors solely by his power of shewing us superhuman persons. On the strength of his decoration and color alone he would hardly have survived his own death twenty years; and even his design would have had only an academic interest; but as a painter of prophets and sibyls he is greatest among the very greatest in his craft, because we aspire to a world of prophets and sybils. Beethoven never heard of radio-activity nor of electrons dancing in vortices of inconceivable energy; but pray can anyone explain the last movement of his Hammerklavier Sonata, Opus 106, otherwise than as a musical picture of these whirling electrons? His contemporaries said he was mad, partly perhaps because the movement was so hard to play; but we, who can make a pianola play it to us over and over until it is as familiar as Pop Goes the Weasel, know that it is sane and methodical. As such, it must represent something; and as all Beethoven's serious compositions represent some process within himself, some nerve storm or soul storm, and the storm here is clearly one of physical movement, I should much like to know what other storm than the atomic storm could have driven him to this oddest of all those many expressions of cyclonic energy which have given him the same distinction among musicians that Michael Angelo has among draughtsmen.

In Beethoven's day the business of art was held to be "the sublime and beautiful." In our day it has fallen to be the imitative and voluptuous. In both periods the word passionate has been freely employed; but in the eighteenth century passion meant irresistible impulse of the loftiest kind: for example, a passion for astronomy or fo. truth. For us it has come to mean concupiscence and nothing else. One might say to the art of Europe what Antony said to the corpse of Cæsar: "Are all thy conquests, glories, triumphs, spoils, shrunk to this little measure?" But in fact it is the mind of Europe that has shrunk, being, as we have seen, wholly preoccupied with a busy spring-cleaning to get rid of its superstitions before readjusting itself to the new conception of Evolution.

Evolution in the Theatre

On the stage (and here I come at last to my own particular function in the matter), Comedy, as a destructive, derisory, critical, negative art, kept the theatre open when sublime tragedy perished. From Molière to Oscar Wilde we had a line of comedic playwrights who, if they had nothing fundamentally positive to say, were at least in revolt against falsehood and imposture, and were not only, as they claimed, "chastening morals by ridicule," but, in Johnson's phrase, clearing out minds of cant, and thereby shewing an uneasiness in the presence of error which is the surest symptom of intellectual vitality. Meanwhile the name of Tragedy was assumed by plays in which everyone was killed in the last act, just as, in spite of Molière, plays in which everyone was married in the last act called themselves comedies. Now neither tragedies nor comedies can be produced according to a prescription which gives only the last moments of the last act. Shakespear did not make Hamlet out of its final butchery, nor Twelfth Night out of its final matrimony. And he could not become the conscious iconographer of a religion because he had no conscious religion. He had therefore to exercise his extraordinary natural gifts in the very entertaining art of mimicry, giving us the famous "delineation of character" which make his plays, like the novels of Scott, Dumas, and Dickens, so delightful. Also, he developed that curious and questionable art of building us a refuge from despair by disguising the cruelties of Nature as jokes. But with all his gifts, the fact remains that he never found the inspiration to write an original play. He furbished up old plays, and adapted popular stories, and chapters of history from Holinshed's Chronicle and Plutarch's biographies, to the stage. All this he did (or did not; for there are minus quantities in the algebra of art) with a recklessness which shewed that his trade lay far from his conscience. It is true that he never takes his characters from the borrowed story, because it was less trouble and more fun to him to create them afresh; but none the less he heaps the murders and villainies of the borrowed story on his own essentially gentle creations without scruple, no matter how incongruous they may be. And all the time his vital need for a philosophy drives him to seek one by the quaint professional method of introducing philosophers as characters into his plays, and even of making his heroes philosophers; but when they come on the stage they have no philosophy to expound: they are only pessimists and railers; and their occasional would-be philosophic speeches, such as The Seven Ages of Man and The Soliloquy on Suicide, shew how deeply in the dark Shakespear was as to what philosophy means. He forced himself in among the greatest of playwrights without having once entered that region in which Michael Angelo, Beethoven, Goethe, and the antique Athenian stage poets are great. He would really not be great at all if it were not that he had religion enough to be aware that his religionless condition was one of despair. His greatest work, Lear, would be only a melodrama were it not for its express admission that if there is nothing more to be said of the universe than Hamlet has to say, then "as flies to wanton boys so we are to the gods: they kill us for their sport."

Ever since Shakespear, playwrights have been struggling with the same lack of religion; and many of them were forced to become mere panders and sensation-mongers because, though they had higher ambitions, they could find no better subject matter. From Congreve to Sheridan they were so sterile in spite of their wit that they did not achieve between them the output of Molière's single lifetime; and they were all (not without reason) ashamed of their profession, and preferred to be regarded as mere men of fashion with a rakish hobby. Goldsmith's was the only saved soul in that pandemonium.

The leaders among my own contemporaries (now veterans) snatched at minor social problems rather than write entirely without any wider purpose than to win money and fame. One of them expressed to me his envy of the ancient Greek playwrights because the Athenians asked them, not for some "new and original" disguise of the half-dozen threadbare plots of the modern theatre, but for the deepest lesson they could draw from the familiar and sacred legends of their country. "Let us all," he said, "write an Electra, an Antigone, an Agamemnon, and shew what we can do with it." But he did not write any of them, because these legends are no longer religious: Aphrodite and Artemis and Poseidon are deader than their statues. Another, with a commanding position and every trick of British farce and Parisian drama at his fingers' ends, finally could not write without a sermon to preach, and yet could not find texts more fundamental than the hypocrisies of sham Puritanism, or the matrimonial speculation which makes our young actresses as careful of their reputations as of

their complexions. A third, too tender-hearted, to break
our spirits with the realities of a bitter experience,
coaxed a wistful pathos and a dainty fun out of the
fairy cloudland that lay between him and the empty
heavens. The giants of the theatre of our time, Ibsen
and Strindberg, had no greater comfort for the world
than we: indeed much less; for they refused us even the
Shakespearian-Dickensian consolation of laughter at
mischief, accurately called comic relief. Our emanci-
pated young successors scorn us, very properly. But
they will be able to do no better whilst the drama remains
pre-Evolutionist. Let them consider the great exception
of Goethe. He, no richer than Shakespear, Ibsen, or
Strindberg in specific talent as a playwright, is in the
empyrean whilst they are gnashing their teeth in im-
potent fury in the mud, or at best finding an acid enjoy-
ment in the irony of their predicament. Goethe is
Olympian: the other giants are infernal in everything
but their veracity and their repudiation of the irreligion
of their time: that is, they are bitter and hopeless. It
is not a question of mere dates. Goethe was an
Evolutionist in 1830: many playwrights, even young
ones, are still untouched by Creative Evolution in 1920.
Ibsen was Darwinized to the extent of exploiting
heredity on the stage much as the ancient Athenian playwrights exploited the Eumenides; but there is no trace
in his plays of any faith in or knowledge of Creative
Evolution as a modern scientific fact, though the poetic
aspiration is plain enough in his Emperor or Galilean;
and as it is one of Ibsen's great distinctions that nothing
was valid for him but science, he left that vision of the
future which his Roman seer calls "the third Empire"
behind him as a Utopian dream when he settled down to
his serious grapple with realities in those plays of
modern life with which he overcame Europe and broke

the dusty windows of every dry-rotten theatre in it from Moscow to Manchester.

My Own Part in the Matter

In my own activities as a playwright I found this state of things intolerable. The fashionable theatre prescribed one serious subject: clandestine adultery: the dullest of all subjects for a serious author, whatever it may be for audiences who read the police intelligence and skip the reviews and leading articles. I tried slumlandlordism, doctrinaire Free Love (pseudo-Ibsenism), prostitution, militarism, marriage, history, current politics, natural Christianity, national and individual character, paradoxes of conventional society, husbandhunting, questions of conscience, professional delusions and impostures, all worked into a series of comedies of manners in the classic fashion, which was then very much out of fashion, the mechanical tricks of Parisian "construction" being *de rigueur* in the theatre. But this, though it occupied me and established me professionally, did not constitute me an iconographer of the religion of my time, and thus fulfil my natural function as an artist. I was quite conscious of this; for I had always known that civilization needs a religion as a matter of life or death; and as the conception of Creative Evolution developed I saw that we were at last within reach of a faith which complied with the first condition of all the religions that have ever taken hold of humanity: namely, that it must be, first and fundamentally, a science of metabiology. This was a crucial point with me; for I had seen Bible fetichism, after standing up to all the rationalistic batteries of Hume, Voltaire, and the rest, collapse before the onslaught of much less gifted Evolutionists, solely because they discredited it as a biological document; so that from that moment it lost its hold, and left literate Christendom faithless. My own Irish eighteenth-centuryism made it impossible for me to believe anything until I could conceive it as a scientific hypothesis, even though the abominations, quackeries, impostures, venalities, credulities, and delusions of the camp followers of science, and the brazen lies and priestly pretensions of the pseudo-scientific cure-mongers, all sedulously inculcated by modern "secondary education," were so monstrous that I was sometimes forced to make a verbal distinction between science and knowledge lest I should mislead my readers. But I never forgot that without knowledge even wisdom is more dangerous than mere opportunist ignorance, and that somebody must take the Garden of Eden in hand and weed it properly.

Accordingly, in 1901, I took the legend of Don Juan in its Mozartian form and made it a dramatic parable of Creative Evolution. But being then at the height of my invention and comedic talent, I decorated it too brilliantly and lavishly. I surrounded it with a comedy of which it formed only one act, and that act was so completely episodical (it was a dream which did not affect the action of the piece) that the comedy could be detached and played by itself: indeed it could hardly be played at full length owing to the enormous length of the entire work, though that feat has been performed a few times in Scotland by Mr. Esmé Percy, who led one of the forlorn hopes of the advanced drama at that time. Also I supplied the published work with an imposing framework consisting of a preface, an appendix called The Revolutionist's Handbook, and a final display of aphoristic fireworks. The effect was so vertiginous, apparently, that nobody noticed the new religion in the centre of the intellectual whirlpool. Now I protest I did not cut these cerebral capers in mere inconsiderate exuberance. I did it because the worst convention of the criticism of the theatre current at that time was that intellectual seriousness is out of place on the stage; that the theatre is a place of shallow amusement; that people go there to be soothed after the enormous intellectual strain of a day in the city: in short, that a playwright is a person whose business it is to make unwholesome confectionery out of cheap emotions. My answer to this was to put all my intellectual goods in the shop window under the sign of Man and Superman. That part of my design succeeded. By good luck and acting, the comedy triumphed on the stage; and the book was a good deal discussed. Since then the sweet-shop view of the theatre has been out of countenance; and its critical exponents have been driven to take an intellectual pose which, though often more trying than their old intellectually nihilistic vulgarity, at least concedes the dignity of the theatre, not to mention the usefulness of those who live by criticizing it. And the younger playwrights are not only taking their art seriously, but being taken seriously themselves. The critic who ought to be a newsboy is now comparatively rare.

I now find myself inspired to make a second legend of Creative Evolution without distractions and embellishments. My sands are running out; the exuberance of 1901 has aged into the garrulity of 1920; and the war has been a stern intimation that the matter is not one to be trifled with. I abandon the legend of Don Juan with its erotic associations, and go back to the legend of the Garden of Eden. I exploit the eternal interest of the philosopher's stone which enables men to live for ever. I am not, I hope, under more illusion than is humanly inevitable as to the crudity of this my beginning of a

Bible for Creative Evolution. I am doing the best I can at my age. My powers are waning; but so much the better for those who found me unbearably brilliant when I was in my prime. It is my hope that a hundred apter and more elegant parables by younger hands will soon leave mine as far behind as the religious pictures of the fifteenth century left behind the first attempts of the early Christians at iconography. In that hope I withdraw and ring up the curtain.

CONTENTS

In the Beginning: B.C. 4004 (In the Garden of Eden) 1

The Gospel of the Brothers Barnabas: Present Day 39

The Thing Happens: A.D. 2170 101

Tragedy of an Elderly Gentleman: A.D. 3000 . 155

As Far as Thought Can Reach: A.D. 31,920 . . 233

CONTENTS

PART I
IN THE BEGINNING
XXXII

IN THE BEGINNING

ACT I

*The Garden of Eden. Afternoon. An immense
serpent is sleeping with her head buried in a thick bed of
Johnswort, and her body coiled in apparently endless
rings through the branches of a tree, which is already
well grown; for the days of creation have been longer
than our reckoning. She is not yet visible to anyone
unaware of her presence, as her colors of green and
brown make a perfect camouflage. Near her head a low
rock shews above the Johnswort.*

*The rock and tree are on the border of a glade in
which lies a dead fawn all awry, its neck being broken.
Adam, crouching with one hand on the rock, is staring
in consternation at the dead body. He has not noticed
the serpent on his left hand. He turns his face to his
right and calls excitedly.*

ADAM. Eve! Eve!

EVE'S VOICE. What is it, Adam?

ADAM. Come here. Quick. Something has happened.

EVE [*running in*] What? Where? [*Adam points to
the fawn.*] Oh! [*She goes to it; and he is emboldened
to go with her.*] What is the matter with its eyes?

ADAM. It is not only its eyes. Look. [*He kicks it.*]

EVE. Oh dont! Why doesnt it wake?

ADAM. I dont know. It is not asleep.

EVE. Not asleep?

ADAM. Try.

1

EVE [*trying to shake it and roll it over*] It is stiff and cold.

ADAM.   Nothing will wake it.

EVE.   It has a queer smell.   Pah!   [*She dusts her hands, and draws away from it.*]   Did you find it like that?

ADAM.   No.   It was playing about; and it tripped and went head over heels.   It never stirred again.   Its neck is wrong.   [*He stoops to lift the neck and shew her.*]

EVE.   Dont touch it.   Come away from it.

[*They both retreat, and contemplate it from a few steps' distance with growing repulsion.*]

EVE.   Adam.

ADAM.   Yes?

EVE.   Suppose you were to trip and fall, would you go like that?

ADAM.   Ugh!   [*He shudders and sits down on the rock.*]

EVE [*throwing herself on the ground beside him, and grasping his knee*] You must be careful.   Promise me you will be careful.

ADAM.   What is the good of being careful?   We have to live here for ever.   Think of what for ever means! Sooner or later I shall trip and fall.   It may be tomorrow; it may be after as many days as there are leaves in the garden and grains of sand by the river.   No matter: some day I shall forget and stumble.

EVE.   I too.

ADAM [*horrified*] Oh no, no.   I should be alone. Alone for ever.   You must never put yourself in danger of stumbling.   You must not move about.   You must sit still.   I will take care of you and bring you what you want.

EVE [*turning away from him with a shrug, and hug-*

ging her ankles] I should soon get tired of that. Besides, if it happened to you, *I* should be alone. I could not sit still then. And at last it would happen to me too.

ADAM.   And then?

EVE.   Then we should be no more. There would be only the things on all fours, and the birds, and the snakes.

ADAM.   That must not be.

EVE.   Yes: that must not be. But it might be.

ADAM.   No. I tell you it must not be. I know that it must not be.

EVE.   We both know it. How do we know it?

ADAM.   There is a voice in the garden that tells me things.

EVE.   The garden is full of voices sometimes. They put all sorts of thoughts into my head.

ADAM.   To me there is only one voice. It is very low; but it is so near that it is like a whisper from within myself. There is no mistaking it for any voice of the birds or beasts, or for your voice.

EVE.   It is strange that I should hear voices from all sides and you only one from within. But I have some thoughts that come from within me and not from the voices. The thought that we must not cease to be comes from within.

ADAM [*despairingly*] But we shall cease to be. We shall fall like the fawn and be broken. [*Rising and moving about in his agitation*] I cannot bear this knowledge. I will not have it. It must not be, I tell you. Yet I do not know how to prevent it.

EVE.   That is just what I feel; but it is very strange that you should say so: there is no pleasing you. You change your mind so often.

ADAM [*scolding her*] Why do you say that? How have I changed my mind?

EVE. You say we must not cease to exist. But you used to complain of having to exist always and for ever. You sometimes sit for hours brooding and silent, hating me in your heart. When I ask you what I have done to you, you say you are not thinking of me, but of the horror of having to be here for ever. But I know very well that what you mean is the horror of having to be here with me for ever.

ADAM. Oh! That is what you think, is it? Well, you are wrong. [*He sits down again, sulkily.*] It is the horror of having to be with myself for ever. I like you; but I do not like myself. I want to be different; to be better; to begin again and again; to shed myself as a snake sheds its skin. I am tired of myself. And yet I must endure myself, not for a day or for many days, but for ever. That is a dreadful thought. That is what makes me sit brooding and silent and hateful. Do you never think of that?

EVE. No: I do not think about myself: what is the use? I am what I am: nothing can alter that. I think about you.

ADAM. You should not. You are always spying on me. I can never be alone. You always want to know what I have been doing. It is a burden. You should try to have an existence of your own, instead of occupying yourself with my existence.

EVE. I have to think about you. You are lazy: you are dirty: you neglect yourself: you are always dreaming: you would eat bad food and become disgusting if I did not watch you and occupy myself with you. And now some day, in spite of all my care, you will fall on your head and become dead.

ADAM. Dead? What word is that?

EVE [*pointing to the fawn*] Like that. I call it dead.

ADAM [*rising and approaching it slowly*] There is something uncanny about it.

EVE [*joining him*] Oh! It is changing into little white worms.

ADAM. Throw it into the river. It is unbearable.

EVE. I dare not touch it.

ADAM. Then I must, though I loathe it. It is poisoning the air. [*He gathers its hooves in his hand and carries it away in the direction from which Eve came, holding it as far from him as possible.*]

[*Eve looks after them for a moment; then, with a shiver of disgust, sits down on the rock, brooding. The body of the serpent becomes visible, glowing with wonderful new colors. She rears her head slowly from the bed of Johnswort, and speaks into Eve's ear in a strange seductively musical whisper.*]

THE SERPENT. Eve.

EVE [*startled*] Who is that?

THE SERPENT. It is I. I have come to shew you my beautiful new hood. See [*she spreads a magnificent amethystine hood*]!

EVE [*admiring it*] Oh! But who taught you to speak?

THE SERPENT. You and Adam. I have crept through the grass, and hidden, and listened to you.

EVE. That was wonderfully clever of you.

THE SERPENT. I am the most subtle of all the creatures of the field.

EVE. Your hood is most lovely. [*She strokes it and pets the serpent.*] Pretty thing! Do you love your godmother Eve?

THE SERPENT. I adore her. [*She licks Eve's neck with her double tongue.*]

EVE [*petting her*] Eve's wonderful darling snake

Eve will never be lonely now that her snake can talk to her.

THE SNAKE. I can talk of many things. I am very wise. It was I who whispered the word to you that you did not know. Dead. Death. Die.

EVE [*shuddering*] Why do you remind me of it? I forgot it when I saw your beautiful hood. You must not remind me of unhappy things.

THE SERPENT. Death is not an unhappy thing when you have learnt how to conquer it.

EVE. How can I conquer it?

THE SERPENT. By another thing, called birth.

EVE. What? [*Trying to pronounce it*] B-birth?

THE SERPENT. Yes, birth.

EVE. What is birth?

THE SERPENT. The serpent never dies. Some day you shall see me come out of this beautiful skin, a new snake with a new and lovelier skin. That is birth.

EVE. I have seen that. It is wonderful.

THE SERPENT. If I can do that, what can I not do? I tell you I am very subtle. When you and Adam talk, I hear you say "Why?" Always "Why?" You see things; and you say "Why?" But I dream things that never were; and I say "Why not?" I made the word dead to describe my old skin that I cast when I am renewed. I call that renewal being born.

EVE. Born is a beautiful word.

THE SERPENT. Why not be born again and again as I am, new and beautiful every time?

EVE. I! It does not happen: that is why.

THE SERPENT. That is how; but it is not why. Why not?

EVE. But I should not like it. It would be nice to be new again; but my old skin would lie on the ground

looking just like me; and Adam would see it shrivel up
and—

THE SERPENT.   No. He need not. There is a second
birth.

EVE.   A second birth?

THE SERPENT.   Listen. I will tell you a great secret.
I am very subtle; and I have thought and thought and
thought. And I am very wilful, and must have what
I want; and I have willed and willed and willed. And
I have eaten strange things: stones and apples that you
are afraid to eat.

EVE.   You dared.

THE SERPENT.   I dared everything. And at last I
found a way of gathering together a part of the life in
my body—

EVE.   What is the life?

THE SERPENT.   That which makes the difference between the dead fawn and the live one.

EVE.   What a beautiful word! And what a wonderful thing! Life is the loveliest of all the new words.

THE SERPENT.   Yes: it was by meditating on Life
that I gained the power to do miracles.

EVE.   Miracles? Another new word.

THE SERPENT.   A miracle is an impossible thing that
is nevertheless possible. Something that never could
happen, and yet does happen.

EVE.   Tell me some miracle that you have done.

THE SERPENT.   I gathered a part of the life in my
body, and shut it into a tiny white case made of the
stones I had eaten.

EVE.   And what good was that?

THE SERPENT.   I shewed the little case to the sun, and
left it in its warmth. And it burst; and a little snake
came out; and it became bigger and bigger from day to
day until it was as big as I. That was the second birth.

EVE. Oh! That is too wonderful. It stirs inside me. It hurts.

THE SERPENT. It nearly tore me asunder. Yet I am alive, and can burst my skin and renew myself as before. Soon there will be as many snakes in Eden as there are scales on my body. Then death will not matter: this snake and that snake will die; but the snakes will live.

EVE. But the rest of us will die sooner or later, like the fawn. And then there will be nothing but snakes, snakes, snakes everywhere.

THE SERPENT. That must not be. I worship you, Eve. I must have something to worship. Something quite different to myself, like you. There must be something greater than the snake.

EVE. Yes: it must not be. Adam must not perish. You are very subtle: tell me what to do.

THE SERPENT. Think. Will. Eat the dust. Lick the white stone: bite the apple you dread. The sun will give life.

EVE. I do not trust the sun. I will give life myself. I will tear another Adam from my body if I tear my body to pieces in the act.

THE SERPENT. Do. Dare it. Everything is possible: everything. Listen. I am old. I am the old serpent, older than Adam, older than Eve. I remember Lilith, who came before Adam and Eve. I was her darling as I am yours. She was alone: there was no man with her. She saw death as you saw it when the fawn fell; and she knew then that she must find out how to renew herself and cast the skin like me. She had a mighty will: she strove and strove and willed and willed for more moons than there are leaves on all the trees of the garden. Her pangs were terrible: her groans drove sleep from Eden. She said it must never be again: that the burden of renewing life was past bearing: that it was too much for one. And when she cast the skin, lo! there was not one new Lilith but two: one like herself, the other like Adam. You were the one: Adam was the other.

EVE. But why did she divide into two, and make us different?

THE SERPENT. I tell you the labor is too much for one. Two must share it.

EVE. Do you mean that Adam must share it with me? He will not. He cannot bear pain, nor take trouble with his body.

THE SERPENT. He need not. There will be no pain for him. He will implore you to let him do his share. He will be in your power through his desire.

EVE. Then I will do it. But how? How did Lilith work this miracle?

THE SERPENT. She imagined it.

EVE. What is imagined?

THE SERPENT. She told it to me as a mervellous story of something that never happened to a Lilith that never was. She did not know then that imagination is the beginning of creation. You imagine what you desire; you will what you imagine; and at last you create what you will.

EVE. How can I create out of nothing?

THE SERPENT. Everything must have been created out of nothing. Look at that thick roll of hard flesh on your strong arm! That was not always there: you could not climb a tree when I first saw you. But you willed and tried and willed and tried; and your will created out of nothing the roll on your arm until you had your desire, and could draw yourself up with one hand and seat yourself on the bough that was above your head.

EVE. That was practice.

THE SERPENT. Things wear out by practice: they do not grow by it. Your hair streams in the wind as if it were trying to stretch itself further and further. But it does not grow longer for all its practice in streaming, because you have not willed it so. When Lilith told me what she had imagined in our silent language (for there were no words then) I bade her desire it and will it; and then, to our great wonder, the thing she had desired and willed created itself in her under the urging of her will. Then I too willed to renew myself as two instead of one; and after many days the miracle happened, and I burst from my skin with another snake interlaced with me; and now there are two imaginations, two desires, two wills to create with.

EVE. To desire, to imagine, to will, to create. That is too long a story. Find me one word for it all: you, who are so clever at words.

THE SERPENT. In one word, to conceive. That is the word that means both the beginning in imagination and the end in creation.

EVE. Find me a word for the story Lilith imagined and told you in your silent language: the story that was too wonderful to be true, and yet came true.

THE SERPENT. A poem.

EVE. Find me another word for what Lilith was to me.

THE SERPENT. She was your mother.

EVE. And Adam's mother?

THE SERPENT. Yes.

EVE [about to rise] I will go and tell Adam to conceive.

THE SERPENT [laughs] ! ! !

EVE [jarred and startled] What a hateful noise! What is the matter with you? No one has ever uttered such a sound before.

THE SERPENT.   Adam cannot conceive.

EVE.   Why?

THE SERPENT.   Lilith did not imagine him so. He can imagine: he can will: he can desire: he can gather his life together for a great spring towards creation: he can create all things except one; and that one is his own kind.

EVE.   Why did Lilith keep this from him?

THE SERPENT.   Because if he could do that he could do without Eve.

EVE   That is true. It is I who must conceive.

THE SERPENT.   Yes. By that he is tied to you.

EVE.   And I to him!

THE SERPENT.   Yes, until you create another Adam.

EVE.   I had not thought of that. You are very subtle. But if I create another Eve he may turn to her and do without me. I will not create any Eves, only Adams.

THE SERPENT.   They cannot renew themselves without Eves. Sooner or later you will die like the fawn; and the new Adams will be unable to create without new Eves. You can imagine such an end; but you cannot desire it, therefore cannot will it, therefore cannot create Adams only.

EVE.   If I am to die like the fawn, why should not the rest die too? What do I care?

THE SERPENT.   Life must not cease. That comes before everything. It is silly to say you do not care. You do care. It is that care that will prompt your imagination; inflame your desires; make your will irresistible; and create out of nothing.

EVE [thoughtfully] There can be no such thing as nothing. The garden is full, not empty.

THE SERPENT.   I had not thought of that. That is a great thought. Yes: there is no such thing as nothing, only things we cannot see. The chameleon eats the air.

EVE. I have another thought: I must tell it to Adam. [*Calling*] Adam! Adam! Coo-ee!

ADAM'S VOICE. Coo-ee!

EVE. This will please him, and cure his fits of melancholy.

THE SERPENT. Do not tell him yet. I have not told you the great secret.

EVE. What more is there to tell? It is I who have to do the miracle.

THE SERPENT. No: he, too, must desire and will. But he must give his desire and his will to you.

EVE. How?

THE SERPENT. That is the great secret. Hush! he is coming.

ADAM [*returning*] Is there another voice in the garden besides our voices and the Voice? I heard a new voice.

EVE [*rising and running to him*] Only think, Adam! Our snake has learnt to speak by listening to us.

ADAM [*delighted*] Is it so? [*He goes past her to the stone, and fondles the serpent.*]

THE SERPENT [*responding affectionately*] It is so, dear Adam.

EVE. But I have more wonderful news than that. Adam: we need not live for ever.

ADAM [*dropping the snake's head in his excitement*] What! Eve: do not play with me about this. If only there may be an end some day, and yet no end! If only I can be relieved of the horror of having to endure myself for ever! If only the care of this terrible garden may pass on to some other gardener! If only the sentinel set by the Voice can be relieved! If only the rest and sleep that enable me to bear it from day to day could grow after many days into an eternal rest, an eternal sleep, then I could face my days, however long they may last. Only, there must be some end, some end: I am not strong enough to bear eternity.

THE SERPENT. You need not live to see another summer; and yet there shall be no end.

ADAM. That cannot be.

THE SERPENT. It can be.

EVE. It shall be.

THE SERPENT. It is. Kill me; and you will find another snake in the garden tomorrow. You will find more snakes than there are fingers on your hands.

EVE. I will make other Adams, other Eves.

ADAM. I tell you you must not make up stories about this. It cannot happen.

THE SERPENT. I can remember when you were yourself a thing that could not happen. Yet you are.

ADAM [*struck*] That must be true. [*He sits down on the stone.*]

THE SERPENT. I will tell Eve the secret; and she will tell it to you.

ADAM. The secret! [*He turns quickly towards the serpent, and in doing so puts his foot on something sharp.*] Oh!

EVE. What is it?

ADAM [*rubbing his foot*] A thistle. And there, next to it, a briar. And nettles, too! I am tired of pulling these things up to keep the garden pleasant for us for ever.

THE SERPENT. They do not grow very fast. They will not overrun the whole garden for a long time: not until you have laid down your burden and gone to sleep for ever. Why should you trouble yourself? Let the new Adams clear a place for themselves.

ADAM. That is very true. You must tell us your

secret. You see, Eve, what a splendid thing it is not to have to live for ever.

EVE [*throwing herself down discontentedly and plucking at the grass*] That is so like a man. The moment you find we need not last for ever, you talk as if we were going to end today. You must clear away some of those horrid things, or we shall be scratched and stung whenever we forget to look where we are stepping.

ADAM. Oh yes, some of them, of course. But only some. I will clear them away tomorrow.

THE SERPENT [*laughs*] ! ! !

ADAM. That is a funny noise to make. I like it.

EVE. I do not. Why do you make it again?

THE SERPENT. Adam has invented something new. He has invented tomorrow. You will invent things every day now that the burden of immortality is lifted from you.

EVE. Immortality? What is that?

THE SERPENT. My new word for having to live for ever.

EVE. The serpent has made a beautiful word for being. Living.

ADAM. Make me a beautiful word for doing things tomorrow; for that surely is a great and blessed invention.

THE SERPENT. Procrastination.

EVE. That is a sweet word. I wish I had a serpent's tongue.

THE SERPENT. That may come too. Everything is possible.

ADAM [*springing up in sudden terror*] Oh!

EVE. What is the matter now?

ADAM. My rest! My escape from life.

THE SERPENT. Death. That is the word.

ADAM. There is a terrible danger in this procrastination.

EVE. What danger?

ADAM. If I put off death until tomorrow, I shall never die. There is no such day as tomorrow, and never can be.

THE SERPENT. I am very subtle; but Man is deeper in his thought than I am. The woman knows that there is no such thing as nothing: the man knows that there is no such day as tomorrow. I do well to worship them.

ADAM. If I am to undertake death, I must appoint a real day, not a tomorrow. When shall I die.

EVE. You may die when I have made another Adam. Not before. But then, as soon as you like. [*She rises, and passing behind him, strolls off carelessly to the tree and leans against it, stroking a ring of the snake.*]

ADAM. There need be no hurry even then.

EVE. I see you will put it off until tomorrow.

ADAM. And you? Will you die the moment you have made a new Eve?

EVE. Why should I? Are you eager to be rid of me? Only just now you wanted me to sit still and never move lest I should stumble and die like the fawn. Now you no longer care.

ADAM. It does not matter so much now.

EVE [*angrily to the snake*] This death that you have brought into the garden is an evil thing. He wants me to die.

THE SERPENT [*to Adam*] Do you want her to die?

ADAM. No. It is I who am to die. Eve must not die before me. I should be lonely.

EVE. You could get one of the new Eves.

ADAM. That is true. But they might not be quite the same. They could not: I feel sure of that. They would not have the same memories. They would be—I want a word for them.

THE SERPENT.   Strangers.

ADAM.   Yes: that is a good hard word. Strangers.

EVE.   When there are new Adams and Eves we shall live in a garden of strangers. We shall need each other. [*She comes quickly behind him and turns up his face to her.*] Do not forget that, Adam. Never forget it.

ADAM.   Why should I forget it? It is I who have thought of it.

EVE.   I, too, have thought of something. The fawn stumbled and fell and died. But you could come softly up behind me and [*she suddenly pounces on his shoulders and throws him forward on his face*] throw me down so that I should die. I should not dare to sleep if there were no reason why you should not make me die.

ADAM [*scrambling up in horror*] Make you die! ! ! What a frightful thought!

THE SERPENT.   Kill, kill, kill, kill. That is the word.

EVE.   The new Adams and Eves might kill us. I shall not make them. [*She sits on the rock and pulls him down beside her, clasping him to her with her right arm.*]

THE SERPENT.   You must. For if you do not there will be an end.

ADAM.   No: they will not kill us: they will feel as I do. There is something against it. The Voice in the garden will tell them that they must not kill, as it tells me.

THE SERPENT.   The voice in the garden is your own voice.

ADAM.   It is; and it is not. It is something greater than me: I am only a part of it.

EVE.   The Voice does not tell me not to kill you. Yet

I do not want you to die before me. No voice is needed to make me feel that.

ADAM [*throwing his arm round her shoulder with an expression of anguish*] Oh no: that is plain without any voice. There is something that holds us together, something that has no word—

THE SERPENT. Love. Love. Love.

ADAM. That is too short a word for so long a thing.

THE SERPENT [*laughs*] ! ! !

EVE [*turning impatiently to the snake*] That heart-biting sound again! Do not do it. Why do you do it?

THE SERPENT. Love may be too long a word for so short a thing soon. But when it is short it will be very sweet.

ADAM [*ruminating*] You puzzle me. My old trouble was heavy; but it was simple. These wonders that you promise to do may tangle up my being before they bring me the gift of death. I was troubled with the burden of eternal being; but I was not confused in my mind. If I did not know that I loved Eve, at least I did not know that she might cease to love me, and come to love some other Adam and desire my death. Can you find a name for that knowledge?

THE SERPENT. Jealousy. Jealousy. Jealousy.

ADAM. A hideous word.

EVE [*shaking him*] Adam: you must not brood. You think too much.

ADAM [*angrily*] How can I help brooding when the future has become uncertain? Anything is better than uncertainty. Life has become uncertain. Love is uncertain. Have you a word for this new misery?

THE SERPENT. Fear. Fear. Fear.

ADAM. Have you a remedy for it?

THE SERPENT. Yes. Hope. Hope. Hope.

ADAM. What is hope?

THE SERPENT. As long as you do not know the future you do not know that it will not be happier than the past. That is hope.

ADAM. It does not console me. Fear is stronger in me than hope. I must have certainty. [*He rises threateningly.*] Give it to me; or I will kill you when next I catch you asleep.

EVE [*throwing her arms round the serpent*] My beautiful snake. Oh no. How can you even think such a horror?

ADAM. Fear will drive me to anything. The serpent gave me fear. Let it now give me certainty or go in fear of me.

THE SERPENT. Bind the future by your will. Make a vow.

ADAM. What is a vow?

THE SERPENT. Choose a day for your death; and resolve to die on that day. Then death is no longer uncertain but certain. Let Eve vow to love you until your death. Then love will be no longer uncertain.

ADAM. Yes: that is splendid: that will bind the future.

EVE [*displeased, turning away from the serpent*] But it will destroy hope.

ADAM [*angrily*] Be silent, woman. Hope is wicked. Happiness is wicked. Certainty is blessed.

THE SERPENT. What is wicked? You have invented a word.

ADAM. Whatever I fear to do is wicked. Listen to me, Eve; and you, snake, listen too, that your memory may hold my vow. I will live a thousand sets of the four seasons—

THE SERPENT. Years. Years.

ADAM. I will live a thousand years; and then I will

endure no more: I will die and take my rest. And I will love Eve all that time and no other woman.

EVE. And if Adam keeps his vow I will love no other man until he dies.

THE SERPENT. You have both invented marriage. And what he will be to you and not to any other woman is husband; and what you will be to him and not to any other man is wife.

ADAM [*instinctively moving his hand towards her*] Husband and wife.

EVE [*slipping her hand into his*] Wife and husband.

THE SERPENT [*laughs*]!!!

EVE [*snatching herself loose from Adam*] Do not make that odious noise, I tell you.

ADAM. Do not listen to her: the noise is good: it lightens my heart. You are a jolly snake. But you have not made a vow yet. What vow do you make?

THE SERPENT. I make no vows. I take my chance.

ADAM. Chance? What does that mean?

THE SERPENT. It means that I fear certainty as you fear uncertainty. It means that nothing is certain but uncertainty. If I bind the future I bind my will. If I bind my will I strangle creation.

EVE. Creation must not be strangled. I tell you I will create, though I tear myself to pieces in the act.

ADAM. Be silent, both of you. I will bind the future. I will be delivered from fear. [*To Eve*] We have made our vows; and if you will create, you shall create within the bounds of those vows. You shall not listen to that snake any more. Come [*he seizes her by the hair to drag her away*].

EVE. Let me go, you fool. It has not yet told me the secret.

ADAM [*releasing her*] That is true. What is a fool?

EVE. I do not know: the word came to me. It was

what you are when you forget and brood and are filled with fear. Let us listen to the snake.

ADAM. No: I am afraid of it. I feel as if the ground were giving way under my feet when it speaks. Do you stay and listen to it.

THE SERPENT [*laughs*]! ! !

ADAM [*brightening*] That noise takes away fear. Funny. The snake and the woman are going to whisper secrets. [*He chuckles and goes away slowly, laughing his first laugh.*]

EVE. Now the secret. The secret. [*She sits on the rock and throws her arms round the serpent, who begins whispering to her.*]

[*Eve's face lights up with intense interest, which increases until an expression of overwhelming repugnance takes its place. She buries her face in her hands.*]

ACT II

A few centuries later. Morning. An oasis in Mesopotamia. Close at hand the end of a log house abuts on a kitchen garden. Adam is digging in the middle of the garden. On his right, Eve sits on a stool in the shadow of a tree by the doorway, spinning flax. Her wheel, which she turns by hand, is a large disc of heavy wood, practically a fly-wheel. At the opposite side of the garden is a thorn brake with a passage right through it barred by a hurdle.

The two are scantily and carelessly dressed in rough linen and leaves. They have lost their youth and grace; and Adam has an unkept beard and jaggedly cut hair; but they are strong and in the prime of life. Adam looks worried, like a farmer. Eve, better humored (having given up worrying), sits and spins and thinks.

A MAN'S VOICE. Hallo, mother!

EVE [*looking across the garden towards the hurdle*] Here is Cain.

ADAM [*uttering a grunt of disgust*] ! ! ! [*He goes on digging without raising his head.*]

[*Cain kicks the hurdle out of his way, and strides into the garden. In pose, voice, and dress he is insistently warlike. He is equipped with huge spear and broad brass-bound leather shield; his casque is a tiger's head with bull's horns; he wears a scarlet cloak with gold brooch over a lion's skin with the claws dangling; his feet are in sandals with brass ornaments; his shins are in brass*

21

*greaves; and his bristling military moustache glistens
with oil. To his parents he has the self-assertive, not-
quite-at-ease manner of a revolted son who knows that he
is not forgiven nor approved of.*]

CAIN [*to Adam*] Still digging? Always dig, dig, dig.
Sticking in the old furrow. No progress! no advanced
ideas! no adventures! What should I be if I had stuck
to the digging you taught me?

ADAM. What are you now, with your shield and
spear, and your brother's blood crying from the ground
against you?

CAIN. I am the first murderer: you are only the first
man. Anybody could be the first man: it is as easy as
to be the first cabbage. To be the first murderer one
must be a man of spirit.

ADAM. Begone. Leave us in peace. The world is
wide enough to keep us apart.

EVE. Why do you want to drive him away? He is
mine. I made him out of my own body. I want to see
my work sometimes.

ADAM. You made Abel also. He killed Abel. Can
you bear to look at him after that?

CAIN. Whose fault was it that I killed Abel? Who
invented killing? Did *I?* No: he invented it himself.
I followed your teaching. I dug and dug and dug.
I cleared away the thistles and briars. I ate the fruits
of the earth. I lived in the sweat of my brow, as you
do. I was a fool. But Abel was a discoverer, a
man of ideas, of spirit: a true Progressive. He was the
discoverer of blood. He was the inventor of killing.
He found out that the fire of the sun could be brought
down by a dewdrop. He invented the altar to keep the
fire alive. He changed the beasts he killed into meat by
the fire on the altar. He kept himself alive by eating
meat. His meal cost him a day's glorious health-giving

sport and an hour's amusing play with the fire. You
learnt nothing from him: you drudged and drudged and
drudged, and dug and dug and dug, and made me do
the same. I envied his happiness, his freedom. I
despised myself for not doing as he did instead of what
you did. He became so happy that he shared his meal
with the Voice that had whispered all his inventions to
him. He said that the Voice was the voice of the fire
that cooked his food, and that the fire that could cook
could also eat. It was true: I saw the fire consume the
food on his altar. Then I, too, made an altar, and
offered my food on it, my grains, my roots, my fruit.
Useless: nothing happened. He laughed at me; and
then came my great idea: why not kill him as he killed
the beasts? I struck; and he died, just as they did.
Then I gave up your old silly drudging ways, and lived
as he had lived, by the chase, by the killing, and by the
fire. Am I not better than you? stronger, happier,
freer?

ADAM. You are not stronger: you are shorter in the
wind: you cannot endure. You have made the beasts
afraid of us; and the snake has invented poison to protect herself against you. I fear you myself. If you
take a step towards your mother with that spear of
yours I will strike you with my spade as you struck
Abel.

EVE. He will not strike me. He loves me.

ADAM. He loved his brother. But he killed him.

CAIN. I do not want to kill women. I do not want to
kill my mother. And for her sake I will not kill you,
though I could send this spear through you without
coming within reach of your spade. But for her, I
could not resist the sport of trying to kill you, in spite
of my fear that you would kill me. I have striven with
a boar and with a lion as to which of us should kill the

other. I have striven with a man: spear to spear and shield to shield. It is terrible; but there is no joy like it. I call it fighting. He who has never fought has never lived. That is what has brought me to my mother today.

ADAM. What have you to do with one another now? She is the creator, you the destroyer.

CAIN. How can I destroy unless she creates? I want her to create more and more men: aye, and more and more women, that they may in turn create more men. I have imagined a glorious poem of many men, or more men than there are leaves on a thousand trees. I will divide them into two great hosts. One of them I will lead; and the other will be led by the man I fear most and desire to fight and kill most. And each host shall try to kill the other host. Think of that! all those multitudes of men fighting, fighting, killing, killing! The four rivers running with blood! The shouts of triumph! the howls of rage! the curses of despair! the shrieks of torment! That will be life indeed: life lived to the very marrow: burning, overwhelming life. Every man who has not seen it, heard it, felt it, risked it, will feel a humbled fool in the presence of the man who has.

EVE. And I! I am to be a mere convenience to make men for you to kill!

ADAM. Or to kill you, you fool.

CAIN. Mother: the making of men is your right, your risk, your agony, your glory, your triumph. You make my father here your mere convenience, as you call it, for that. He has to dig for you, sweat for you, plod for you, like the ox who helps him to tear up the ground or the ass who carries his burdens for him. No woman shall make me live my father's life. I will hunt: I will fight and strive to the very bursting of my sinews. When I have slain the boar at the risk of my life, I will

throw it to my woman to cook, and give her a morsel of
it for her pains. She shall have no other food; and that
will make her my slave. And the man that slays me
shall have her for his booty. Man shall be the master
of Woman, not her baby and her drudge.

*Adam throws down his spade, and stands looking
darkly at Eve.*

EVE.   Are you tempted, Adam? Does this seem a
better thing to you than love between us.

CAIN.   What does he know of love? Only when he
has fought, when he has faced terror and death, when
he has striven to the spending of the last rally of his
strength, can he know what it is to rest in love in the
arms of a woman. Ask that woman whom you made,
who is also my wife, whether she would have me as I was
in the days when I followed the ways of Adam, and was
a digger and a drudge?

EVE [*angrily throwing down her distaff*] What! You
dare come here boasting about that good-for-nothing
Lua, the worst of daughters and the worst of wives!
You her master! You are more her slave than Adam's
ox or your own sheep-dog. Forsooth, when you have
slain the boar at the risk of your life, you will throw
her a morsel of it for her pains! Ha! Poor wretch: do
you think I do not know her, and know you, better than
that? Do you risk your life when you trap the ermine
and the sable and the blue fox to hang on her lazy
shoulders and make her look more like an animal than
a woman? When you have to snare the little tender
birds because it is too much trouble for her to chew
honest food, how much of a great warrior do you feel
then? You slay the tiger at the risk of your life; but
who gets the striped skin you have run that risk for?
She takes it to lie on, and flings you the carrion flesh
you cannot eat. You fight because you think that your

fighting makes her admire and desire you.   Fool: she
makes you fight because you bring her the ornaments
and the treasures of those you have slain, and because
she is courted and propitiated with power and gold by
the people who fear you.   You say that *I* make a mere
convenience of Adam: I who spin and keep the house,
and bear and rear children, and am a woman and not a
pet animal to please men and prey on them!   What are
you, you poor slave of a painted face and a bundle of
skunk's fur?   You were a man-child when I bore you.
Lua was a woman-child when I bore her.   What have
you made of yourselves?

CAIN [*letting his spear fall into the crook of his shield
arm, and twirling his moustache*] There is something
higher than man.   There is hero and superman.

EVE.   Superman!   You are no superman: you are
Anti-Man: you are to other men what the stoat is to the
rabbit; and she is to you what the leech is to the stoat.
You despise your father; but when he dies the world will
be the richer because he lived.   When you die, men will
say, "He was a great warrior; but it would have been
better for the world if he had never been born."   And of
Lua they will say nothing; but when they think of her
they will spit.

CAIN.   She is a better sort of woman to live with than
you.   If Lua nagged at me as you are nagging, and as
you nag at Adam, I would beat her black and blue from
head to foot.   I have done it too, slave as you say I am.

EVE.   Yes, because she looked at another man.   And
then you grovelled at her feet, and cried, and begged
her to forgive you, and were ten times more her slave
than ever; and she, when she had finished screaming and
the pain went off a little, she forgave you, did she not?

CAIN.   She loved me more than ever.   That is the true
nature of woman.

EVE [*now pitying him maternally*] Love! You call
that love! You call that the nature of woman! My
boy: this is neither man nor woman nor love nor life.
You have no real strength in your bones nor sap in your
flesh.

CAIN. Ha! [*He seizes his spear and swings it mus-
cularly*].

EVE. Yes: you have to twirl a stick to feel your
strength: you cannot taste life without making it bitter
and boiling hot: you cannot love Lua until her face is
painted, nor feel the natural warmth of her flesh until
you have stuck a squirrel's fur on it. You can feel nothing but a torment, and believe nothing but a lie. You
will not raise your head to look at all the miracles of
life that surround you; but you will run ten miles to see
a fight or a death.

ADAM. Enough said. Let the boy alone.

CAIN. Boy! Ha! ha!

EVE [*to Adam*] You think, perhaps, that his way of
life may be better than yours after all. You are still
tempted. Well, will you pamper me as he pampers his
woman? Will you kill tigers and bears until I have a
heap of their skins to lounge on? Shall I paint my face
and let my arms waste into pretty softness, and eat
partridges and doves, and the flesh of kids whose milk
you will steal for me?

ADAM. You are hard enough to bear with as you are.
Stay as you are; and I will stay as I am.

CAIN. You neither of you know anything about life.
You are simple country folk. You are the nurses and
valets of the oxen and dogs and asses you have tamed to
work for you. I can raise you out of that. I have a
plan. Why not tame men and women to work for us?
Why not bring them up from childhood never to know
any other lot, so that they may believe that we are gods,

and that they are here only to make life glorious for us?

ADAM [*impresssd*] That is a great thought, certainly.

EVE [*contemptuously*] Great thought!

ADAM. Well, as the serpent used to say, why not?

EVE. Because I would not have such wretches in my house. Because I hate creatures with two heads, or with withered limbs, or that are distorted and perverted and unnatural. I have told Cain already that he is not a man and that Lua is not a woman: they are monsters. And now you want to make still more unnatural monsters, so that you may be utterly lazy and worthless, and that your tamed human animals may find work a blasting curse. A fine dream, truly! [*To Cain*]. Your father is a fool skin deep; but you are a fool to your very marrow; and your baggage of a wife is worse.

ADAM. Why am I a fool? How am I a greater fool than you?

EVE. You said there would be no killing because the Voice would tell our children that they must not kill. Why did it not tell Cain that?

CAIN. It did; but I am not a child to be afraid of a Voice. The Voice thought I was nothing but my brother's keeper. It found that I was myself, and that it was for Abel to be himself also, and look to himself. He was not my keeper any more than I was his: why did he not kill me? There was no more to prevent him than there was to prevent me: it was man to man; and I won. I was the first conqueror.

ADAM. What did the Voice say to you when you thought all that?

CAIN. Why, it gave me right. It said that my deed was as a mark on me, a burnt-in mark such as Abel put on his sheep, that no man should slay me. And here I stand unslain, whilst the cowards who have never slain, the men who are content to be their brothers' keepers instead of their masters, are despised and rejected, and slain like rabbits. He who bears the brand of Cain shall rule the earth. When he falls, he shall be avenged seven-fold: the Voice has said it; so beware how you plot against me, you and all the rest.

ADAM. Cease your boasting and bullying, and tell the truth. Does not the Voice tell you that as no man dare slay you for murdering your brother, you ought to slay yourself?

CAIN. No.

ADAM. Then there is no such thing as divine justice, unless you are lying.

CAIN. I am not lying: I dare all truths. There is divine justice. For the Voice tells me that I must offer myself to every man to be killed if he can kill me. With-out danger I cannot be great. That is how I pay for Abel's blood. Danger and fear follow my steps every-where. Without them courage would have no sense. And it is courage, courage, courage, that raises the blood of life to crimson splendor.

ADAM [*picking up his spade and preparing to dig again*] Take yourself off then. This splendid life of yours does not last for a thousand years; and I must last for a thousand years. When you fighters do not get killed in fighting one another or fighting the beasts, you die from mere evil in yourselves. Your flesh ceases to grow like man's flesh: it grows like a fungus on a tree. Instead of breathing, you sneeze, or cough up your insides, and wither and perish. Your bowels become rotten; your hair falls from you; your teeth blacken and drop out; and you die before your time, not because you will, but because you must. I will dig, and live.

CAIN. And pray, what use is this thousand years of life to you, you old vegetable? Do you dig any better because you have been digging for hundreds of years?

I have not lived as long as you; but I know all there is to be known, of the craft of digging. By quitting it I have set myself free to learn nobler crafts of which you know nothing. I know the craft of fighting and of hunting: in a word, the craft of killing. What certainty have you of your thousand years? I could kill both of you; and you could no more defend yourselves than a couple of sheep. I spare you; but others may kill you. Why not live bravely, and die early and make room for others? Why, I—I! that know many more crafts than either of you, am tired of myself when I am not fighting or hunting. Sooner than face a thousand years of it I should kill myself, as the Voice sometimes tempts me to do already.

ADAM.   Liar: you denied just now that it called on you to pay for Abel's life with your own.

CAIN.   The Voice does not speak to me as it does to you. I am a man: you are only a grown-up child. One does not speak to a child as to a man. And a man does not listen and tremble in silence. He replies: he makes the Voice respect him: in the end he dictates what the Voice shall say.

ADAM.   May your tongue be accurst for such blasphemy!

EVE.   Keep a guard on your own tongue; and do not curse my son. It was Lilith who did wrong when she shared the labor of creation so unequally between man and wife. If you, Cain, had had the trouble of making Abel, or had had to make another man to replace him when he was gone, you would not have killed him: you would have risked your own life to save his. That is why all this empty talk of yours, which tempted Adam just now when he threw down his spade and listened to you for a while, went by me like foul wind that has passed over a dead body. That is why there is enmity between Woman the creator and Man the destroyer. I know you: I am your mother. You are idle: you are selfish. It is long and hard and painful to create life: it is short and easy to steal the life others have made. When you dug, you made the earth live and bring forth as I live and bring forth. It was for that that Lilith set you free from the travail of women, not for theft and murder.

CAIN.   The Devil thank her for it! I can make better use of my time than to play the husband to the clay beneath my feet.

ADAM.   Devil? What new word is that?

CAIN.   Hearken to me, old fool. I have never in my soul listened willingly when you have told me of the Voice that whispers to you. There must be two Voices: one that gulls and despises you, and another that trusts and respects me. I call yours the Devil. Mine I call the Voice of God.

ADAM.   Mine is the Voice of Life: yours the Voice of Death.

CAIN.   Be it so. For it whispers to me that death is not really death: that it is the gate of another life; a life infinitely splendid and intense: a life of the soul alone: a life without clods or spades, hunger or fatigue—

EVE.   Selfish and idle, Cain. I know.

CAIN.   Selfish, yes: a life in which no man is his brother's keeper, because his brother can keep himself. But am I idle? In rejecting your drudgery, have I not embraced evils and agonies of which you know nothing? The arrow is lighter in the hand than the spade; but the energy that drives it through the breast of a fighter is as fire to water compared with the strength that drives the spade into the harmless dirty clay. My strength is as the strength of ten because my heart is pure.

ADAM.   What is that word? What is pure?

CAIN. Turned from the clay. Turned upward to the sun, to the clear clean heavens.

ADAM. The heavens are empty, child. The earth is fruitful. The earth feeds us. It gives us the strength by which we made you and all mankind. Cut off from the clay which you despise, you would perish miserably.

CAIN. I revolt against the clay. I revolt against the food. You say it gives strength: does it not also turn into filth and smite us with diseases? I revolt against these births that you and mother are so proud of. They drag us down to the level of the beasts. If that is to be the last thing as it has been the first, let mankind perish. If I am to eat like a bear, if Lua is to bring forth cubs like a bear, then I had rather be a bear than a man; for the bear is not ashamed: he knows no better. If you are content, like the bear, I am not. Stay with the woman who gives you children: I will go to the woman who gives me dreams. Grope in the ground for your food: I will bring it from the skies with my arrows, or strike it down as it roams the earth in the pride of its life. If I must have food or die, I will at least have it at as far a remove from the earth as I can. The ox shall make it something nobler than grass before it comes to me. And as the man is nobler than the ox, I shall some day let my enemy eat the ox; and then I will slay and eat him.

ADAM. Monster! You hear this, Eve?

EVE. So that is what comes of turning your face to the clean clear heavens! Man-eating! Child-eating! For that is what it would come to, just as it came to lambs and kids when Abel began with sheep and goats. You are a poor silly creature after all. Do you think I never have these thoughts: I! who have the labor of the child-bearing: I! who have the drudgery of preparing the food? I thought for a moment that perhaps this strong brave son of mine, who could imagine some-

thing better, and could desire what he imagined, might
also be able to will what he desired until he created it.
And all that comes of it is that he wants to be a bear
and eat children. Even a bear would not eat a man if
it could get honey instead.

CAIN. I do not want to be a bear. I do not want to
eat children. I do not know what I want, except that I
want to be something higher and nobler than this stupid
old digger whom Lilith made to help you to bring me
into the world, and whom you despise now that he has
served your turn.

ADAM [in sullen rage] I have half a mind to shew you
that my spade can split your undutiful head open, in
spite of your spear.

CAIN. Undutiful! Ha! ha! [Flourishing his spear].
Try it, old everybody's father. Try a taste of fighting.

EVE. Peace, peace, you two fools. Sit down and be
quiet; and listen to me. [Adam with a weary shrug,
throws down his spade. Cain, with a laughing one
throws down his shield and spear. Both sit on the
ground]. I hardly know which of you satisfies me least,
you with your dirty digging, or he with his dirty killing.
I cannot think it was for either of these cheap ways of
life that Lilith set you free. [To Adam]. You dig
roots and coax grains out of the earth: why do you not
draw down a divine sustenance from the skies? He steals
and kills for his food; and makes up idle poems of life
after death; and dresses up his terror-ridden life with
fine words and his disease-ridden body with fine clothes,
so that men may glorify and honor him instead of cursing him as murderer and thief. All you men, except
only Adam, are my sons, or my sons' sons, or my sons'
sons' sons: you all come to see me: you all shew off
before me: all your little wisdoms and accomplishments
are trotted out before mother Eve. The diggers come:

the fighters and killers come: they are both very dull;
for they either complain to me of the last harvest, or
boast to me of the last fight; and one harvest is just
like another, and the last fight only a repetition of the
first.   Oh, I have heard it all a thousand times.   They
tell me too of their last-born: the clever thing the darling
child said yesterday, and how much more wonderful or
witty or quaint it is than any child that ever was born
before.   And I have to pretend to be surprised, delighted,
interested; though the last child is like the first, and has
said and done nothing that did not delight Adam and me
when you and Abel said it.   For you were the first children in the world, and filled us with such wonder and
delight as no couple can ever again feel while the world
lasts.   When I can bear no more, I go to our old garden,
that is now a mass of nettles and thistles, in the hope
of finding the serpent to talk to.   But you have made
the serpent our enemy: she has left the garden, or is
dead: I never see her now.   So I have to come back and
listen to Adam saying the same thing for the ten-thou-
sandth time, or to receive a visit from the last great-
great-grandson who has grown up and wants to impress
me with his importance.   Oh, it is dreary, dreary!   And
there is yet nearly seven hundred years of it to endure.

   CAIN.   Poor mother!   You see, life is too long.   One
tires of everything.   There is nothing new under the
sun.

   ADAM [*to Eve, grumpily*] Why do you live on, if you
can find nothing better to do than complain?

   EVE.   Because there is still hope.

   CAIN.   Of what?

   EVE.   Of the coming true of your dreams and mine.
Of newly created things.   Of better things.   My sons
and my sons' sons are not all diggers and fighters.   Some
of them will neither dig nor fight: they are more useless

than either of you: they are weaklings and cowards: they are vain; yet they are dirty and will not take the trouble to cut their hair. They borrow and never pay; but one gives them what they want, because they tell beautiful lies in beautiful words. They can remember their dreams. They can dream without sleeping. They have not will enough to create instead of dreaming; but the serpent said that every dream could be willed into creation by those strong enough to believe in it. There are others who cut reeds of different lengths and blow through them, making lovely patterns of sound in the air; and some of them can weave the patterns together, sounding three reeds at the same time, and raising my soul to things for which I have no words. And others make little mammoths out of clay, or make faces appear on flat stones, and ask me to create women for them with such faces. I have watched those faces and willed; and then I have made a woman-child that has grown up quite like them. And others think of numbers without having to count on their fingers, and watch the sky at night, and give names to the stars, and can foretell when the sun will be covered with a black saucepan lid. And there is Tubal, who made his wheel for me which has saved me so much labor. And there is Enoch, who walks on the hills, and hears the Voice continually, and has given up his will to do the will of the Voice, and has some of the Voice's greatness. When they come, there is always some new wonder, or some new hope: something to live for. They never want to die, because they are always learning and always creating either things or wisdom, or at least dreaming of them. And then you, Cain, come to me with your stupid fighting and destroying, and your foolish boasting: and you want me to tell you that it is all splendid, and that you are heroic, and that nothing but death or the dread of death makes life worth living. Away with you, naughty child; and do you, Adam, go on with your work and not waste your time listening to him.

CAIN. I am not, perhaps, very clever; but—

EVE [*interrupting him*] Perhaps not; but do not begin to boast of that. It is no credit to you.

CAIN. For all that, mother, I have an instinct which tells me that death plays its part in life. Tell me this: who invented death?

Adam springs to his feet. Eve drops her distaff. Both shew the greatest consternation.

CAIN. What is the matter with you both?

ADAM. Boy: you have asked us a terrible question.

EVE. You invented murder. Let that be enough for you.

CAIN. Murder is not death. You know what I mean. Those whom I slay would die if I spared them. If I am not slain, yet I shall die. Who put this upon me? I say, who invented death?

ADAM. Be reasonable, boy. Could you bear to live for ever? You think you could, because you know that you will never have to make your thought good. But I have known what it is to sit and brood under the terror of eternity, of immortality. Think of it, man! to have no escape! to be Adam, Adam, Adam through more days than there are grains of sand by the two rivers, and then be as far from the end as ever! I, who have so much in me that I hate and long to cast off! Be thankful to your parents, who enabled you to hand on your burden to new and better men, and won for you an eternal rest; for it was we who invented death.

CAIN [*rising*] You did well: I, too, do not want to live for ever. But if you invented death, why do you blame me, who am a minister of death?

ADAM.   I do not blame you. Go in peace. Leave me
to my digging, and your mother to her spinning.

CAIN.   Well, I will leave you to it, though I have
shewn you a better way. [*He picks up his shield and
spear*]. ·I will go back to my brave warrior friends and
their splendid women. [*He strides to the thorn brake*].
When Adam delved and Eve span, where was then the
gentleman? [*He goes away roaring with laughter,
which ceases as he cries from the distance*]. Good-bye,
mother.

ADAM [*grumbling*] He might have put the hurdle
back, lazy hound! [*He replaces the hurdle across the
passage*].

EVE.   Through him and his like, death is gaining on
life. Already most of our grandchildren die before they
have sense enough to know how to live.

ADAM.   No matter. [*He spits on his hands, and takes
up the spade again*].   Life is still long enough to learn
to dig, short as they are making it.

EVE [*musing*] Yes, to dig. And to fight. But is it
long enough for the other things, the great things?
Will they live long enough to eat manna?

ADAM.   What is manna?

EVE.   Food drawn down from heaven, made out of the
air, not dug dirtily from the earth. Will they learn all
the ways of all the stars in their little time? It took
Enoch two hundred years to learn to intercept the will
of the Voice. When he was a mere child of eighty, his
babyish attempts to understand the Voice were more
dangerous than the wrath of Cain. If they shorten
their lives, they will dig and fight and kill and die; and
their baby Enochs will tell them that it is the will of the
Voice that they should dig and fight and kill and die
for ever.

ADAM.   If they are lazy and have a will towards death

I cannot help it. I will live my thousand years: if they will not, let them die and be damned.

EVE. Damned? What is that?

ADAM. The state of them that love death more than life. Go on with your spinning; and do not sit there idle while I am straining my muscles for you.

EVE [*slowly taking up her distaff*] If you were not a fool you would find something better for both of us to live by than this spinning and digging.

ADAM. Go on with your work, I tell you; or you shall go without bread.

EVE. Man need not always live by bread alone. There is something else. We do not yet know what it is; but some day we shall find out; and then we will live on that alone; and there shall be no more digging nor spinning, nor fighting nor killing.

She spins resignedly: he digs impatiently.

PART II

THE GOSPEL
OF THE BROTHERS BARNABAS

XXXIII

THE GOSPEL
OF THE BROTHERS BARNABAS

In the first years after the war an impressive-looking gentleman of 50 is seated writing in a well-furnished spacious study. He is dressed in black. His coat is a frock-coat; his tie is white; and his waistcoat, though it is not quite a clergyman's waistcoat, and his collar, though it buttons in front instead of behind, combine with the prosperity indicated by his surroundings, and his air of personal distinction, to suggest the clerical dignitary. Still, he is clearly neither dean nor bishop; he is rather too starkly intellectual for a popular Free Church enthusiast; and he is not careworn enough to be a great headmaster.

The study windows, which have broad comfortable window seats, overlook Hampstead Heath towards London. Consequently, it being a fine afternoon in spring, the room is sunny. As you face these windows, you have on your right the fireplace, with a few logs smouldering in it, and a couple of comfortable library chairs on the hearth-rug; beyond it and beside it the door; before you the writing-table, at which the clerical gentleman sits a little to your left facing the door with his right profile presented to you; on your left a settee; and on your right a couple of Chippendale chairs. There is also an upholstered square stool in the middle of the room, against the writing-table. The walls are covered with bookshelves above and lockers beneath.

The door opens; and another gentleman, shorter than the clerical one, within a year or two of the same age, dressed in a well-worn tweed lounge suit, with a short beard and much less style in his bearing and carriage, looks in.

THE CLERICAL GENTLEMAN [*familiar and by no means cordial*] Hallo! I didnt expect you until the five o'clock train.

THE TWEEDED GENTLEMAN [*coming in very slowly*] I have something on my mind. I thought I'd come early.

THE CLERICAL GENTLEMAN [*throwing down his pen*] What is on your mind?

THE TWEEDED GENTLEMAN [*sitting down on the stool, heavily preoccupied with his thought*] I have made up my mind at last about the time. I make it three hundred years.

THE CLERICAL GENTLEMAN [*sitting up energetically*] Now that is extraordinary. Most extraordinary. The very last words I wrote when you interrupted me were "at least three centuries." [*He snatches up his manuscript and points to it*]. Here it is: [*reading*] "the term of human life must be extended to at least three centuries."

THE TWEEDED GENTLEMAN. How did you arrive at it?

A parlor maid opens the door, ushering in a young clergyman.

THE PARLOR MAID. Mr Haslam. [*She withdraws*].

The visitor is so very unwelcome that his host forgets to rise; and the two brothers stare at the intruder, quite unable to conceal their dismay. Haslam, who has nothing clerical about him except his collar, and wears a snuff-colored suit, smiles with a frank schoolboyishness that makes it impossible to be unkind to him, and explodes into obviously unpremeditated speech.

HASLAM.   I'm afraid I'm an awful nuisance.   I'm the rector; and I suppose one ought to call on people.

THE TWEEDED GENTLEMAN [*in ghostly tones*] We're not Church people, you know.

HASLAM.   Oh, I dont mind that, if you dont.   The Church people here are mostly as dull as ditch-water.   I have heard such a lot about you; and there are so jolly few people to talk to.   I thought you perhaps wouldnt mind.   Do you mind? for of course I'll go like a shot if I'm in the way.

THE CLERICAL GENTLEMAN [*rising, disarmed*] Sit down Mr—er?

HASLAM.   Haslam.

THE CLERICAL GENTLEMAN.   Mr Haslam.

THE TWEEDED GENTLEMAN [*rising and offering him the stool*] Sit down.   [*He retreats towards the Chippendale chairs*].

HASLAM [*sitting down on the stool*] Thanks awfully.

THE CLERICAL GENTLEMAN [*resuming his seat*] This is my brother Conrad, Professor of Biology at Jarrowfields University: Dr Conrad Barnabas.   My name is Franklyn: Franklyn Barnabas.   I was in the Church myself for some years.

HASLAM [*sympathizing*] Yes: one cant help it.   If theres a living in the family, or one's Governor knows a patron, one gets shoved into the Church by one's parents.

CONRAD [*sitting down on the furthest Chippendale with a snort of amusement*] Mp!

FRANKLYN.   One gets shoved out of it, sometimes, by one's conscience.

HASLAM.   Oh yes; but where is a chap like me to go? I'm afraid I'm not intellectual enough to split straws when theres a job in front of me, and nothing better for me to do.   I daresay the Church was a bit thick for you;

but it's good enough for me. It will last my time, any-how. [*He laughs good-humoredly*].

FRANKLYN [*with renewed energy*] There again! You see, Con. It will last his time. Life is too short for men to take it seriously.

HASLAM. Thats a way of looking at it, certainly.

FRANKLYN. I was not shoved into the Church, Mr Haslam: I felt it to be my vocation to walk with God, like Enoch. After twenty years of it I realized that I was walking with my own ignorance and self-conceit, and that I was not within a hundred and fifty years of the experience and wisdom I was pretending to.

HASLAM. Now I come to think of it, old Methuselah must have had to think twice before he took on anything for life. If I thought I was going to live nine hundred and sixty years, I dont think I should stay in the Church.

FRANKLYN. If men lived even a third of that time, the Church would be very different to the thing it is.

CONRAD. If I could count on nine hundred and sixty years I could make myself a real biologist, instead of what I am now: a child trying to walk. Are you sure you might not become a good clergyman if you had a few centuries to do it in?

HASLAM. Oh, theres nothing much the matter with me: it's quite easy to be a decent parson. It's the Church that chokes me off. I couldnt stick it for nine hundred years. I should chuck it. You know, some-times, when the bishop, who is the most priceless of fossils, lets off something more than usually out-of-date, the bird starts in my garden.

FRANKLYN. The bird?

HASLAM. Oh yes. Theres a bird there that keeps on singing "Stick it or chuck it: stick it or chuck it"—just like that—for an hour on end in the spring. I wish my father had found some other shop for me.

The parlor maid comes back.

THE PARLOR MAID.   Any letters for the post, sir?

FRANKLYN.   These.   [*He proffers a basket of letters. She comes to the table and takes them*].

HASLAM [*to the maid*] Have you told Mr Barnabas yet?

THE PARLOR MAID [*flinching a little*] No, sir.

FRANKLYN.   Told me what?

HASLAM.   She is going to leave you?

FRANKLYN.   Indeed? I'm sorry. Is it our fault, Mr Haslam?

HASLAM.   Not a bit. She is jolly well off here.

THE PARLOR MAID [*reddening*] I have never denied it, sir: I couldnt ask for a better place. But I have only one life to live; and I maynt get a second chance. Excuse me, sir; but the letters must go to catch the post. [*She goes out with the letters*].

The two brothers look enquiringly at Haslam.

HASLAM.   Silly girl! Going to marry a village woodman and live in a hovel with him and a lot of kids tumbling over one another, just because the fellow has poetic-looking eyes and a moustache.

CONRAD [*demurring*] She said it was because she had only one life.

HASLAM.   Same thing, poor girl! The fellow persuaded her to chuck it; and when she marries him she'll have to stick it. Rotten state of things, I call it.

CONRAD.   You see, she hasnt time to find out what life really means. She has to die before she knows.

HASLAM [*agreeably*] Thats it.

FRANKLYN.   She hasnt time to form a well-instructed conscience.

HASLAM [*still more cheerfully*] Quite.

FRANKLYN. It goes deeper. She hasnt time to form a genuine conscience at all. Some romantic points of honor and a few conventions. A world without conscience: that is the horror of our condition.

HASLAM [*beaming*] Simply fatuous. [*Rising*]. Well, I suppose I'd better be going. It's most awfully good of you to put up with my calling.

CONRAD [*in his former low ghostly tone*] You neednt go, you know, if you are really interested.

HASLAM [*fed up*] Well, I'm afraid I ought to—I really must get back—I have something to do in the—

FRANKLYN [*smiling benignly and rising to proffer his hand*] Good-bye.

CONRAD [*gruffly, giving him up as a bad job*] Good-bye.

HASLAM. Good-bye. Sorry—er—

As the rector moves to shake hands with Franklyn, feeling that he is making a frightful mess of his departure, a vigorous sunburnt young lady with hazel hair cut to the level of her neck, like an Italian youth in a Gozzoli picture, comes in impetuously. She seems to have nothing on but her short skirt, her blouse, her stockings, and a pair of Norwegian shoes: in short, she is a Simple-Lifer.

THE SIMPLE-LIFER [*swooping on Conrad and kissing him*] Hallo, Nunk. Youre before your time.

CONRAD. Behave yourself. Theres a visitor.

She turns quickly and sees the rector. She instinctively switches at her Gozzoli fringe with her fingers, but gives it up as hopeless.

FRANKLYN. Mr Haslam, our new rector. [*To Haslam*]. My daughter Cynthia.

CONRAD. Usually called Savvy, short for Savage.

SAVVY. I usually call Mr Haslam Bill, short for

William. [*She strolls to the hearth-rug, and surveys them calmly from that commanding position*].

FRANKLYN.   You know him?

SAVVY.   Rather.   Sit down, Bill.

FRANKLYN.   Mr Haslam is going, Savvy.   He has an engagement.

SAVVY.   I know.   I'm the engagement.

CONRAD.   In that case, would you mind taking him into the garden while I talk to your father?

SAVVY [*to Haslam*] Tennis?

HASLAM.   Rather!

SAVVY.   Come on.   [*She dances out.   He runs out boyishly after her*].

FRANKLYN [*leaving his table and beginning to walk up and down the room discontentedly*] Savvy's manners jar on me.   They would have horrified her grandmother.

CONRAD [*obstinately*] They are happier manners than Mother's manners.

FRANKLYN.   Yes: they are franker, wholesomer, better in a hundred ways.   And yet I squirm at them.   I cannot get it out of my head that Mother was a well-mannered woman, and that Savvy has no manners at all.

CONRAD.   There wasnt any pleasure in Mother's fine manners.   That makes a biological difference.

FRANKLYN.   But there was beauty in Mother's manners, grace in them, style in them: above all, decision in them.   Savvy is such a cub.

CONRAD.   So she ought to be, at her age.

FRANKLYN.   There it comes again!   Her age! her age!

CONRAD.   You want her to be fully grown at eighteen.   You want to force her into a stuck-up, artificial, premature self-possession before she has any self to possess.   You just let her alone: she is right enough for her years.

FRANKLYN.   I have let her alone; and look at the result! Like all the other young people who have been let alone, she becomes a Socialist. That is, she becomes hopelessly demoralized.

CONRAD. Well, arnt you a Socialist?

FRANKLYN. Yes; but that is not the same thing. You and I were brought up in the old bourgeois morality. We were taught bourgeois manners and bourgeois points of honor. Bourgeois manners may be snobbish manners: there may be no pleasure in them, as you say; but they are better than no manners. Many bourgeois points of honor may be false; but at least they exist. The women know what to expect and what is expected of them. Savvy doesnt. She is a Bolshevist and nothing else. She has to improvize her manners and her conduct as she goes along. It's often charming, no doubt; but sometimes she puts her foot in it frightfully; and then I feel that she is blaming me for not teaching her better.

CONRAD. Well, you have something better to teach her now, at all events.

FRANKLYN. Yes; but it is too late. She doesnt trust me now. She doesnt talk about such things to me. She doesnt read anything I write. She never comes to hear me lecture. I am out of it as far as Savvy is concerned. [*He resumes his seat at the writing-table*].

CONRAD. I must have a talk to her.

FRANKLYN. Perhaps she will listen to you. You are not her father.

CONRAD. I sent her my last book. I can break the ice by asking her what she made of it.

FRANKLYN. When she heard you were coming, she asked me whether all the leaves were cut, in case it fell into your hands. She hasnt read a word of it.

CONRAD [*rising indignantly*] What!

FRANKLYN [*inexorably*] Not a word of it.

CONRAD [*beaten*] Well, I suppose it's only natural. Biology is a dry subject for a girl; and I am a pretty dry old codger. [*He sits down again resignedly*].

FRANKLYN. Brother: if that is so; if biology as you have worked at it, and religion as I have worked at it, are dry subjects like the old stuff they taught under these names, and we two are dry old codgers, like the old preachers and professors, then the Gospel of the Brothers Barnabas is a delusion. Unless this withered thing religion, and this dry thing science, have come alive in our hands, alive and intensely interesting, we may just as well go out and dig the garden until it is time to dig our graves. [*The parlor maid returns. Franklyn is impatient at the interruption*]. Well? what is it now?

THE PARLOR MAID. Mr Joyce Burge on the telephone, sir. He wants to speak to you.

FRANKLYN [*astonished*] Mr Joyce Burge!

THE PARLOR MAID. Yes, sir.

FRANKLYN [*to Conrad*] What on earth does this mean? I havnt heard from him nor exchanged a word with him for years. I resigned the chairmanship of the Liberal Association and shook the dust of party politics from my feet before he was Prime Minister in the Coalition. Of course, he dropped me like a hot potato.

CONRAD. Well, now that the Coalition has chucked him out, and he is only one of the half-dozen leaders of the Opposition, perhaps he wants to pick you up again.

THE PARLOR MAID [*warningly*] He is holding the line, sir.

FRANKLYN. Yes: all right. [*He hurries out*].

The parlor maid goes to the hearthrug to make up the fire. Conrad rises and strolls to the middle of the room, where he stops and looks quizzically down at her.

CONRAD. So you have only one life to live, eh?

THE PARLOR MAID [*dropping on her knees in conster-nation*] I meant no offence, sir.

CONRAD. You didnt give any. But you know you could live a devil of a long life if you really wanted to.

THE PARLOR MAID [*sitting down on her heels*] Oh dont say that, sir. It's so unsettling.

CONRAD. Why? Have you been thinking about it?

THE PARLOR MAID. It would never have come into my head if you hadnt put it there, sir. Me and cook had a look at your book.

CONRAD. What!

> You and cook
> Had a look
> At my book!

And my niece wouldnt open it! The prophet is without honor in his own family. Well, what do you think of living for several hundred years? Are you going to have a try for it?

THE PARLOR MAID. Well, of course youre not in earnest, sir. But it does set one thinking, especially when one is going to be married.

CONRAD. What has that to do with it? He may live as long as you, you know.

THE PARLOR MAID. That's just it, sir. You see, he must take me for better for worse, til death do us part. Do you think he would be so ready to do that, sir, if he thought it might be for several hundred years?

CONRAD. That's true. And what about yourself?

THE PARLOR MAID. Oh, I tell you straight out, sir, I'd never promise to live with the same man as long as that. I wouldnt put up with my own children as long as that. Why, cook figured it out, sir, that when you were only 200, you might marry your own great-great-great-great-great-great-grandson and not even know who he was.

CONRAD. Well, why not? For all you know, the man you are going to marry may be your great-great-great-great-great-great-grandmother's great-great-great-great-great-great-grandson.

THE PARLOR MAID. But do you think it would ever be thought respectable, sir?

CONRAD. My good girl, all biological necessities have to be made respectable whether we like it or not; so you neednt worry yourself about that.

Franklyn returns and crosses the room to his chair, but does not sit down. The parlor maid goes out.

CONRAD. Well, what does Joyce Burge want?

FRANKLYN. Oh, a silly misunderstanding. I have promised to address a meeting in Middlesborough; and some fool has put it into the papers that I am "coming to Middlesborough," without any explanation. Of course, now that we are on the eve of a general election, political people think I am coming there to contest the parliamentary seat. Burge knows that I have a following, and thinks I could get into the House of Commons and head a group there. So he insists on coming to see me. He is staying with some people at Dollis Hill, and can be here in five or ten minutes, he says.

CONRAD. But didn't you tell him that it's a false alarm?

FRANKLYN. Of course I did; but he wont believe me.

CONRAD. Called you a liar, in fact?

FRANKLYN. No: I wish he had: any sort of plain speaking is better than the nauseous sham goodfellowship our democratic public men get up for shop use. He pretends to believe me, and assures me his visit is quite disinterested; but why should he come if he has no axe to grind? These chaps never believe anything they say themselves; and naturally they cannot believe anything anyone else says.

CONRAD [*rising*] Well, I shall clear out. It was hard enough to stand the party politicians before the war; but now that they have managed to half kill Europe between them, I cant be civil to them, and I dont see why I should be.

FRANKLYN. Wait a bit. We have to find out how the world will take our new gospel. [*Conrad sits down again*]. Party politicians are still unfortunately an important part of the world. Suppose we try it on Joyce Burge.

CONRAD. How can you? You can tell things only to people who can listen. Joyce Burge has talked so much that he has lost the power of listening. He doesnt listen even in the House of Commons.

Savvy rushes in breathless, followed by Haslam, who remains timidly just inside the door.

SAVVY [*running to Franklyn*] I say! Who do you think has just driven up in a big car?

FRANKLYN. Mr Joyce Burge, perhaps.

SAVVY [*disappointed*] Oh, they know, Bill. Why didnt you tell us he was coming? I have nothing on.

HASLAM. I'd better go, hadnt I?

CONRAD. You just wait here, both of you. When you start yawning, Joyce Burge will take the hint, perhaps.

SAVVY [*to Franklyn*] May we?

FRANKLYN. Yes, if you promise to behave yourself.

SAVVY [*making a wry face*] That will be a treat, wont it?

THE PARLOR MAID [*entering and announcing*] Mr Joyce Burge. [*Haslam hastily moves to the fireplace; and the parlor maid goes out and shuts the door when the visitor has passed in*].

FRANKLYN [*hurrying past Savvy to his guest with the false cordiality he has just been denouncing*] Oh!

Here you are. Delighted to see you. [*He shakes Burge's hand, and introduces Savvy*] My daughter.

SAVVY [*not daring to approach*] Very kind of you to come.

Joyce Burge stands fast and says nothing; but he screws up his cheeks into a smile at each introduction, and makes his eyes shine in a very winning manner. He is a well-fed man turned fifty, with broad forehead, and grey hair which, his neck being short, falls almost to his collar.

FRANKLYN. Mr Haslam, our rector.

Burge conveys an impression of shining like a church window; and Haslam seizes the nearest library chair on the hearth, and swings it round for Burge between the stool and Conrad. He then retires to the window seat at the other side of the room, and is joined by Savvy. They sit there, side by side, hunched up with their elbows on their knees and their chins on their hands, providing Burge with a sort of Strangers' Gallery during the ensuing sitting.

FRANKLYN. I forget whether you know my brother Conrad. He is a biologist.

BURGE [*suddenly bursting into energetic action and shaking hands heartily with Conrad*] By reputation only, but very well, of course. How I wish I could have devoted myself to biology! I have always been interested in rocks and strata and volcanoes and so forth: they throw such a light on the age of the earth. [*With conviction*] There is nothing like biology. "The cloud-capped towers, the solemn pinnacles, the gorgeous temples, the great globe itself: yea, all that it inherit shall dissolve, and, like this influential pageant faded, leave not a rack behind." That's biology, you know: good sound biology. [*He sits down. So do the others, Franklyn on the stool, and Conrad on his Chippendale*].

Well, my dear Barnabas, what do you think of the situation? Dont you think the time has come for us to make a move?

FRANKLYN. The time has always come to make a move.

BURGE. How true! But what is the move to be? You are a man of enormous influence. We know that. Weve always known it. We have to consult you whether we like it or not. We—

FRANKLYN [*interrupting firmly*] I never meddle in party politics now.

SAVVY. It's no use saying you have no influence, daddy. Heaps of people swear by you.

BURGE [*shining at her*] Of course they do. Come! let me prove to you what we think of you. Shall we find you a first-rate constituency to contest at the next election? One that wont cost you a penny. A metropolitan seat. What do you say to the Strand?

FRANKLYN. My dear Burge, I am not a child. Why do you go on wasting your party funds on the Strand? You know you cannot win it.

BURGE. We cannot win it; but you—

FRANKLYN. Oh, please!

SAVVY. The Strand's no use, Mr. Burge. I once canvassed for a Socialist there. Cheese it.

BURGE. Cheese it!

HASLAM [*spluttering with suppressed laughter*] Priceless!

SAVVY. Well, I suppose I shouldnt say cheese it to a Right Honorable. But the Strand, you know! Do come off it.

FRANKLYN. You must excuse my daughter's shocking manners, Burge; but I agree with her that popular democratic statesmen soon come to believe that everyone they speak to is an ignorant dupe and a born fool into the bargain.

BURGE [*laughing genially*] You old aristocrat, you! But believe me, the instinct of the people is sound—

CONRAD [*cutting in sharply*] Then why are you in the Opposition instead of in the Government?

BURGE [*showing signs of temper under this heckling*] I deny that I am in the Opposition morally. The Government does not represent the country. I was chucked out of the Coalition by a Tory conspiracy. The people want me back. I dont want to go back.

FRANKLYN [*gently remonstrant*] My dear Burge: of course you do.

BURGE [*turning on him*] Not a bit of it. I want to cultivate my garden. I am not interested in politics: I am interested in roses. I havent a scrap of ambition. I went into politics because my wife shoved me into them, bless her! But I want to serve my country. What else am I for? I want to save my country from the Tories. They dont represent the people. The man they have made Prime Minister has never represented the people; and you know it. Lord Dunreen is the bitterest old Tory left alive. What has he to offer to the people?

FRANKLYN [*cutting in before Burge can proceed—as he evidently intends—to answer his own question*] I will tell you. He has ascertainable beliefs and principles to offer. The people know where they are with Lord Dunreen. They know what he thinks right and what he thinks wrong. With your followers they never know where they are. With you they never know where they are.

BURGE [*amazed*] With me!

FRANKLYN. Well, where are you? What are you?

BURGE. Barnabas: you must be mad. You ask me what I am?

FRANKLYN. I do.

BURGE. I am, if I mistake not, Joyce Burge, pretty well known throughout Europe, and indeed throughout the world, as the man who—unworthily perhaps, but not quite unsuccessfully—held the helm when the ship of State weathered the mightiest hurricane that has ever burst with earth-shaking violence on the land of our fathers.

FRANKLYN. I know that. I know who you are. And the earth-shaking part of it to me is that though you were placed in that enormously responsible position, neither I nor anyone else knows what your beliefs are, or even whether you have either beliefs or principles. What we did know was that your Government was formed largely of men who regarded you as a robber of henroosts, and whom you regarded as enemies of the people.

BURGE [adroitly, as he thinks] I agree with you. I agree with you absolutely. I dont believe in coalition governments.

FRANKLYN. Precisely. Yet you formed two.

BURGE. Why? Because we were at war. That is what you fellows never would realize. The Hun was at the gate. Our country, our lives, the honor of our wives and mothers and daughters, the tender flesh of our innocent babes, were at stake. Was that a time to argue about principles?

FRANKLYN. I should say it was the time of all others to confirm the resolution of our own men and gain the confidence and support of public opinion throughout the world by a declaration of principle. Do you think the Hun would ever have come to the gate if he had known that it would be shut in his face on principle? Did he not hold his own against you until America boldly affirmed the democratic principle and came to our rescue? Why did you let America snatch that honor from England?

BURGE. Barnabas: America was carried away by words, and had to eat them at the Peace Conference. Beware of eloquence: it is the bane of popular speakers like you.

FRANKLYN ⎰[*exclaiming*]⎱ Well!!
SAVVY   ⎱   *all*   ⎰ I like that!
HASLAM ⎰ *together*]⎱ Priceless!

BURGE [*continuing remorselessly*] Come down to facts. It wasnt principle that won the war: it was the British fleet and the blockade. America found the talk: I found the shells. You cannot win wars by principles; but you can win elections by them. There I am with you. You want the next election to be fought on principles: that is what it comes to, doesnt it?

FRANKLYN. I dont want it to be fought at all? An election is a moral horror, as bad as a battle except for the blood: a mud bath for every soul concerned in it. You know very well that it will not be fought on principle.

BURGE. On the contrary it will be fought on nothing else. I believe a program is a mistake. I agree with you that principle is what we want.

FRANKLYN. Principle without program, eh?

BURGE. Exactly. There it is in three words.

FRANKLYN. Why not in one word? Platitudes. That is what principle without program means.

BURGE [*puzzled but patient, trying to get at Franklyn's drift in order to ascertain his price*] I have not made myself clear. Listen. I am agreeing with you. I am on your side. I am accepting your proposal. There isnt going to be any more coalition. This time there wont be a Tory in the Cabinet. Every candidate will have to pledge himself to Free Trade, slightly modified by consideration for our Overseas Dominions; to Disestablishment; to Reform of the House of Lords; to a revised scheme of Taxation of Land Values; and to doing something or other to keep the Irish quiet. Does that satisfy you?

FRANKLYN. It does not even interest me. Suppose your friends do commit themselves to all this! What does it prove about them except that they are hopelessly out of date even in party politics? that they have learnt nothing and forgotten nothing since 1885? What is it to me that they hate the Church and hate the landed gentry; that they are jealous of the nobility, and have shipping shares instead of manufacturing businesses in the Midlands? I can find you hundreds of the most sordid rascals, or the most densely stupid reactionaries, with all these qualifications.

BURGE. Personal abuse proves nothing. Do you suppose the Tories are all angels because they are all members of the Church of England?

FRANKLYN. No; but they stand together as members of the Church of England, whereas your people, in attacking the Church, are all over the shop. The supporters of the Church are of one mind about religion: its enemies are of a dozen minds. The Churchmen are a phalanx: your people are a mob in which atheists are jostled by Plymouth Brethren, and Positivists by Pillars of Fire. You have with you all the crudest unbelievers and all the crudest fanatics.

BURGE. We stand, as Cromwell did, for liberty of conscience, if that is what you mean.

FRANKLYN. How can you talk such rubbish over the graves of your conscientious objectors? All law limits liberty of conscience: if a man's conscience allows him to steal your watch or to shirk military service, how much liberty do you allow it? Liberty of conscience is not my point.

BURGE [*testily*] I wish you would come to your point. Half the time you are saying that you must have principles; and when I offer you principles you say they wont work.

FRANKLYN. You have not offered me any principles. Your party shibboleths are not principles. If you get into power again you will find yourself at the head of a rabble of Socialists and anti-Socialists, of Jingo Imperialists and Little Englanders, of cast-iron Materialists and ecstatic Quakers, of Christian Scientists and Compulsory Inoculationists, of Syndicalists and Bureaucrats: in short, of men differing fiercely and irreconcilably on every principle that goes to the root of human society and destiny; and the impossibility of keeping such a team together will force you to sell the pass again to the solid Conservative Opposition.

BURGE [*rising in wrath*] Sell the pass again! You accuse me of having sold the pass!

FRANKLYN. When the terrible impact of real warfare swept your parliamentary sham warfare into the dustbin, you had to go behind the backs of your followers and make a secret agreement with the leaders of the Opposition party to keep you in power on condition that you dropped all legislation of which they did not approve. And you could not even hold them to their bargain; for they presently betrayed the secret and forced the coalition on you.

BURGE. I solemnly declare that this is a false and monstrous accusation.

FRANKLYN. Do you deny that the thing occurred? Were the uncontradicted reports false? Were the published letters forgeries?

BURGE. Certainly not. But *I* did not do it. I was not Prime Minister then. It was that old dotard, that played-out old humbug Lubin. He was Prime Minister then, not I.

FRANKLYN. Do you mean to say you did not know?

BURGE [*sitting down again with a shrug*] Oh, I had to be told. But what could I do? If we had refused we might have had to go out of office.

FRANKLYN. Precisely.

BURGE. Well, could we desert the country at such a crisis? The Hun was at the gate. Everyone has to make a sacrifice for the sake of the country at such moments. We had to rise above party; and I am proud to say we never gave party a second thought. We stuck to——

CONRAD. Office?

BURGE [*turning on him*] Yes, sir, to office: that is, to responsibility, to danger, to heart-sickening toil, to abuse and misunderstanding, to a martyrdom that made us envy the very soldiers in the trenches. If you had had to live for months on aspirin and bromide of potassium to get a wink of sleep, you wouldnt talk about office as if it were a catch.

FRANKLYN. Still, you admit that under our parliamentary system Lubin could not have helped himself?

BURGE. On that subject my lips are closed. Nothing will induce me to say one word against the old man. I never have; and I never will. Lubin is old: he has never been a real statesman: he is as lazy as a cat on a hearthrug: you cant get him to attend to anything; he is good for nothing but getting up and making speeches with a peroration that goes down with the back benches. But I say nothing against him. I gather that you do not think much of me as a statesman: but at all events I can

get things done. I can hustle: even you will admit that.
But Lubin! Oh my stars, Lubin!! If you only knew—

*The parlor maid opens the door and announces a
visitor.*

THE PARLOR MAID. Mr. Lubin.

BURGE [*bounding from his chair*] Lubin! Is this a
conspiracy?

*They all rise in amazement, staring at the door.
Lubin enters: a man at the end of his sixties, a Yorkshireman with the last traces of Scandinavian flax still
in his white hair, undistinguished in stature, unassum-
ing in his manner, and taking his simple dignity for
granted, but wonderfully comfortable and quite self-
assured in contrast to the intellectual restlessness of
Franklyn and the mesmeric self-assertiveness of Burge.
His presence suddenly brings out the fact that they are
unhappy men, ill at ease, square pegs in round holes,
whilst he flourishes like a primrose.*

The parlor maid withdraws.

LUBIN [*coming to Franklyn*] How do you do, Mr
Barnabas? [*He speaks very comfortably and kindly,
much as if he were the host, and Franklyn an embarrassed but welcome guest*]. I had the pleasure of meeting you once at the Mansion House. I think it was to
celebrate the conclusion of the hundred years peace with
America.

FRANKLYN [*shaking hands*] It was long before that:
a meeting about Venezuela, when we were on the point of
going to war with America.

LUBIN [*not at all put out*] Yes: you are quite right.
I knew it was something about America. [*He pats
Franklyn's hand*]. And how have you been all this
time? Well, eh?

FRANKLYN [*smiling to soften the sarcasm*] A few
vicissitude of health naturally in so long a time.

LUBIN. Just so. Just so. [*Looking round at Savvy*] The young lady is——?

FRANKLYN. My daughter, Savvy.

Savvy comes from the window between her father and Lubin.

LUBIN [*taking her hand affectionately in both his*] And why has she never come to see us?

BURGE. I dont know whether you have noticed, Lubin, that I am present.

Savvy takes advantage of this diversion to slip away to the settee, where she is stealthily joined by Haslam, who sits down on her left.

LUBIN [*seating himself in Burge's chair with ineffable comfortableness*] My dear Burge: if you imagine that it is possible to be within ten miles of your energetic presence without being acutely aware of it, you do yourself the greatest injustice. How are you? And how are your good newspaper friends? [*Burge makes an explosive movement; but Lubin goes on calmly and sweetly*] And what are you doing here with my old friend Barnabas, if I may ask?

BURGE [*sitting down in Conrad's chair, leaving him standing uneasily in the corner*] Well, just what you are doing, if you want to know. I am trying to enlist Mr Barnabas's valuable support for my party.

LUBIN. Your party, eh? The newspaper party?

BURGE. The Liberal Party. The party of which I have the honor to be leader.

LUBIN. Have you now? Thats very interesting; for I thought *I* was the leader of the Liberal Party. However, it is very kind of you to take it off my hands, if the party will let you.

BURGE. Do you suggest that I have not the support and confidence of the party?

LUBIN. I dont suggest anything, my dear Burge.

Mr Barnabas will tell you that we all think very highly
of you.   The country owes you a great deal.   During
the war, you did very creditably over the munitions; and
if you were not quite so successful with the peace, nobody doubted that you meant well.

BURGE.   Very kind of you, Lubin.   Let me remark
that you cannot lead a progressive party without getting a move on.

LUBIN.   You mean you cannot.   I did it for ten
years without the least difficulty.   And very comfortable,
prosperous, pleasant years they were.

BURGE.   Yes; but what did they end in?

LUBIN.   In you, Burge.   You dont complain of that,
do you?

BURGE [*fiercely*] In plague, pestilence, and famine;
battle, murder, and sudden death.

LUBIN [*with an appreciative chuckle*] The Noncon-
formist can quote the prayer-book for his own purposes,
I see.   How you enjoyed yourself over that business,
Burge!   Do you remember the Knock-Out Blow?

BURGE.   It came off: dont forget that.   Do you remember fighting to the last drop of your blood?

LUBIN [*unruffled, to Franklyn*] By the way, I remember your brother Conrad—a wonderful brain and a dear
good fellow—explaining to me that I couldnt fight to the
last drop of my blood, because I should be dead long
before I came to it.   Most interesting, and quite true.
He was introduced to me at a meeting where the suf-
fragettes kept disturbing me.   They had to be carried
out kicking and making a horrid disturbance.

CONRAD.   No: it was later, at a meeting to support
the Franchise Bill which gave them the vote.

LUBIN [*discovering Conrad's presence for the first
time*] Youre right: it was.   I knew it had something
to do with women.   My memory never deceives me

Thank you. Will you introduce me to this gentleman, Barnabas?

CONRAD [*not at all affably*] I am the Conrad in question. [*He sits down in dudgeon on the vacant Chippendale*].

LUBIN. Are you? [*Looking at him pleasantly*] Yes: of course you are. I never forget a face. But [*with an arch turn of his eyes to Savvy*] your pretty niece engaged all my powers of vision.

BURGE. I wish youd be serious, Lubin. God knows we have passed through times terrible enough to make any man serious.

LUBIN. I do not think I need to be reminded of that. In peace time I used to keep myself fresh for my work by banishing all worldly considerations from my mind on Sundays; but war has no respect for the Sabbath; and there have been Sundays within the last few years on which I had to play as many as sixty-six games of bridge to keep my mind off the news from the front.

BURGE [*scandalized*] Sixty-six games of bridge on Sunday ! ! !

LUBIN. You probably sang sixty-six hymns. But as I cannot boast either your admirable voice or your spiritual fervor, I had to fall back on bridge.

FRANKLYN. If I may go back to the subject of your visit, it seems to me that you may both be completely superseded by the Labor Party.

BURGE. But I am in the truest sense myself a Labor leader. I— [*he stops, as Lubin has risen with a half-suppressed yawn, and is already talking calmly, but without a pretence of interest*].

LUBIN. The Labor Party! Oh no, Mr Barnabas. No, no, no, no, no. [*He moves in Savvy's direction*]. There will be no trouble about that. Of course we must give them a few seats: more, I quite admit, than we should have dreamt of leaving to them before the war; but— [*by this time he has reached the sofa where Savvy and Haslam are seated. He sits down between them; takes her hand; and drops the subject of Labor*]. Well, my dear young lady? What is the latest news? Whats going on? Have you seen Shoddy's new play? Tell me all about it, and all about the latest books, and all about everything.

SAVVY.   You have not met Mr Haslam.   Our Rector.

LUBIN [*who has quite overlooked Haslam*] Never heard of him.   Is he any good?

FRANKLYN.   I was introducing him.   This is Mr Haslam.

HASLAM.   How d'ye do!

LUBIN.   I beg your pardon, Mr Haslam. Delighted to meet you.   [*To Savvy*] Well, now, how many books have you written?

SAVVY [*rather overwhelmed but attracted*] None.   I dont write.

LUBIN.   You dont say so!   Well, what do you do? Music?   Skirt-dancing?

SAVVY.   I dont do anything.

LUBIN.   Thank God!   You and I were born for one another.   Who is your favorite poet, Sally?

SAVVY.   Savvy.

LUBIN.   Savvy!   I never heard of him. Tell me all about him.   Keep me up to date.

SAVVY.   It's not a poet.   *I* am Savvy, not Sally.

LUBIN.   Savvy!   Thats a funny name, and very pretty.   Savvy.   It sounds Chinese.   What does it mean?

CONRAD.   Short for Savage.

LUBIN [*patting her hand*] La belle Sauvage.

HASLAM [*rising and surrendering Savvy to Lubin by*

crossing to the fireplace] I suppose the Church is out of it as far as progressive politics are concerned.

BURGE.   Nonsense!   That notion about the Church being unprogressive is one of those shibboleths that our party must drop.   The Church is all right essentially. Get rid of the establishment; get rid of the bishops; get rid of the candlesticks; get rid of the 39 articles; and the Church of England is just as good as any other Church; and I dont care who hears me say so.

LUBIN.   It doesnt matter a bit who hears you say so, my dear Burge.   [*To Savvy*] Who did you say your favorite poet was?

SAVVY.   I dont make pets of poets.   Who's yours?

LUBIN.   Horace.

SAVVY.   Horace who?

LUBIN.   Quintus Horatius Flaccus: the noblest Roman of them all, my dear.

SAVVY.   Oh, if he is dead, that explains it.   I have a theory that all the dead people we feel especially interested in must have been ourselves.   You must be Horace's reincarnation.

LUBIN [*delighted*] That is the very most charming and penetrating and intelligent thing that has ever been said to me.   Barnabas: will you exchange daughters with me?   I can give you your choice of two.

FRANKLYN.   Man proposes.   Savvy disposes.

LUBIN.   What does Savvy say?

BURGE.   Lubin: I came here to talk politics.

LUBIN.   Yes: you have only one subject, Burge.   I came here to talk to Savvy.   Take Burge into the next room, Barnabas; and let him rip.

BURGE [*half-angrily, half-indulgent*] No; but really, Lubin, we are at a crisis—

LUBIN.   My dear Burge, life is a disease; and the only difference between one man and another is the stage

of the disease at which he lives. You are always at the
crisis: I am always in the convalescent stage. I enjoy
convalescence. It is the part that makes the illness
worth while.

SAVVY [*half-rising*] Perhaps I'd better run away. I
am distracting you.

LUBIN [*making her sit down again*] Not at all, my
dear. You are only distracting Burge. Jolly good
thing for him to be distracted by a pretty girl. Just
what he needs.

BURGE. I sometimes envy you, Lubin. The great
movement of mankind, the giant sweep of the ages,
passes you by and leaves you standing.

LUBIN. It leaves me sitting, and quite comfortable,
thank you. Go on sweeping. When you are tired of it,
come back; and you will find England where it was, and
me in my accustomed place, with Miss Savvy telling me
all sorts of interesting things.

SAVVY [*who has been growing more and more restless*]
Dont let him shut you up, Mr Burge. You know, Mr
Lubin, I am frightfully interested in the Labor movement, and in Theosophy, and in reconstruction after the
war, and all sorts of things. I daresay the flappers in
your smart set are tremendously flattered when you sit
beside them and are nice to them as you are being nice
to me; but I am not smart; and I am no use as a flapper.
I am dowdy and serious. I want you to be serious. If
you refuse, I shall go and sit beside Mr Burge, and ask
him to hold my hand.

LUBIN. He wouldnt know how to do it, my dear.
Burge has a reputation as a profligate—

BURGE [*starting*] Lubin: this is monstrous. I—

LUBIN [*continuing*] —but he is really a model of
domesticity. His name is coupled with all the most
celebrated beauties; but for him there is only one

woman; and that is not you, my dear, but his very charming wife.

BURGE.   You are destroying my character in the act of pretending to save it.   Have the goodness to confine yourself to your own character and your own wife. Both of them need all your attention.

LUBIN.   I have the privilege of my age and of my transparent innocence.   I have not to struggle with your volcanic energy.

BURGE [*with an immense sense of power*] No, by George!

FRANKLYN.   I think I shall speak both for my brother and myself, and possibly also for my daughter, if I say that since the object of your visit and Mr Joyce Burge's is to some extent political, we should hear with great interest something about your political aims, Mr Lubin.

LUBIN [*assenting with complete good humor, and becoming attentive, clear, and businesslike in his tone*] By all means, Mr Barnabas.   What we have to consider first, I take it, is what prospect there is of our finding you beside us in the House after the next election.

FRANKLYN.   When I speak of politics, Mr Lubin, I am not thinking of elections, or available seats, or party funds, or the registers, or even, I am sorry to have to add, of parliament as it exists at present.   I had much rather you talked about bridge than about electioneering: it is the more interesting game of the two.

BURGE.   He wants to discuss principles, Lubin.

LUBIN [*very cool and clear*] I understand Mr Barnabas quite well.   But elections are unsettled things: principles are settled things.

CONRAD [*impatiently*] Great Heavens!—

LUBIN [*interrupting him with quiet authority*] One moment, Dr Barnabas.   The main principles on which modern civilized society is founded are pretty well

understood among educated people.   That is what our
dangerously half-educated masses and their pet—dema-
gogues—if Burge will excuse that expression—

BURGE.   Dont mind me.   Go on.   I shall have something to say presently.

LUBIN.   —that is what our dangerously half-educated people do not realize.   Take all this fuss about
the Labor Party, with its imaginary new principles and
new politics.   The Labor members will find that the immutable laws of political economy take no more notice
of their ambitions and aspirations than the law of gravitation.   I speak, if I may say so, with knowledge; for I
have made a special study of the Labor question.

FRANLYN [*with interest and some surprise*] Indeed?

LUBIN.   Yes.   It occurred quite at the beginning of
my career.   I was asked to deliver an address to the
students at the Working Men's College; and I was
strongly advised to comply, as Gladstone and Morley
and others were doing that sort of thing at the moment.
It was rather a troublesome job, because I had not gone
into political economy at the time.   As you know, at the
university I was a classical scholar; and my profession
was the Law.   But I looked up the text-books, and got
up the case most carefully.   I found that the correct
view is that all this Trade Unionism and Socialism and
so forth is founded on the ignorant delusion that wages
and the production and distribution of wealth can be
controlled by legislation or by any human action whatever.   They obey fixed scientific laws, which have been
ascertained and settled finally by the highest economic
authorities.   Naturally I do not at this distance of time
remember the exact process of reasoning; but I can get
up the case again at any time in a couple of days; and
you may rely on me absolutely, should the occasion
arise, to deal with all these ignorant and unpractical

people in a conclusive and convincing way, except, of course, as far as it may be advisable to indulge and flatter them a little so as to let them down without creating ill feeling in the working-class electorate. In short, I can get that lecture up again almost at a moment's notice.

SAVVY.   But, Mr Lubin, I have had a university education too; and all this about wages and distribution being fixed by immutable laws of political economy is obsolete rot.

FRANKLYN [*shocked*] Oh, my dear! That is not polite.

LUBIN.   No, no, no. Dont scold her. She mustnt be scolded. [*To Savvy*] I understand. You are a disciple of Karl Marx.

SAVVY.   No, no. Karl Marx's economies are all rot.

LUBIN [*at last a little taken aback*] Dear me!

SAVVY.   You must excuse me, Mr Lubin; but it's like hearing a man talk about the Garden of Eden.

CONRAD.   Why shouldnt he talk about the Garden of Eden? It was a first attempt at biology anyhow.

LUBIN [*recovering his self-possession*] I am sound on the Garden of Eden. I have heard of Darwin.

SAVVY.   But Darwin is all rot.

LUBIN.   What! Already!

SAVVY.   It's no good your smiling at me like a Cheshire cat, Mr Lubin; and I am not going to sit here mumchance like an old-fashioned goody-goody wife while you men monopolize the conversation and pay out the very ghastliest exploded drivel as the latest thing in politics. I am not giving you my own ideas, Mr Lubin, but just the regular orthodox science of to-day. Only the most awful old fossils think that Socialism is bad economics and that Darwin invented Evolution. Ask Papa. Ask Uncle. Ask the first person you meet in the street. [*She rises and crosses to Haslam*]. Give me a cigaret, Bill, will you?

HASLAM. Priceless. [*He complies*].

FRANKLYN. Savvy has not lived long enough to have any manners, Mr Lubin; but that is where you stand with the younger generation. Dont smoke, dear.

Savvy, with a shrug of rather mutinous resignation, throws the cigaret into the fire. Haslam, on the point of lighting one for himself, changes his mind.

LUBIN [*shrewd and serious*] Mr Barnabas: I confess I am surprised; and I will not pretend that I am convinced. But I am open to conviction. I may be wrong.

BURGE [*in a burst of irony*] Oh no. Impossible! Impossible!

LUBIN. Yes, Mr Barnabas, though I do not possess Burge's genius for being always wrong, I have been in that position once or twice. I could not conceal from you, even if I wished to, that my time has been so completely filled by my professional work as a lawyer, and later on by my duties as leader of the House of Commons in the days when Prime Ministers were also leaders—

BURGE [*stung*] Not to mention bridge and smart society.

LUBIN. —not to mention the continual and trying effort to make Burge behave himself, that I have not been able to keep my academic reading up to date. I have kept my classics brushed up out of sheer love for them; but my economics and my science, such as they were, may possibly be a little rusty. Yet I think I may say that if you and your brother will be so good as to put me on the track of the necessary documents, I will undertake to put the case to the House or to the country to your entire satisfaction. You see, as long as you can shew these troublesome half-educated people who

want to turn the world upside down that they are talking nonsense, it really does not matter very much
whether you do it in terms of what Miss Barnabas calls
obsolete rot or in terms of what her granddaughter will
probably call unmitigated tosh.   I have no objection
whatever to denounce Karl Marx.   Anything I can say
against Darwin will please a large body of sincerely
pious voters.   If it will be easier to carry on the business of the country on the understanding that the
present state of things is to be called Socialism, I have
no objection in the world to call it Socialism.   There is
the precedent of the Emperor Constantine, who saved
the society of his own day by agreeing to call his Im-
perialism Christianity.   Mind: I must not go ahead of
the electorate.   You must not call a voter a Socialist
until—

FRANKLYN.   Until he is a Socialist.   Agreed.

LUBIN.   Oh, not at all.   You need not wait for that.
You must not call him a Socialist until he wishes to be
called a Socialist: that is all.   Surely you would not say
that I must not address my constituents as gentlemen
until they are gentlemen.   I address them as gentlemen
because they wish to be so addressed.   [*He rises from
the sofa and goes to Franklyn, placing a reassuring
hand on his shoulder*].   Do not be afraid of Socialism,
Mr Barnabas.   You need not tremble for your property
or your position or your dignity.   England will remain
what England is, no matter what new political names
may come into vogue.   I do not intend to resist the
transition to Socialism.   You may depend on me to guide
it, to lead it, to give suitable expression to its aspirations, and to steer it clear of Utopian absurdities.   I can
honestly ask for your support on the most advanced
Socialist grounds no less than on the soundest Liberal
ones.

BURGE. In short, Lubin, youre incorrigible. You
dont believe anything is going to change. The millions
are still to toil—the people—my people—for I am a
man of the people—

LUBIN [*interrupting him contemptuously*] Dont be
ridiculous, Burge. You are a country solicitor, further
removed from the people, more foreign to them, more
jealous of letting them up to your level, than any duke
or any archbishop.

BURGE [*hotly*] I deny it. You think I have never been
poor. You think I have never cleaned my own boots.
You think my fingers have never come out through the
soles when I was cleaning them. You think—

LUBIN. I think you fall into the very common mistake of supposing that it is poverty that makes the
proletarian and money that makes the gentleman. You
are quite wrong. You never belonged to the people:
you belonged to the impecunious. Impecuniosity and
broken boots are the lot of the unsuccessful middle class,
and the commonplaces of the early struggles of the professional and younger son class. I defy you to find a
farm laborer in England with broken boots. Call a
mechanic one of the poor, and he'll punch your head.
When you talk to your constituents about the toiling
millions, they dont consider that you are referring to
them. They are all third cousins of somebody with a
title or a park. I am a Yorkshireman, my friend. I
know England; and you dont. If you did you would
know—

BURGE. What do you know that I don't know?

LUBIN. I know that we are taking up too much of
Mr. Barnabas's time. [*Franklyn rises*]. May I take it.
my dear Barnabas, that I may count on your support if
we succeed in forcing an election before the new register
is in full working order?

BURGE [*rising also*] May the party count on your support? I say nothing about myself. Can the party depend on you? Is there any question of yours that I have left unanswered?

CONRAD.   We havent asked you any, you know.

BURGE.   May I take that as a mark of confidence?

CONRAD.   If I were a laborer in your constituency, I should ask you a biological question?

LUBIN.   No you wouldnt, my dear Doctor. Laborers never ask questions.

BURGE.   Ask it now. I have never flinched from being heckled. Out with it. Is it about the land?

CONRAD.   No.

BURGE.   Is it about the Church?

CONRAD.   No.

BURGE.   Is it about the House of Lords?

CONRAD.   No.

BURGE.   Is it about Proportional Representation?

CONRAD.   No.

BURGE.   Is it about Free Trade?

CONRAD.   No.

BURGE.   Is it about the priest in the school?

CONRAD.   No.

BURGE.   Is it about Ireland?

CONRAD.   No.

BURGE.   Is it about Germany?

CONRAD.   No.

BURGE.   Well, is it about Republicanism? Come! I wont flinch. Is it about the Monarchy?

CONRAD.   No.

BURGE.   Well, what the devil is it about, then?

CONRAD.   You understand that I am asking the question in the character of a laborer who earned thirteen shillings a week before the war and earns thirty now, when he can get it?

BURGE.   Yes: I understand that. I am ready for you. Out with it.

CONRAD.   And whom you propose to represent in parliament?

BURGE.   Yes, yes, yes. Come on.

CONRAD.   The question is this. Would you allow your son to marry my daughter, or your daughter to marry my son?

BURGE [*taken aback*] Oh, come! Thats not a political question.

CONRAD.   Then, as a biologist, I dont take the slightest interest in your politics! and I shall not walk across the street to vote for you or anyone else at the election. Good evening.

LUBIN.   Serve you right, Burge! Dr Barnabas: you have my assurance that my daughter shall marry the man of her choice, whether he be lord or laborer. May I count on your support?

BURGE [*hurling the epithet at him*] Humbug!

SAVVY.   Stop. [*They all stop short in the movement of leavetaking to look at her*]. Daddy: are you going to let them off like this? How are they to know anything if nobody ever tells them? If you dont, I will.

CONRAD.   You cant. You didnt read my book; and you know nothing about it. You just hold your tongue.

SAVVY.   I just wont, Nunk. I shall have a vote when I am thirty; and I ought to have it now. Why are these two ridiculous people to be allowed to come in and walk over us as if the world existed only to play their silly parliamentary game?

FRANKLYN [*severely*] Savvy: you really must not be uncivil to our guests.

SAVVY.   I'm sorry. But Mr Lubin didnt stand on much ceremony with me, did he? And Mr Burge hasnt addressed a single word to me. I'm not going to stand it. You and Nunk have a much better program than either of them. It's the only one we are going to vote for; and they ought to be told about it for the credit of the family and the good of their own souls. You just tip them a chapter from the gospel of the brothers Barnabas, Daddy.

Lubin and Burge turn enquiringly to Franklyn, suspecting a move to form a new party.

FRANKLYN. It is quite true, Mr Lubin, that I and my brother have a little program of our own which—

CONRAD [*interrupting*] It's not a little program: it's an almighty big one. It's not our own: it's the program of the whole of civilization.

BURGE. Then why split the party before you have put it to us? For God's sake let us have no more splits. I am here to learn. I am here to gather your opinions and represent them. I invite you to put your views before me. I offer myself to be heckled. You have asked me only an absurd non-political question.

FRANKLYN. Candidly, I fear our program will be thrown away on you. It would not interest you.

BURGE [*with challenging audacity*] Try. Lubin can go if he likes; but I am still open to new ideas, if only I can find them.

FRANKLYN [*to Lubin*] Are you prepared to listen, Mr Lubin; or shall I thank you for your very kind and welcome visit, and say good evening?

LUBIN [*sitting down resignedly on the settee, but involuntarily making a movement which looks like the stifling of a yawn*] With pleasure, Mr Barnabas. Of course you know that before I can adopt any new plank in the party platform, it will have to reach me through the National Liberal Federation, which you can approach through your local Liberal and Radical Association.

FRANKLYN. I could recall to you several instances of the addition to your party program of measures of which no local branch of your Federation had ever dreamt. But I understand that you are not really interested. I will spare you, and drop the subject.

LUBIN [*waking up a little*] You quite misunderstand me. Please do not take it in that way. I only—

BURGE [*talking him down*] Never mind the Federation: *I* will answer for the Federation. Go on, Barnabas: go on. Never mind Lubin [*he sits down in the chair from which Lubin first displaced him*].

FRANKLYN. Our program is only that the term of human life shall be extended to three hundred years.

LUBIN [*softly*] Eh?

BURGE [*explosively*] What!

SAVVY. Our election cry is "Back to Methuselah!"

HASLAM. Priceless!

Lubin and Burge look at one another.

CONRAD. No. We are not mad.

SAVVY. Theyre not joking either. They mean it.

LUBIN [*cautiously*] Assuming that, in some sense which I am for the moment unable to fathom, you are in earnest, Mr Barnabas, may I ask what this has to do with politics?

FRANKLYN. The connexion is very evident. You are now, Mr Lubin, within immediate reach of your seventieth year. Mr Joyce Burge is your junior by about eleven years. You will go down to posterity as one of a European group of immature statesmen and monarchs who, doing the very best for your respective countries of which you were capable, succeeded in all-but-wrecking the civilization of Europe, and did, in effect, wipe out of existence many billions of its inhabitants.

BURGE. Less than a million.

FRANKLYN. That was our loss alone.

BURGE. Oh, if you count foreigners—!

HASLAM. God counts foreigners, you know.

SAVVY [*with intense satisfaction*] Well said, Bill.

FRANKLYN. I am not blaming you. Your task was beyond human capacity. What with our huge armaments, our terrible engines of destruction, our systems of coercion manned by an irresistible police, you were called on to control powers so gigantic that one shudders at the thought of their being entrusted even to an infinitely experienced and benevolent God, much less to mortal men whose whole life does not last a hundred years.

BURGE. We won the war: dont forget that.

FRANKLYN. No: the soldiers and sailors won it, and left you to finish it. And you were so utterly incompetent that the multitudes of children slain by hunger in the first years of peace made us all wish we were at war again.

CONRAD. It's no use arguing about it. It is now absolutely certain that the political and social problems raised by our civilization cannot be solved by mere human mushrooms who decay and die when they are just beginning to have a glimmer of the wisdom and knowledge needed for their own government.

LUBIN. Quite an interesting idea, Doctor. Extravagant. Fantastic. But quite interesting. When I was young I used to feel my human limitations very acutely.

BURGE. God knows I have often felt that I could not go on if it had not been for the sense that I was only an instrument in the hands of a Power above us.

CONRAD. I'm glad you both agree with us, and with one another.

LUBIN. I have not gone so far as that, I think.

After all, we have had many very able political leaders even within your recollection and mine.

FRANKLYN.   Have you read the recent biographies—Dilke's, for instance—which revealed the truth about them?

LUBIN.   I did not discover any new truth revealed in these books, Mr Barnabas.

FRANKLYN.   What! Not the truth that England was governed all that time by a little woman who knew her own mind?

SAVVY.   Hear, hear!

LUBIN.   That often happens. Which woman do you mean?

FRANKLYN.   Queen Victoria, to whom your Prime Ministers stood in the relation of naughty children whose heads she knocked together when their tempers and quarrels became intolerable. Within thirteen years of her death Europe became a hell.

BURGE.   Quite true. That was because she was piously brought up, and regarded herself as an instrument. If a statesman remembers that he is only an instrument, and feels quite sure that he is rightly interpreting the divine purpose, he will come out all right, you know.

FRANKLYN.   The Kaiser felt like that. Did he come out all right?

BURGE.   Well, let us be fair, even to the Kaiser. Let us be fair.

FRANKLYN.   Were you fair to him when you won an election on the program of hanging him?

BURGE.   Stuff! I am the last man alive to hang anybody; but the people wouldnt listen to reason. Besides, I knew the Dutch wouldnt give him up.

SAVVY.   Oh, dont start arguing about poor old Bill. Stick to our point. Let these two gentlemen settle the

question for themselves. Mr Burge: do you think Mr
Lubin is fit to govern England?

BURGE. No. Frankly, I dont.

LUBIN [*remonstrant*] Really!

CONRAD. Why?

BURGE. Because he has no conscience: thats why.

LUBIN [*shocked and amazed*] Oh!

FRANKLYN. Mr Lubin: do you consider Joyce Burge
qualified to govern England?

LUBIN [*with dignified emotion, wounded, but without
bitterness*] Excuse me, Mr Barnabas; but before I
answer that question I want to say this. Burge: we have
had differences of opinion; and your newspaper friends
have said hard things of me. But we worked together
for years; and I hope I have done nothing to justify
you in the amazing accusation you have just brought
against me. Do you realize that you said that I have
no conscience?

BURGE. Lubin: I am very accessible to an appeal to
my emotions; and you are very cunning in making such
appeals. I will meet you to this extent. I dont mean
that you are a bad man. I dont mean that I dislike you,
in spite of your continual attempts to discourage and
depress me. But you have a mind like a looking-glass.
You are very clear and smooth and lucid as to what is
standing in front of you. But you have no foresight
and no hindsight. You have no vision and no memory.
You have no continuity; and a man without continuity
can have neither conscience nor honor from one day to
another. The result is that yau have always been a
damned bad minister; and you have sometimes been a
damned bad friend. Now you can answer Barnabas'
question and take it out of me to your heart's content.
He asked you was I fit to govern England.

LUBIN [*recovering himself*] After what has just

passed I sincerely wish I could honestly say yes, Burge.
But it seems to me that you have condemned yourself
out of your own mouth. You represent something
which has had too much influence and popularity in this
country since Joseph Chamberlain set the fashion; and
that is mere energy without intellect and without knowledge. Your mind is not a trained mind: it has not been
stored with the best information, nor cultivated by
intercourse with educated minds at any of our great
seats of learning. As I happen to have enjoyed that
advantage, it follows that you do not understand my
mind. Candidly, I think that disqualifies you. The
peace found out your weaknesses.

BURGE. Oh! What did it find out in you?

LUBIN. You and your newspaper confederates took
the peace out of my hands. The peace did not find me
out because it did not find me in.

FRANKLYN. Come! Confess, both of you. You
were only flies on the wheel. The war went England's
way; but the peace went its own way, and not England's
way nor any of the ways you had so glibly appointed
for it. Your peace treaty was a scrap of paper before
the ink dried on it. The statesmen of Europe were incapable of governing Europe. What they needed was a
couple of hundred years training and experience: what
they actually had was a few years at the bar or in a
counting-house or on the grouse moors and golf courses.
And now we are waiting, with monster cannons trained
on every city and seaport, and huge aeroplanes ready
to spring into the air and drop bombs every one of
which will obliterate a whole street, and poison gases
that will strike multitudes dead with a breath, until one
of you gentlemen rises in his helplessness to tell us, who
are as helpless as himself, that we are at war again.

CONRAD. Aha! What consolation will it be for us

then that you two are able to tell off one another's defects so cleverly in your afternoon chat?

BURGE [*angrily*] If you come to that, what consolation will it be that you two can sit there and tell both of us off? you, who have had no responsibility! you, who havnt lifted a finger, as far as I know, to help us through this awful crisis which has left me ten years older than my proper age! Can you tell me a single thing you did to help us during the whole infernal business?

CONRAD. We're not blaming you: you hadnt lived long enough. No more had we. Cant you see that three-score-and-ten, though it may be long enough for a very crude sort of village life, isnt long enough for a complicated civilization like ours? Flinders Petrie has counted nine attempts at civilization made by people exactly like us; and everyone of them failed just as ours is failing. They failed because the citizens and statesmen died of old age or overeating before they had grown out of schoolboy games and savage sports and cigars and champagne. The signs of the end are always the same: Democracy, Socialism, and Votes for Women. We shall go to smash within the lifetime of men now living unless we recognize that we must live longer.

LUBIN. I am glad you agree with me that Socialism and Votes for Women are signs of decay.

FRANKLYN. Not at all: they are only the difficulties that overtax your capacity. If you cannot organize Socialism you cannot organize civilized life; and you will relapse into barbarism accordingly.

SAVVY. Hear, hear!

BURGE. A useful point. We cannot put back the clock.

HASLAM. *I* can. Ive often done it.

LUBIN. Tut tut! My dear Burge: what are you dreaming of? Mr. Barnabas: I am a very patient man. But will you tell me what earthly use or interest there is in a conclusion that cannot be realized? I grant you that if we could live three hundred years we should all be, perhaps wiser, certainly older. You will grant me in return, I hope, that if the sky fell we should all catch larks.

FRANKLYN. Your turn now, Conrad. Go ahead.

CONRAD. I dont think it's any good. I dont think they want to live longer than usual.

LUBIN. Although I am a mere child of 69, I am old enough to have lost the habit of crying for the moon.

BURGE. Have you discovered the elixir of life or have you not? If not, I agree with Lubin that you are wasting our time.

CONRAD. Is your time of any value?

BURGE [*unable to believe his ears*] My time of any value! What do you mean?

LUBIN [*smiling comfortably*] From your high scientific point of view, I daresay, none whatever, Professor. In any case I think a little perfectly idle discussion would do Burge good. After all, we might as well hear about the elixir of life as read novels, or whatever Burge does when he is not playing golf on Walton Heath. What is your elixir, Dr Barnabas? Lemons? Sour milk? Or what is the latest?

BURGE. We were just beginning to talk seriously; and now you snatch at the chance of talking rot. [*He rises*]. Good evening. [*He turns to the door*].

CONRAD [*rudely*] Die as soon as you like. Good evening.

BURGE [*hesitating*] Look here. I took sour milk twice a day until Metchnikoff died. He thought it would keep him alive "or ever; and he died of it.

CONRAD. You might as well have taken sour beer.

BURGE. You believe in lemons?

CONRAD. I wouldnt eat a lemon for ten pounds.

BURGE [*sitting down again*] What do you recommend?

CONRAD [*rising with a gesture of despair*] Whats the use of going on, Frank? Because I am a doctor, and because they think I have a bottle to give them that will make them live for ever, they are listening to me for the first time with their mouths open and their eyes shut. Thats their notion of science.

SAVVY. Steady, Nunk! Hold the fort.

CONRAD [*growls and sits down*] ! ! !

LUBIN. You volunteered the consultation, Doctor. I may tell you that, far from sharing the credulity as to science which is now the fashion, I am prepared to demonstrate that during the last fifty years, though the Church has often been wrong, and even the Liberal Party has not been infallible, the men of science have always been wrong.

CONRAD. Yes: the fellows you call men of science. The people who make money by it, and their medical hangers-on. But has anybody been right?

LUBIN. The poets and story tellers, especially the classical poets and story tellers, have been, in the main, right. I will ask you not to repeat this as my opinion outside; for the vote of the medical profession and its worshippers is not to be trifled with.

FRANKLYN. You are quite right: the poem is our real clue to biological science. The most scientific document we possess at present is, as your grandmother would have told you quite truly, the story of the Garden of Eden.

BURGE [*pricking up his ears*] Whats that? If you can establish that, Barnabas, I am prepared to hear you

out with my very best attention. I am listening.
Go on.

FRANKLYN. Well, you remember, dont you, that in
the Garden of Eden Adam and Eve were not created
mortal, and that natural death, as we call it, was not a
part of life, but a later and quite separate invention?

BURGE. Now you mention it, thats true. Death came
afterwards.

LUBIN. What about accidental death? That was
always possible.

FRANKLYN. Precisely. Adam and Eve were hung up
between two frightful possibilities. One was the extinction of mankind by their accidental death. The other
was the prospect of living for ever. They could bear
neither. They decided that they would just take a short
turn of a thousand years, and meanwhile hand on their
work to a new pair. Consequently, they had to invent
natural birth and natural death, which are, after all,
only modes of perpetuating life without putting on any
single creature the terrible burden of immortality.

LUBIN. I see. The old must make room for the new.

BURGE. Death is nothing but making room. Thats
all there is in it or ever has been in it.

FRANKLYN. Yes; but the old must not desert their
posts until the new are ripe for them. They desert them
now two hundred years too soon.

SAVVY. I believe the old people are the new people re-
incarnated, Nunk. I suspect I am Eve. I am very fond
of apples; and they always disagree with me.

CONRAD. You are Eve, in a sense. The Eternal Life
persists; only It wears out Its bodies and minds and gets
new ones, like new clothes. You are only a new hat and
frock on Eve.

FRANKLYN. Yes. Bodies and minds ever better and
better fitted to carry out Its eternal pursuit.

LUBIN [*with quiet scepticism*] What pursuit, may one ask, Mr Barnabas?

FRANKLYN. The pursuit of omnipotence and omniscience. Greater power and greater knowledge: these are what we are all pursuing even at the risk of our lives and the sacrifice of our pleasures. Evolution is that pursuit and nothing else. It is the path of godhead. A man differs from a microbe only in being further on the path.

LUBIN. And how soon do you expect this modest end to be reached?

FRANKLYN. Never, thank God! As there is no limit to power and knowledge there can be no end. "The power and the glory, world without end": have those words meant nothing to you?

BURGE [*pulling out an old envelope*] I should like to make a note of that. [*He does so*].

CONRAD. There will always be something to live for.

BURGE [*pocketing his envelope and becoming more and more business like*] Right: I have got that. Now what about sin? What about the Fall? How do you work them in?

CONRAD. I dont work in the Fall. The Fall is outside Science. But I daresay Frank can work it in for you.

BURGE [*to Franklyn*] I wish you would, you know. It's important. Very important.

FRANKLYN. Well, consider it this way. It is clear that when Adam and Eve were immortal it was necessary that they should make the earth an extremely comfortable place to live in.

BURGE. True. If you take a house on a ninety-nine years lease, you spend a good deal of money on it. If you take it for three months you generally have a bill for dilapidations to pay at the end of them.

FRANKLYN. Just so. Consequently, when Adam had the Garden of Eden on a lease for ever, he took care to make it what the house agents call a highly desirable country residence. But the moment he invented death, and became a tenant for life only, the place was no longer worth the trouble. It was then that he let the thistles grow. Life was so short that it was no longer worth his while to do anything thoroughly well.

BURGE. Do you think that is enough to constitute what an average elector would consider a Fall? Is it tragic enough?

FRANKLYN. That is only the first step of the Fall. Adam did not fall down that step only: he fell down a whole flight. For instance, before he invented birth he dared not have lost his temper; for if he had killed Eve he would have been lonely and barren to all eternity. But when he invented birth, and anyone who was killed could be replaced, he could afford to let himself go. He undoubtedly invented wife-beating; and that was another step down. One of his sons invented meat-eating. The other was horrified at the innovation. With the ferocity which is still characteristic of bulls and other vegetarians, he slew his beefsteak-eating brother, and thus invented murder. That was a very steep step. It was so exciting that all the others began to kill one another for sport, and thus invented war, the steepest step of all. They even took to killing animals as a means of killing time, and then, of course, ate them to save the long and difficult labor of agriculture. I ask you to contemplate our fathers as they came crashing down all the steps of this Jacob's ladder that reached from paradise to a hell on earth in which they had multiplied the chances of death from violence, accident, and disease until they could hardly count on three score and ten years of life, much less the thousand that Adam had been ready to face! With that picture before you, will you now ask me where was the Fall? You might as well stand at the foot of Snowden and ask me where is the mountain. The very children see it so plainly that they compress its history into a two line epic:

Old Daddy Long Legs wouldnt say his prayers:
Take him by the hind legs and throw him downstairs.

LUBIN [*still immovably sceptical*] And what does Science say to this fairy tale, Doctor Barnabas? Surely Science knows nothing of Genesis, or of Adam and Eve.

CONRAD. Then it isnt Science: thats all. Science has to account for everything; and everything includes the Bible.

FRANKLYN. The Book of Genesis is a part of nature like any other part of nature. The fact that the tale of the Garden of Eden has survived and held the imagination of men spellbound for centuries, whilst hundreds of much more plausible and amusing stories have gone out of fashion and perished like last year's popular song, is a scientific fact; and Science is bound to explain it. You tell me that Science knows nothing of it. Then Science is more ignorant than the children at any village school.

CONRAD. Of course if you think it more scientific to say that what we are discussing is not Adam and Eve and Eden, but the phylogeny of the blastoderm—

SAVVY. You neednt swear, Nunk.

CONRAD. Shut up, you: I am not swearing. [*To Lubin*]. If you want the professional humbug of re-writing the Bible in words of four syllables, and pre-tending it's something new, I can humbug you to your heart's content. I can call Genesis Phylogenesis. Let the Creator say, if you like, "I will establish an antipathetic symbiosis between thee and the female, and between thy blastoderm and her blastoderm." Nobody will understand you; and Savvy will think you are swearing. The meaning is the same.

HASLAM.   Priceless.   But it's quite simple.   The one version is poetry: the other is science.

FRANKLYN.   The one is classroom jargon: the other is inspired human language.

LUBIN [calmly reminiscent] One of the few modern authors into whom I have occasionally glanced is Rousseau, who was a sort of Deist like Burge—

BURGE [interrupting him forcibly] Lubin: has this stupendously important communication which Professor Barnabas has just made to us: a communication for which I shall be indebted to him all my life long: has this, I say, no deeper effect on you than to set you pulling my leg by trying to make out that I am an infidel?

LUBIN.   It's very interesting and amusing, Burge; and I think I see a case in it.   I think I could undertake to argue it in an ecclesiastical court.   But important is hardly a word I should attach to it.

BURGE.   Good God!   Here is this professor: a man utterly removed from the turmoil of our political life: devoted to pure learning in its most abstract phases; and I solemnly declare he is the greatest politician, the most inspired party leader, in the kingdom.   I take off my hat to him.   I, Joyce Burge, give him best.   And you sit there purring like an Angora cat, and can see nothing in it!

CONRAD [opening his eyes widely] Hallo!   What have I done to deserve this tribute?

BURGE.   Done!   You have put the Liberal Party into power for the next thirty years, Doctor: thats what youve done.

CONRAD. God forbid!

BURGE. It's all up with the Church now. Thanks to you, we go to the country with one cry and one only: Back to the Bible! Think of the effect on the Nonconformist vote. You gather that in with one hand; and you gather in the modern scientific sceptical professional vote with the other. The village atheist and the first cornet in the local Salvation Army band meet on the village green and shake hands. You take your school children, your Bible class under the Cowper-Temple clause, into the museum. You shew the kids the Piltdown skull; and you say, "Thats Adam. Thats Eve's husband." You take the spectacled science student from the laboratory in Owens College; and when he asks you for a truly scientific history of Evolution, you put into his hand The Pilgrim's Progress. You—[*Savvy and Haslam explode into shrieks of merriment*]. What are you two laughing at?

SAVVY. Oh, go on, Mr Burge. Dont stop.

CONRAD. Priceless!

FRANKLYN. Would thirty years of office for the Liberal Party seem so important to you, Mr Burge, if you had another two and a half centuries to live?

BURGE [*decisively*] No. You will have to drop that part of it. The constituencies wont swallow it.

LUBIN [*seriously*] I am not so sure of that, Burge. I am not sure that it may not prove the only point they will swallow.

BURGE. It will be no use to us even if they do. It's not a party point. It's as good for the other side as for us.

LUBIN. Not necessarily. If we get in first with it, it will be associated in the public mind with our party. Suppose I put it forward as a plank in our program that we advocate the extension of human life to three hundred years! Dunreen, as leader of the opposite party, will be bound to oppose me: to denounce me as a visionary and so forth. By doing so he will place himself in the position of wanting to rob the people of two hundred and thirty years of their natural life. The Unionists will become the party of Premature Death; and we shall become the Longevity party.

BURGE [*shaken*] You really think the electorate would swallow it?

LUBIN. My dear Burge: is there anything the electorate will not swallow if it is judiciously put to them? But we must make sure of our ground. We must have the support of the men of science. Is there serious agreement among them, Doctor, as to the possibility of such an evolution as you have described?

CONRAD. Yes. Ever since the reaction against Darwin set in at the beginning of the present century, all scientific opinion worth counting has been converging rapidly upon Creative Evolution.

FRANKLYN. Poetry has been converging on it: philosophy has been converging on it: religion has been converging on it. It is going to be the religion of the twentieth century: a religion that has its intellectual roots in philosophy and science just as medieval Christianity had its intellectual roots in Aristotle.

LUBIN. But surely any change would be so extremely gradual that—

CONRAD. Dont deceive yourself. It's only the politicians who improve the world so gradually that nobody can see the improvement. The notion that Nature does not proceed by jumps is only one of the budget of plausible lies that we call classical education. Nature always proceeds by jumps. She may spend twenty thousand years making up her mind to jump; but when she makes it up at last, the jump is big enough to take us into a new age.

LUBIN [*impressed*] Fancy my being leader of the party for the next three hundred years!

BURGE. What! ! !

LUBIN. Perhaps hard on some of the younger men. I think in fairness I shall have to step aside to make room after another century or so: that is, if Mimi can be persuaded to give up Downing Street.

BURGE. This is too much. Your collossal conceit blinds you to the most obvious necessity of the political situation.

LUBIN. You mean my retirement. I really cannot see that it is a necessity. I could not see it when I was almost an old man—or at least an elderly one. Now that it appears that I am a young man, the case for it breaks down completely. [*To Conrad*]. May I ask are there any alternative theories? Is there a scientific Opposition?

CONRAD. Well, some authorities hold that the human race is a failure, and that a new form of life, better adapted to high civilization, will supersede us as we have superseded the ape and the elephant.

BURGE. The superman: eh?

CONRAD. No. Some being quite different from us.

LUBIN. Is that altogether desirable?

FRANKLYN. I fear so. However that may be, we may be quite sure of one thing. We shall not be let alone. The force behind evolution, call it what you will, is determined to solve the problem of civilization; and if it cannot do it through us, it will produce some more capable agents. Man is not God's last word: God can still create. If you cannot do His work He will produce some being who can.

BURGE [*with zealous reverence*] What do we know

about Him, Barnabas? What does anyone know about Him?

CONRAD. We know this about Him with absolute certainty. The power my brother calls God proceeds by the method of Trial and Error; and if we turn out to be one of the errors, we shall go the way of the mastodon and the megatherium and all the other scrapped experiments.

LUBIN [*rising and beginning to walk up and down the room with his considering cap on*] I admit that I am impressed, gentlemen. I will go so far as to say that your theory is likely to prove more interesting than ever Welsh Disestablishment was. But as a practical politician—hm! Eh, Burge?

CONRAD. We are not practical politicians. We are out to get something done. Practical politicians are people who have mastered the art of using parliament to prevent anything being done.

FRANKLYN. When we get matured statesmen and citizens—

LUBIN [*stopping short*] Citizens! Oh! Are the citizens to live three hundred years as well as the statesmen?

COKRAD. Of course.

LUBIN. I confess that had not occurred to me. [*He sits down abruptly, evidently very unfavorably affected by this new light*].

Savvy and Haslam look at one another with unspeakable feelings.

BURGE. Do you think it would be wise to go quite so far at first? Surely it would be more prudent to begin with the best men.

FRANKLYN. You need not be anxious about that. It will begin with the best men.

LUBIN. I am glad to hear you say so. You see, we must put this into a practical parliamentary shape.

BURGE. We shall have to draft a Bill: that is the long and the short of it. Until you have your Bill drafted you dont know what you are really doing: that is my experience.

LUBIN. Quite so. My idea is that whilst we should interest the electorate in this as a sort of religious aspiration and personal hope, using it at the same time to remove their prejudices against those of us who are getting on in years, it would be in the last degree upsetting and even dangerous to enable everyone to live longer than usual. Take the mere question of the manufacture of the specific, whatever it may be! There are forty millions of people in the country. Let me assume for the sake of illustration that each person would have to consume, say, five ounces a day of the elixir. That would be—let me see—five times three hundred and sixty-five is—um—twenty-five—thirty-two—eighteen— eighteen hundred and twenty-five ounces a year: just two ounces over the hundredweight.

BURGE. Two million tons a year, in round numbers, of stuff that everyone would clamor for: that men would trample down women and children in the streets to get at. You couldnt produce it. There would be blue murder. It's out of the question. We must keep the actual secret to ourselves.

CONRAD [*staring at them*] The actual secret! What on earth is the man talking about?

BURGE. The stuff. The powder. The bottle. The tabloid. Whatever it is. You said it wasnt lemons.

CONRAD. My good sir: I have no powder, no bottle, no tabloid. I am not a quack: I am a biologist. This is a thing thats going to happen.

LUBIN [*completely let down*] Going to happen!   Oh!
Is that all?   [*He looks at his watch*].

BURGE.   Going to happen!   What do you mean?   Do
you mean that you cant make it happen?

CONRAD.   No   more   than   I   could   have   made   you
happen?

FRANKLYN.   We can put it into men's heads that there
is nothing to prevent its happening but their own will to
die before their work is done, and their own ignorance of
the splendid work there is for them to do.

CONRAD.   Spread that knowledge and that conviction; and as surely as the sun will rise tomorrow, the
thing will happen.

FRANKLYN.   We dont know where or when or to whom
it will happen.   It may happen first to someone in this
room.

HASLAM.   It would happen to me: thats jolly sure.

CONRAD.   It might happen to anyone.   It might happen to the parlormaid.   How do we know?

SAVVY.   The parlormaid!   Oh, thats nonsense, Nunk.

LUBIN [*once more quite comfortable*] I think Miss
Savvy has delivered the final verdict.

BURGE.   Do you mean to say that you have nothing
more practical to offer than the mere wish to live longer?
Why, if people could live by merely wishing to, we
should all be living for ever already!   Everybody would
like to live for ever.   Why dont they?

CONRAD.   Pshaw!   Everybody would like to have a
million of money.   Why havnt they?   Because the men
who would like to be millionaires wont save sixpence even
with the chance of starvation staring them in the face.
The men who want to live for ever wont cut off a glass
of beer or a pipe of tobacco, though they believe the
teetotallers and non-smokers live longer.   That sort of

liking is not willing. See what they do when they know
they must.

FRANKLYN. Do not mistake mere idle fancies for the
tremendous miracle-working force of Will nerved to
creation by a conviction of Necessity. I tell you men
capable of such willing, and realizing its necessity, will
do it reluctantly, under inner compulsion, as all great
efforts are made. They will hide what they are doing
from themselves: they will take care not to know what
they are doing. They will live three hundred years, not
because they would like to, but because the soul deep
down in them will know that they must, if the world is
to be saved.

LUBIN [*turning to Franklyn and patting him almost
paternally*] Well, my dear Barnabas, for the last thirty
years the post has brought me at least once a week a
plan from some crank or other for the establishment of
the millennium. I think you are the maddest of all the
cranks; but you are much the most interesting. I am
conscious of a very curious mixture of relief and disap-
pointment in finding that your plan is all moonshine, and
that you have nothing practical to offer us. But what
a pity! It is such a fascinating idea! I think you are
too hard on us practical men; but there are men in every
Government, even on the Front Bench, who deserve all
you say. And now, before dropping the subject, may I
put just one question to you? An idle question, since
nothing can come of it; but still—

FRANKLYN. Ask your question.

LUBIN. Why do you fix three hundred years as the
exact figure?

FRANKLYN. Because we must fix some figure. Less
would not be enough; and more would be more than we
dare as yet face.

LUBIN. Pooh! I am quite prepared to face three thousand not to say three million.

CONRAD. Yes. because you dont believe you will be called on to make good your word.

FRANKLYN [*gently*] Also, perhaps, because you have never been troubled much by visions of the future.

BURGE [*with intense conviction*] The future does not exist for Henry Hopkins Lubin.

LUBIN. If by the future you mean the millenial delusions which you use as a bunch of carrots to lure the uneducated British donkey to the polling booth to vote for you, it certainly does not.

BURGE. I can see the future not only because, if I may say so in all humility, I have been gifted with a certain power of spiritual vision, but because I have practised as a solicitor. A solicitor has to advise families. He has to think of the future and know the past. His office is the real modern confessional. Among other things he has to make people's wills for them. He has to shew them how to provide for their daughters after their deaths. Has it occurred to you, Lubin, that if you live three hundred years, your daughters will have to wait a devilish long time for their money?

FRANKLYN. The money may not wait for them. Few investments flourish for three hundred years.

SAVVY. And what about before your death? Suppose they didn't get married! Imagine a girl living at home with her mother and on her father for three hundred years! Theyd murder her if she didnt murder them first.

LUBIN. By the way, Barnabas, is your daughter to keep her good looks all the time?

FRANKLYN. Will it matter? Can you conceive the most hardened flirt going on flirting for three centuries? At the end of half the time we shall hardly notice whether it is a woman or a man we are speaking to.

LUBIN [*not quite relishing this ascetic prospect*] Hm! [*He rises*]. Ah, well: you must come and tell my wife and my young people all about it; and you will bring your daughter with you, of course. [*He shakes hands with Savvy*]. Good-bye. [*He shakes hands with Franklyn*]. Good-bye, Doctor. [*He shakes hands with Conrad*]. Come on Burge; you must really tell me what line you are going to take about the Church at the election?

BURGE. Havnt you heard? Havnt you taken in the revelation that has been vouchsafed to us? The line I am going to take is Back to Methuselah.

LUBIN [*decisively*] Dont be ridiculous, Burge. You dont suppose, do you, that our friends here are in earnest, or that our very pleasant conversation has had anything to do with practical politics! They have just been pulling our legs very wittily. Come along. [*He goes out, Franklyn politely going with him, but shaking his head in mute protest*].

BURGE [*shaking Conrad's hand*] It's beyond the old man, Doctor. No spiritual side to him: only a sort of classical side that goes down with his own set. Besides, he's done, gone, past, burnt out, burst up; thinks he is our leader and is only our rag and bottle department. But you may depend on me. I will work this stunt of yours in. I see its value. [*He begins moving towards the door with Conrad*]. Of course I cant put it exactly in your way; but you are quite right about our needing something fresh; and I believe an election can be fought on the death rate and on Adam and Eve as scientific facts. It will take the Opposition right out of its depth. And if we win there will be an O.M. for somebody when the first honors list comes round. [*By this time he has talked himself out of the room and out of earshot, Conrad accompanying him].*

Savvy and Haslam, left alone, seize each other in an ecstasy of amusement, and jazz to the settee, where they sit down again side by side.

HASLAM [*caressing her*] Darling! What a priceless humbug old Lubin is!

SAVVY. Oh, sweet old thing! I love him. Burge is a flaming fraud if you like.

HASLAM. Did you notice one thing? It struck me as rather curious.

SAVVY. What?

HASLAM. Lubin and your father have both survived the war. But their sons were killed in it.

SAVVY [*sobered*] Yes. Jim's death killed mother.

HASLAM. And they never said a word about it!

SAVVY. Well, why should they? The subject didnt come up. *I* forgot about it too; and I was very fond of Jim.

HASLAM. I didnt forget it, because I'm of military age; and if I hadnt been a parson I'd have had to go out and be killed too. To me the awful thing about their political incompetence was that they had to kill their own sons. It was the war casualty lists and the starvation afterwards that finished me up with politics and the Church and everything else except you.

SAVVY. Oh, I was just as bad as any of them. I sold flags in the streets in my best clothes; and—hsh! [*She jumps up and pretends to be looking for a book on the shelves behind the settee].*

Franklyn and Conrad return, looking weary and glum.

CONRAD. Well, thats how the gospel of the brothers Barnabas is going to be received! [*He drops into Burge's chair].*

FRANKLYN [*going back to his seat at the table*] It's no use. Were you convinced, Mr Haslam?

HASLAM. About our being able to live three hundred years? Frankly, no.

CONRAD [*to Savvy*] Nor you, I suppose?

SAVVY. Oh, I dont know. I thought I was for a moment. I can believe, in a sort of way, that people might live for three hundred years. But when you came down to tin tacks, and said that the parlormaid might, then I saw how absurd it was.

FRANKLYN. Just so. We had better hold our tongues about it, Con. We should only be laughed at, and lose the little credit we earned on false pretences in the days of our ignorance.

CONRAD. I daresay. But Creative Evolution doesnt stop while people are laughing. Laughing may even lubricate its job.

SAVVY. What does that mean?

CONRAD. It means that the first man to live three hundred years maynt have the slightest notion that he is going to do it, and may be the loudest laugher of the lot.

SAVVY. Or the first woman?

CONRAD [*assenting*] Or the first woman.

HASLAM. Well, it wont be one of us, anyhow.

FRANKLYN. How do you know?

This is unanswerable. None of them have anything more to say.

PART III
THE THING HAPPENS
XXXIV

THE THING HAPPENS

*A summer afternoon in the year 2170 A.D. The offi-
cial parlor of the President of the British Islands. A
board table, long enough for three chairs at each side
besides the presidential chair at the head and an ordinary
chair at the foot, occupies the breadth of the room. On
the table, opposite every chair, a small switchboard with
a dial. There is no fireplace. The end wall is a silvery
screen nearly as large as a pair of folding doors. The
door is on your left as you face the screen; and there is
a row of thick pegs, padded and covered with velvet,
beside it.*

*A stoutish middle-aged man, good-looking and breez-
ily general, dressed in a silk smock, stockings, hand-
somely ornamented sandals, and a gold fillet round his
brows, comes in. He is like Joyce Burge, yet also like
Lubin, as if Nature had made a composite photograph
of the two men. He takes off the fillet and hangs it on
a peg; then sits down in the presidential chair at the
head of the table, which is at the end farthest from the
door. He puts a peg into his switchboard; turns the
pointer on the dial; puts another peg in; and presses a
button. Immediately the silvery screen vanishes; and
in its place appears, in reverse from right to left, another office similarly furnished, with a thin, unamiable
man similarly dressed, but in duller colors, turning over
some documents at the table. His gold fillet is hanging*

*up on a similar peg beside the door.   He is rather like
Conrad Barnabas, but younger, and much more commonplace.*

BURGE-LUBIN.   Hallo, Barnabas!

BARNABAS [*without looking round*] What number?

BURGE-LUBIN. Five double x three two games. Burge-
Lubin.

*Barnabas puts a plug in number five; turns his
pointer to double x; puts another plug in 32; presses a
button and looks round at Burge-Lubin, who is now
visible to him as well as audible.*

BARNABAS [*curtly*] Oh! That you, President?

BURGE-LUBIN.   Yes. They told me you wanted me
to ring you up.   Anything wrong?

BARNABAS [*harsh and querulous*] I wish to make a
protest.

BURGE-LUBIN [*good-humored and mocking*] What!
Another protest! Whats wrong now?

BARNABAS.   If you only knew all the protests I
havent made, you would be surprised at my patience.
It is you who are always treating me with the grossest
want of consideration.

BURGE-LUBIN.   What have I done now?

BARNABAS.   You have put me down to go to the
Record Office to-day to receive that American fellow, and
do the honors of a ridiculous cinema show.   That is not
the business of the Accountant General: it is the business of the President.   It is an outrageous waste of my
time, and an unjustifiable shirking of your duty at my
expense.   I refuse to go.   You must go.

BURGE-LUBIN.   My dear boy, nothing would give me
greater pleasure than to take the job off your hands—

BARNABAS.   Then do it.   Thats all I want [*he is
about to switch off*].

BURGE-LUBIN. Dont switch off. Listen. This
American has invented a method of breathing under
water.

BARNABAS. What do I care? I dont want to breathe
under water.

BURGE-LUBIN. You may, my dear Barnabas, at any
time. You know you never look where you are going
when you are immersed in your calculations. Some day
you will walk into the Serpentine. This man's invention
may save your life.

BARNABAS [*angrily*] Will you tell me what that has to
do with your putting your ceremonial duties on to my
shoulders? I will not be trifled [*he vanishes and is replaced by the blank screen*]—

BURGE-LUBIN [*indignantly holding down his button*]
Dont cut us off, please: we have not finished. I am the
President, speaking to the Accountant General. What
are you dreaming of?

A WOMAN' VOICE. Sorry. [*The screen shows Barnabas as before*].

BURGE-LUBIN. Since you take it that way, I will go
in your place. It's a pity, because, you see, this American thinks you are the greatest living authority on the
duration of human life; and—

BARNABAS [*interrupting*] The American thinks!
What do you mean? I am the greatest living authority
on the duration of human life. Who dares dispute it?

BURGE-LUBIN. Nobody, dear lad, nobody. Dont fly
out at me. It is evident that you have not read the
American's book.

BARNABAS. Dont tell me that you have, or that you
have read any book except a novel for the last twenty
years; for I wont believe you.

BURGE-LUBIN. Quite right, dear old fellow: I havnt

read it. But I have read what The Times Literary Supplement says about it.

BARNABAS. I dont care two straws what it says about it. Does it say anything about me?

BURGE-LUBIN. Yes.

BARNABAS. Oh! does it? What?

BURGE-LUBIN. It points out that an extraordinary number of first-rate persons like you and me have died by drowning during the last two centuries, and that when this invention of breathing under water takes effect, your estimate of the average duration of human life will be upset.

BARNABAS [alarmed] Upset my estimate! Gracious Heavens! Does the fool realize what that means? Do you realize what that means?

BURGE-LUBIN. I suppose it means that we shall have to amend the Act.

BARNABAS. Amend my Act! Monstrous!

BURGE-LUBIN. But we must. We cant ask people to go on working until they are forty-three unless our figures are unchallengable. You know what a row there was over those last three years, and how nearly the too-old-at-forty people won.

BARNABAS. They would have made the British Islands bankrupt if theyd won. But you dont care for that: you care for nothing but being popular.

BURGE-LUBIN. Oh, well: I shouldnt worry if I were you; for most people complain that there is not enough work for them, and would be only too glad to stick on instead of retiring at forty-three, if only they were asked as a favor instead of having to.

BARNABAS. Thank you: I need no consolation. [He rises determinedly and puts on his fillet].

BURGE-LUBIN. Are you off? Where are you going to?

BARNABAS. To that cinema tomfoolery, of course. I shall put this American imposter in his place. [*He goes out*].

BURGE-LUBIN [*calling after him*] God bless you, dear old chap! [*With a chuckle, he switches off; and the screen becomes blank. He presses a button and holds it down while he calls*] Hallo!

A WOMAN'S VOICE. Hallo!

BURGE-LUBIN [*formally*] The President respectfully solicits the privilege of an interview with the Chief Secretary, and holds himself entirely at his honor's august disposal.

A CHINESE VOICE. He is coming.

BURGE-LUBIN. Oh! That you, Confucius? So good of you. Come along [*he releases the button*].

A man in a yellow gown, presenting the general appearance of a Chinese sage, enters.

BURGE-LUBIN [*jocularly*] Well, illustrious Sage-&-Onions, how are your poor sore feet?

CONFUCIUS [*gravely*] I thank you for your kind enquiries. I am well.

BURGE-LUBIN. Thats right. Sit down and make yourself comfortable. Any business for me today?

CONFUCIUS [*sitting down on the first chair round the corner of the table to the President's right*] None.

BURGE-LUBIN. Have you heard the result of the bye-election?

CONFUCIUS. A walk-over. Only one candidate.

BURGE-LUBIN. Any good?

CONFUCIUS. He was released from the County Lunatic Asylum a fortnight ago. Not mad enough for the lethal chamber: not sane enough for any place but the division lobby. A very popular speaker.

BURGE-LUBIN. I wish the people would take a serious interest in politics.

CONFUCIUS. I do not agree. The Englishman is not fitted by nature to understand politics. Ever since the public services have been manned by Chinese, the country has been well and honestly governed. What more is needed?

BURGE-LUBIN. What I cant make out is that China is one of the worst governed countries on earth.

CONFUCIUS. No. It was badly governed twenty years ago; but since we forbade any Chinaman to take part in our public services, and imported natives of Scotland for that purpose, we have done well. Your information here is always twenty years out of date.

BURGE-LUBIN. People dont seem to be able to govern themselves. I cant understand it. Why should it be so?

CONFUCIUS. Justice is impartiality. Only strangers are impartial.

BURGE-LUBIN. It ends in the public services being so good that the Government has nothing to do but think.

CONFUCIUS. Were it otherwise, the Government would have too much to do to think.

BURGE-LUBIN. Is that any excuse for the English people electing a parliament of lunatics?

CONFUCIUS. The English people always did elect parliaments of lunatics. What does it matter if your permanent officials are honest and competent?

BURGE-LUBIN. You do not know the history of this country. What would my ancestors have said to the menagerie of degenerates that is still called the House of Commons? Confucius: you will not believe me; and I do not blame you for it; but England once saved the liberties of the world by inventing parliamentary government, which was her peculiar and supreme glory.

CONFUCIUS. I know the history of your country perfectly well. It proves the exact contrary.

BURGE-LUBIN. How do you make that out?

CUNFUCIUS. The only power your parliament ever had was the power of withholding supplies from the king.

BURGE-LUBIN. Precisely. That great Englishman Simon de Montfort—

CONFUCIUS. He was not an Englishman: he was a Frenchman. He imported parliaments from France.

BURGE-LUBIN [surprised] You dont say so!

CONFUCIUS. The king and his loyal subjects killed Simon for forcing his French parliament on them. The first thing British parliaments always did was to grant supplies to the king for life with enthusiastic expressions of loyalty, lest they should have any real power, and be expected to do something.

BURGE-LUBIN. Look here, Confucius: you know more history than I do, of course; but democracy—

CONFUCIUS. An institution peculiar to China. And it was never really a success there.

BURGE-LUBIN. But the Habeas Corpus Act!

CONFUCIUS. The English always suspended it when it threatened to be of the slightest use.

BURGE-LUBIN. Well, trial by jury: you cant deny that we established that?

CONFUCIUS. All cases that were dangerous to the governing classes were tried in the Star Chamber or by Court Martial, except when the prisoner was not tried at all, but executed after calling him names enough to make him unpopular.

BURGE-LUBIN. Oh, bother! You may be right in these little details; but in the large we have managed to hold our own as a great race. Well, people who could do nothing couldnt have done that, you know.

CONFUCIUS. I did not say you could do nothing. You could fight. You could eat. You could drink. Until the twentieth century you could produce children.

You could play games. You could work when you were forced to. But you could not govern yourselves.

BURGE-LUBIN. Then how did we get our reputation as the pioneers of liberty?

CUNFUCIUS. By your steadfast refusal to be governed at all. A horse that kicks everyone who tries to harness and guide him may be a pioneer of liberty; but he is not a pioneer of government. In China he would be shot.

BURGE-LUBIN. Stuff! Do you imply that the administration of which I am president is no Government?

CONFUCIUS. I do. *I* am the Government.

BURGE-LUBIN. You! You!! You fat yellow lump of conceit!

CONFUCIUS. Only an Englishman could be so ignorant of the nature of government as to suppose that a capable statesman cannot be fat, yellow, and conceited. Many Englishmen are slim, red-nosed, and modest. Put them in my place, and within a year you will be back in the anarchy and chaos of the nineteenth and twentieth centuries.

BURGE-LUBIN. Oh, if you go back to the dark ages, I have nothing more to say. But we did not perish. We extricated ourselves from that chaos. We are now the best governed country in the world. How did we manage that if we are such fools as you pretend?

CONFUCIUS. You did not do it until the slaughter and ruin produced by your anarchy forced you at last to recognize two inexorable facts. First, that government is absolutely necessary to civilization, and that you could not maintain civilization by merely doing down your neighbor, as you called it, and cutting off the head of your king whenever he happened to be a logical Scot and tried to take his position seriously. Second, that government is an art of which you are congenitally incapable. Accordingly, you imported educated negresses and Chinese to govern you. Since then you have done very well.

BURGE-LUBIN. So have you, you old humbug. All the same, I dont know how you stand the work you do. You seem to me positively to like public business. Why wont you let me take you down to the coast some week-end and teach you marine golf?

CONFUCIUS. It does not interest me. I am not a barbarian.

BURGE-LUBIN. You mean that I am?

CONFUCIUS. That is evident.

BURGE-LUBIN. How?

CONFUCIUS. People like you. They like cheerful good-natured barbarians. They have elected you President five times in succession. They will elect you five times more. *I* like you. You are better company than a dog or a horse because you can speak.

BURGE-LUBIN. Am I a barbarian because you like me?

CONFUCIUS. Surely. Nobody likes me: I am held in awe. Capable persons are never liked. I am not like-able; but I am indispensable.

BURGE-LUBIN. Oh, cheer up, old man; theres nothing so disagreeable about you as all that. I dont dislike you; and if you think I'm afraid of you, you jolly well dont know Burge-Lubin: thats all.

CONFUCIUS. You are brave: yes. It is a form of stupidity.

BURGE-LUBIN. You may not be brave; one doesnt expect it from a Chink. But you have the devil's own cheek.

CONFUCIUS. I have the assured certainty of the man who sees and knows. Your genial bluster, your cheery self-confidence, are pleasant, like the open air. But they are blind: they are vain. I seem to see a great dog wag his tail and bark joyously. But if he leaves my heel he is lost.

BURGE-LUBIN. Thank you for a handsome compliment. I have a big dog; and he is the best fellow I know. If you knew how much uglier you are than a chow, you wouldn't start those comparisons, though. [*Rising*] Well, if you have nothing for me to do, I am going to leave your heel for the rest of the day and enjoy myself. What would you recommend me to do with myself?

CONFUCIUS. Give yourself up to contemplation; and great thoughts will come to you.

BURGE-LUBIN. Will they? If you think I am going to sit here on a fine day like this with my legs crossed waiting for great thoughts, you exaggerate my taste for them. I prefer marine golf. [*Stopping short*] Oh, by the way, I forgot something. I have a word or two to say to the Minister of Health. [*He goes back to his chair*].

CONFUCIUS. Her number is—

BURGE-LUBIN. I know it.

CONFUCIUS [*rising*] I cannot understand her attraction for you. For me a woman who is not yellow does not exist, save as an official. [*He goes out*].

Burge-Lubin operates the .switchboard as before. The screen vanishes; and a dainty room with a bed, a wardrobe, and a dressing-table with a mirror and a switch on it, appears. Seated at it a handsome negress is trying on a brilliant head scarf. Her dressing-gown is thrown back from her shoulders to her chair. She is in corset, knickers, and silk stockings.

BURGE-LUBIN [*horrified*] I beg your pardon a thousand times— [*The startled negress snatches the peg out of her switchboard and vanishes*].

THE NEGRESS'S VOICE. Who it is?

BURGE-LUBIN. Me. The President. Burge-Lubin.
I had no idea your bedroom switch was in. I beg your
pardon.

*The negress reappears. She has pulled the dress-
ing-gown perfunctorily over her shoulders, and continues
her experiments with the scarf, not at all put out, and
rather amused by Burge's prudery.*

THE NEGRESS. Stupid of me. I was talking to another lady this morning; and I left the peg in.

BURGE-LUBIN. But I am so sorry.

THE NEGRESS [*sunnily: still busy with the scarf*]
Why? It was my fault.

BURGE-LUBIN [*embarrassed*] Well—er—er— But I
suppose you were used to it in Africa.

THE NEGRESS. Your delicacy is very touching, Mr
President. It would be funny if it were not so unpleasant, because, like all white delicacy, it is in the
wrong place. How do you think this suits my com-
plexion?

BURGE-LUBIN. How can any really vivid color go
wrong with a black satin skin? It is our women's
wretched pale faces that have to be matched and lighted.
Yours is always right.

THE NEGRESS. Yes: it is a pity your white beauties
have all the same ashy faces, the same colorless drab, the
same age. But look at their beautiful noses and little
lips! They are physically insipid: they have no beauty:
you cannot love them; but how elegant!

BURGE-LUBIN. Cant you find an official pretext for
coming to see me? Isnt it ridiculous that we have never
met? It's so tantalizing to see you and talk to you, and
to know all the time that you are two hundred miles
away, and that I cant touch you?

THE NEGRESS. I cannot live on the East Coast: it is

hard enough to keep my blood warm here. Besides, my friend, it would not be safe. These distant flirtations are very charming; and they teach self-control.

BURGE-LUBIN. Damn self-control! I want to hold you in my arms—to— [*the negress snatches out the peg from the switchboard and vanishes. She is still heard laughing*]. Black devil! [*He snatches out his peg furiously; her laugh is no longer heard*]. Oh, these sex episodes! Why can I not resist them? Disgraceful!

Confucius returns.

CONFUCIUS. I forgot. There is something for you to do this morning. You have to go to the Record Office to receive the American barbarian.

BURGE-LUBIN. Confucius: once for all, I object to this Chinese habit of describing white men as barbarians.

CONFUCIUS [*standing formally at the end of the table with his hands palm to palm*] I make a mental note that you do not wish the Americans to be described as barbarians.

BURGE-LUBIN. Not at all. The Americans are barbarians. But we are not. I suppose the particular barbarian you are speaking of is the American who has invented a means of breathing under water.

CONFUCIUS. He says he has invented such a method. For some reason which is not intelligible in China, Englishmen always believe any statement made by an American inventor, especially one who has never invented anything. Therefore you believe this person and have given him a public reception. Today the Record Office is entertaining him with a display of the cinematographic records of all the eminent Englishmen who have lost their lives by drowning since the cinema was invented. Why not go to see it if you are at a loss for 'omething to do?

BURGE-LUBIN. What earthly interest is there in looking at a moving picture of a lot of people merely because they were drowned? If they had had any sense, they would not have been drowned, probably.

CONFUCIUS. That is not so. It has never been noticed before; but the Record Office has just made two remarkable discoveries about the public men and women who have displayed extraordinary ability during the past century. One is that they retained unusual youthfulness up to an advanced age. The other is that they all met their death by drowning.

BURGE-LUBIN. Yes: I know. Can you explain it?

CONFUCIUS. It cannot be explained. It is not reasonable. Therefore I do not believe it.

The Accountant General rushes in, looking ghastly. He staggers to the middle of the table.

BURGE-LUBIN. Whats the matter? Are you ill?

BARNABAS [*choking*] No. I— [*he collapses into the middle chair*]. I must speak to you in private.

Confucius calmly withdrawns.

BURGE-LUBIN. What on earth is it? Have some oxygen.

BARNABAS. I have had some. Go to the Record Office. You will see men fainting there again and again, and being revived with oxygen, as I have been. They have seen with their own eyes as I have.

BURGE-LUBIN. Seen what?

BARNABAS. Seen the Archbishop of York.

BURGE-LUBIN. Well, why shouldnt they see the Archbishop of York? What are they fainting for? Has he been murdered?

BARNABAS. No: he has been drowned.

BURGE-LUBIN. Good God! Where? When? How? Poor fellow!

RABNABAS. Poor fellow! Poor thief! Poor swindler! Poor robber of his country's Exchequer! **Poor fellow indeed!** Wait til I catch him.

BURGE-LUBIN. How can you catch him when he is dead? Youre mad.

BARNABAS. Dead! Who said he was dead?

BURGE-LUBIN. You did. Drowned.

BARNABAS [*exasperated*] Will you listen to me? Was old Archbishop Haslam, the present man's last predecessor but four, drowned or not?

BURGE-LUBIN. I dont know. Look him up in the Encyclopedia Britannica.

BARNABAS. Yah! Was Archbishop Stickit, who wrote Stickit on the Psalms, drowned or not?

BURGE-LUBIN. Yes, mercifully. He deserved it.

BARNABAS. Was President Dickenson drowned? Was General Bullyboy drowned?

BURGE-LUBIN. Who is denying it?

BARNABAS. Well, weve had moving pictures of all four put on the screen today for this American; and they and the Archbishop are the same man. Now tell me I am mad.

BURGE-LUBIN. I do tell you you are mad. Stark raving mad.

BARNABAS. Am I to believe my own eyes or am I not?

BURGE-LUBIN. You can do as you please. All I can tell you is that *I* dont believe your eyes if they cant see any difference between a live archbishop and two dead ones. [*The apparatus rings, he holds the button down*]. Yes?

THE WOMAN'S VOICE. The Archbishop of York, to see the President.

BARNABAS [*hoarse with rage*] Have him in. I'll talk to the scoundrel.

BURGE-LUBIN [*releasing the button*] Not while you are in this state.

BARNABAS [*reaching furiously for his button and holding it down*] Send the Archbishop in at once.

BURGE-LUBIN.   If you lose your temper, Barnabas, remember that we shall be two to one.

The Archbishop enters. He has a white band round his throat, set in a black stock. He wears a sort of kilt of black ribbons, and soft black boots that button high up on his calves. His costume does not differ otherwise from that of the President and the Accountant General; but its color scheme is black and white. He is older than the Reverend Bill Haslam was when he woed Miss Savvy Barnabas; but he is recognizably the same man. He does not look a day over fifty, and is very well preserved even at that; but his boyishness of manner is quite gone: he now has complete authority and self-possession: in fact the President is a little afraid of him; and it seems quite natural and inevitable that he should speak first.

THE ARCHBISHOP.   Good day, Mr President.

BURGE-LUBIN.   Good day, Mr Archbishop. Be seated.

THE ARCHBISHOP [*sitting down between them*] Good day, Mr Accountant General.

BARNABAS [*malevolently*] Good day to you.   I have a question to put to you, if you dont mind.

THE ARCHBISHOP [*looking curiously at him, jarred by his uncivil tone*] Certainly.   What is it?

BARNABAS   What is your definition of a thief?

THE ARCHBISHOP.   Rather an old-fashioned word, is it not?

BARNABAS.   It survives officially in my department.

THE ARCHBISHOP.   Our departments are full of survivals.   Look at my tie! my apron! my boots!   They are all mere survivals; yet it seems that without them I cannot be a proper Archbishop.

BARNABAS.   Indeed!   Well, in my department the word thief survives, because in the community the thing thief survives. And a very despicable and dishonorable thing he is, too.

THE ARCHBISHOP [*coolly*] I daresay.

BARNABAS. In my department, sir, a thief is a person who lives longer than the statutory expectation of life entitles him to, and goes on drawing public money when, if he were an honest man, he would be dead.

THE ARCHBISHOP. Then let me say, sir, that your department does not understand its own business. If you have miscalculated the duration of human life, that is not the fault of the persons whose longevity you have miscalculated. And if they continue to work and produce, they pay their way, even if they live two or three centuries.

BARNABAS. I know nothing about their working and producing. That is not the business of my department. I am concerned with their expectation of life; and I say that no man has any right to go on living and drawing money when he ought to be dead.

THE ARCHBISHOP. You do not comprehend the relation between income and production.

BARNABAS. I understand my own department.

THE ARCHBISHOP. That is not enough. Your department is part of a synthesis which embraces all the departments.

BURGE-LUBIN. Synthesis! This is an intellectual difficulty. This is a job for Confucius. I heard him use that very word the other day; and I wondered what the devil he meant. [*Switching on*] Hallo! Put me through to the Chief Secretary.

CONFUCIUS'S VOICE. You are speaking to him.

BURGE-LUBIN. An intellectual difficulty, old man. Something we dont understand. Come and help us out.

THE ARCHBISHOP. May I ask how the question has arisen?

BARNABAS. Ah! You begin to smell a rat, do you?
You thought yourself pretty safe. You—

BURGE-LUBIN. Steady, Barnabas. Dont be in a
hurry.

Confucius enters.

THE ARCHBISHOP [*rising*] Good morning, Mr Chief
Secretary.

BURGE-LUBIN [*rising in instinctive imitation of the
Archbishop*] Honor us by taking a seat, O sage.

CONFUCIUS. Ceremony is needless. [*He bows to the
company and takes the chair at the foot of the table*].

*The President and the Archbishop resume their
seats.*

BURGE-LUBIN. We wish to put a case to you, Confucius. Suppose a man, instead of conforming to the
official estimate of his expectation of life, were to live
for more than two centuries and a half, would the
Accountant General be justified in calling him a thief?

CONFUCIUS. No. He would be justified in calling
him a liar.

THE ARCHBISHOP. I think not, Mr Chief Secretary.
What do you suppose my age is?

CONFUCIUS. Fifty.

BURGE-LUBIN. You dont look it. Forty-five; and
young for your age.

THE ARCHBISHOP. My age is two hundred and
eighty-three.

BARNABAS [*morosely triumphant*] Hmp! Mad, am I?

BURGE-LUBIN. Youre both mad. Excuse me, Archbishop; but this is getting a bit—well—

THE ARCHBISHOP [*to Confucius*] Mr Chief Secretary:
will you, to oblige me, assume that I have lived nearly
three centuries? As a hypothesis.

BURGE-LUBIN. What is a hypothesis?

CONFUCIUS. It does not matter. I understand. [*To

the Archbishop] Am I to assume that you have lived in your ancestors, or by metempsychosis—

BURGE-LUBIN. Met—Emp—Sy— Good Lord! What a brain, Confucius! What a brain!

THE ARCHBISHOP. Nothing of that kind. Assume in the ordinary sense that I was born in the year 1887, and that I have worked continuously in one profession or another since the year 1910. Am I a thief?

CONFUCIUS. I do not know. Was that one of your professions?

THE ARCHBISHOP. No. I have been nothing worse than an Archbishop, a President, and a General.

BARNABAS. Has he or has he not robbed the Exchequer by drawing five or six incomes when he was only entitled to one? Answer me that.

CONFUCIUS. Certainly not. The hypothesis is that he has worked continuously since 1910. We are now in the year 2170. What is the official lifetime?

BARNABAS. Seventy-eight. Of course it's an average; and we dont mind a man here and there going on to ninety, or even, as a curiosity, becoming a centenarian. But I say that a man who goes beyond that is a swindler.

CONFUCIUS. Seventy-eight into two hundred and eighty-three goes more than three and a half times. Your department owes the Archbishop two and a half educations and three and a half retiring pensions.

BARNABAS. Stuff! How can that be?

CONFUCIUS. At what age do your people begin to work for the community?

BURGE-LUBIN. Three. They do certain things every day when they are three. Just to break them in, you know. But they become self-supporting, or nearly so, at thirteen.

CONFUCIUS. And at what age do they retire?

BARNABAS.   Forty-three.

CONFUCIUS.   That is, they do thirty years' work; and they receive maintenance and education, without working, for thirteen years of childhood and thirty-five years of superannuation, forty-eight years in all, for each thirty years' work.   The Archbishop has given you 260 years' work, and has received only one education and no superannuation.   You therefore owe him over 300 years of leisure and nearly eight educations.   You are thus heavily in his debt.   In other words, he has effected an enormous national economy by living so long; and you, by living only seventy-eight years, are profiting at his expense.   He is the benefactor: you are the thief. [*Half rising*] May I now withdraw and return to my serious business, as my own span is comparatively short.

BURGE-LUBIN.   Dont be in a hurry, old chap.   [*Confucius sits down again*].   This hypothecary, or whatever you call it, is put up seriously.   I dont believe it; but if the Archbishop and the Accountant General are going to insist that it's true, we shall have either to lock them up or to see the thing through.

BARNABAS.   It's no use trying these Chinese subtleties on me.   I'm a plain man; and though I dont understand metaphysics, and dont believe in them, I understand figures; and if the Archbishop is only entitled to seventy-eight years, and he takes 283, I say he takes more than he is entitled to.   Get over that if you can.

THE ARCHBISHOP.   I have not taken 283 years: I have taken 23 and given 260.

CONFUCIUS.   Do your accounts shew a deficiency or a surplus?

BARNABAS.   A surplus.   Thats what I cant make out. Thats the artfulness of these people.

BURGE-LUBIN.   That settles it.   Whats the use of

arguing? The Chink says you are wrong; and theres an end of it.

BARNABAS. I say nothing against the Chink's arguments. But what about my facts?

CONFUCIUS. If your facts include a case of a man living 283 years, I advise you to take a few weeks at the seaside.

BARNABAS. Let there be an end of this hinting that I am out of my mind. Come and look at the cinema record. I tell you this man is Archbishop Haslam, Archbiship Stickit, President Dickenson, General Bully-boy and himself into the bargain: all five of them.

THE ARCHBISHOP. I do not deny it. I never have denied it. Nobody has ever asked me.

BURGE-LUBIN. But damn it, man—I beg your pardon, Archbishop; but really, really—

THE ARCHBISHOP. Dont mention it. What were you going to say?

BURGE-LUBIN. Well, you were drowned four times over. You are not a cat, you know.

THE ARCHBISHOP. That is very easy to understand. Consider my situation when I first made the amazing discovery that I was destined to live three hundred years! I—

CONFUCIUS [*interrupting him*] Pardon me. Such a discovery was impossible. You have not made it yet. You may live a million years if you have already lived two hundred. There is no question of three hundred years. You have made a slip at the very beginning of your fairy tale, Mr Archbishop.

BURGE-LUBIN. Good, Confucius! [*To the Archbishop*] He has you there. I dont see how you can get over that.

THE ARCHBISHOP. Yes: it is quite a good point. But if the Accountant General will go to the British

Museum library, and search the catalogue, he will find under his own name a curious and now forgotten book, dated 1924, entitled The Gospel of the Brothers Barnabas. That gospel was that men must live three hundred years if civilization is to be saved. It shewed that this extension of individual human life was possible, and how it was likely to come about. I married the daughter of one of the brothers.

BARNABAS. Do you mean to say you claim to be a connection of mine?

THE ARCHBISHOP. I claim nothing. As I have by this time perhaps three or four million cousins of one degree or another, I have ceased to call on the family.

BURGE-LUBIN. Gracious heavens! Four million relatives! Is that calculation correct, Confucius?

CONFUCIUS. In China it might be forty millions if there were no checks on population.

BURGE-LUBIN. This is a staggerer. It brings home to one—but [recovering] it isn't true, you know. Let us keep sane.

CONFUCIUS [to the Archbishop] You wish us to understand that the illustrious ancestors of the Accountant General communicated to you a secret by which you could attain the age of three hundred years.

THE ARCHBISHOP. No. Nothing of the kind. They simply believed that mankind could live any length of time it knew to be absolutely necessary to save civilization from extinction. I did not share their belief: at least I was not conscious of sharing it: I thought I was only amused by it. To me my father-in-law and his brother were a pair of clever cranks who had talked one another into a fixed idea which had become a monomania with them. It was not until I got into serious difficulties with the pension authorities after turning seventy that I began to suspect the truth.

CONFUCIUS. The truth?

THE ARCHBISHOP. Yes, Mr Chief Secretary: the truth. Like all revolutionary truths, it began as a joke. As I shewed no signs of ageing after forty-five, my wife used to make fun of me by saying that I was certainly going to live three hundred years. She was sixty-eight when she died; and the last thing she said to me, as I sat by her bedside holding her hand, was "Bill: you really dont look fifty. I wonder——" She broke off, and fell asleep wondering, and never awoke. Then I began to wonder too. That is the explanation of the three hundred years, Mr Secretary.

CONFUCIUS. It is very ingenious, Mr Archbishop. And very well told.

BURGE-LUBIN. Of course you understand that *I* dont for a moment suggest the very faintest doubt of your absolute veracity, Archbishop. You know that, dont you?

THE ARCHBISHOP. Quite, Mr President. Only you dont believe me: that is all. I do not expect you to. In your place I should not believe. You had better have a look at the films. [*Pointing to the Accountant General*] He believes.

BURGE-LUBIN. But the drowning? What about the drowning? A man might get drowned once, or even twice if he was exceptionally careless. But he couldn't be drowned four times. He would run away from water like a mad dog.

THE ARCHBISHOP. Perhaps Mr Chief Secretary can guess the explanation of that.

CONFUCIUS. To keep your secret, you had to die.

BURGE-LUBIN. But dash it all, man, he isnt dead.

CONFUCIUS. It is socially impossible not to do what everybody else does. One must die at the usual time.

BARNABAS. Of course. A simple point of honor.

CONFUCIUS.   Not at all.   A simple necessity.

BURGE-LUBIN.   Well, I'm hanged if I see it.   I should jolly well live for ever if I could.

THE ARCHBISHOP.   It is not so easy as you think. You, Mr Chief Secretary, have grasped the difficulties of the position.   Let me remind you, Mr President, that I was over eighty before the 1969 Act for the Redistribution of Income entitled me to a handsome retiring pension.   Owing to my youthful appearance I was prosecuted for attempting to obtain public money on false pretences when I claimed it. I could prove nothing; for the register of my birth had been blown to pieces by a bomb dropped on a village church years before in the first of the big modern wars.   I was ordered back to work as a man of forty, and had to work for fifteen years more, the retiring age being then fifty-five.

BURGE-LUBIN.   As late as fifty-five!   How did people stand it?

THE ARCHBISHOP.   They made difficulties about letting me go even then, I still looked so young.   For some years I was in continual trouble.   The industrial police rounded me up again and again, refusing to believe that I was over age.   They began to call me the Wandering Jew.   You see how impossible my position was.   I foresaw that in twenty years more my official record would prove me to be seventy-five; my appearance would make it impossible to believe that I was more than forty-five; and my real age would be one hundred and seventeen. What was I to do?   Bleach my hair?   Hobble about on two sticks?   Mimic the voice of a centenarian?   Better have killed myself.

BARNABAS.   You ought to have killed yourself. As an honest man you were entitled to no more than an honest man's expectation of life.

THE ARCHBISHOP.   I did kill myself.   It was quite

easy. I left a suit of clothes by the seashore during the bathing season, with documents in the pockets to identify me. I then turned up in a strange place, pretending that I had lost my memory, and did not know my name or my age or anything about myself. Under treatment I recovered my health, but not my memory. I have had several careers since I began this routine of life and death. I have been an archbishop three times. When I persuaded the authorities to knock down all our towns and rebuild them from the foundations, or move them, I went into the artillery, and became a general. I have been President.

BURGE-LUBIN. Dickenson?

THE ARCHBISHOP. Yes.

BURGE-LUBIN. But they found Dickenson's body: its ashes are buried in St. Paul's.

THE ARCHBISHOP. They almost always found the body. During the bathing season there are plenty of bodies. I have been cremated again and again. At first I used to attend my own funeral in disguise, because I had read about a man doing that in an old romance by an author named Bennett, from whom I remember borrowing five pounds in 1912. But I got tired of that. I would not cross the street now to read my latest epitaph.

The Chief Secretary and the President look very glum. Their incredulity is vanquished at last.

BURGE-LUBIN. Look here. Do you chaps realize how awful this is? Here we are sitting calmly in the presence of a man whose death is overdue by two centuries. He may crumble into dust before our eyes at any moment.

BARNABAS. Not he. He'll go on drawing his pension until the end of the world.

THE ARCHBISHOP. Not quite that. My expectation of life is only three hundred years.

BARNABAS.   You will last out my time anyhow: thats
enough for me.

THE ARCHBISHOP [*coolly*] How do you know?

BARNABAS [*taken aback*] How do I know!

THE ARCHBISHOP.   Yes: how do you know? I did not
begin even to suspect until I was nearly seventy. I was
only vain of my youthful appearance. I was not quite
serious about it until I was ninety. Even now I am not
sure from one moment to another, though I have given
you my reason for thinking that I have quite unintentionally committed myself to a lifetime of three hundred
years.

BURGE-LUBIN.   But how do you do it? Is it lemons?
Is it Soya beans? Is it—

THE ARCHBISHOP.   I do not do it. It happens. It
may happen to anyone. It may happen to you.

BURGE-LUBIN [*the full significance of this for himself
dawning on him*] Then we three may be in the same boat
with you, for all we know?

THE ARCHBISHOP.   You may. Therefore I advise you
to be very careful how you take any step that will make
my position uncomfortable.

BURGE-LUBIN.   Well, I'm dashed! One of my secre-
taries was remarking only this morning how well and
young I am looking. Barnabas: I have an absolute conviction that I am one of the—the—shall I say one of
the victims?—of this strange destiny.

THE ARCHBISHOP.   Your   great-great-great-great-
great-great-grandfather   formed   the   same   conviction
when he was between sixty and seventy. I knew him.

BURGE-LUBIN [*depressed*] Ah! But he died.

THE ARCHBISHOP.   No.

BURGE-LUBIN [*hopefully*] Do you mean to say he is
still alive?

THE ARCHBISHOP.   No. He was shot. Under the influence of his belief that he was going to live three hundred years he became a changed man. He began to tell people the truth; and they disliked it so much that they took advantage of certain clauses of an Act of Parliament he had himself passed during the Four Years War, and had purposely forgotten to repeal afterwards. They took him to the Tower of London and shot him.

[*The apparatus rings.*]

CONFUCIUS [*answering*] Yes? [*He listens.*]

A WOMAN'S VOICE. The Domestic Minister has called.

BURGE-LUBIN [*not quite catching the answer*] Who does she say had called?

CONFUCIUS. The Domestic Minister.

BARNABAS. Oh, dash it! That awful woman!

BURGE-LUBIN. She certainly is a bit of a terror. I dont know exactly why; for she is not at all bad-looking.

BARNABAS [*out of patience*] For Heaven's sake, dont be frivolous.

THE ARCHBISHOP. He cannot help it, Mr Accountant General. Three of his sixteen great-great-great-grandfathers married Lubins.

BURGE-LUBIN. Tut tut! I am not frivolling. *I* did not ask the lady here. Which of you did?

CONFUCIUS. It is her official duty to report personally to the President once a quarter.

BURGE-LUBIN. Oh, that! Then I suppose it's my official duty to receive her. Theyd better send her in. You dont mind, do you? She will bring us back to real life. I dont know how you fellows feel; but I'm just going dotty.

CONFUCIUS [*into the telephone*] The President will receive the Domestic Minister at once.

They watch the door in silence for the entrance of the Domestic Minister.

BURGE-LUBIN [*suddenly, to the Archbishop*] I suppose you have been married over and over again.

THE ARCHBISHOP. Once. You do not make vows until death when death is three hundred years off.

They relapse into uneasy silence. The Domestic Minister enters. She is a handsome woman, apparently in the prime of life, with elegant, tense, well held-up figure, and the walk of a goddess. Her expression and deportment are grave, swift, decisive, awful, unanswerable. She wears a Dianesque tunic instead of a blouse, and a silver coronet instead of a gold fillet. Her dress otherwise is not markedly different from that of the men, who rise as she enters, and incline their heads with instinctive awe. She comes to the vacant chair between Barnabas and Confucius.

BURGE-LUBIN [*resolutely genial and gallant*] Delighted to see you, Mrs Lutestring.

CONFUCIUS. We are honored by your celestial presence.

BARNABAS. Good day, madam.

THE ARCHBISHOP. I have not had the pleasure of meeting you before. I am the Archbishop of York.

MRS LUTESTRING. Surely we have met, Mr Archbishop. I remember your face. We— [*she checks herself suddenly*] Ah, no: I remember now: it was someone else. [*She sits down*].

They all sit down.

THE ARCHBISHOP [*also puzzled*] Are you sure you are mistaken? I also have some association with your face, Mrs Lutestring. Something like a door opening continually and revealing you. And a smile of welcome when you recognized me. Did you ever open a door for me, I wonder?

MRS LUTESTRING. I often opened a door for the per-

son you have just reminded me of. But he has been
dead many years.

*The rest, except the Archbishop, look at one another
quickly.*

CONFUCIUS.   May I ask how many years?

MRS LUTESTRING [*struck by his tone, looks at him for
a moment with some displeasure; then replies*] It does
not matter.   A long time.

BURGE-LUBIN.   You mustnt rush to conclusions about
the Archbishop, Mrs Lutestring.   He is an older bird
than you think.   Older than you, at all events.

MRS LUTESTRING [*with a melancholy smile*] I think
not, Mr President.   But the subject is a delicate one.
I had rather not pursue it.

CONFUCIUS.   There is a question which has not been
asked.

MRS LUTESTRING [*very decisively*] If it is a question
about my age, Mr Chief Secretary, it had better not be
asked.   All that concerns you about my personal affairs
can be found in the books of the Accountant General.

CONFUCIUS.   The question I was thinking of will not
be addressed to you.   But let me say that your sensitiveness on the point is very strange, coming from a
woman so superior to all common weaknesses as we know
you to be.

MRS LUTESTRING.   I may have reasons which have
nothing to do with common weaknesses, Mr Chief Secretary.   I hope you will respect them.

CONFUCIUS [*after bowing to her in assent*] I will now
put my question.   Have you, Mr Archbishop, any
ground for assuming, as you seem to do, that what has
happened to you has not happened to other people as
well?

BURGE-LUBIN.   Yes, by George!   I never thought of
that.

THE ARCHBISHOP. I have never met any case but my own.

CONFUCIUS. How do you know?

THE ARCHBISHOP. Well, no one has ever told me that they were in this extraordinary position.

CONFUCIUS. That proves nothing. Did you ever tell anybody that you were in it? You never told us. Why did you never tell us?

THE ARCHBISHOP. I am surprised at the question, coming from so astute a mind as yours, Mr Secretary. When you reach the age I reached before I discovered what was happening to me, I was old enough to know and fear the ferocious hatred with which human animals, like all other animals, turn upon any unhappy individual who has the misfortune to be unlike themselves in every respect: to be unnatural, as they call it. You will still find, among the tales of that twentieth-century classic, Wells, a story of a race of men who grew twice as big as their fellows, and another story of a man who fell into the hands of a race of blind men. The big people had to fight the little people for their lives; and the man with eyes would have had his eyes put out by the blind had he not fled to the desert, where he perished miserably. Wells's teaching, on that and other matters, was not lost on me. By the way, he lent me five pounds once which I never repaid; and it still troubles my conscience.

CONFUCIUS. And were you the only reader of Wells? If there were others like you, had they not the same reason for keeping the secret?

THE ARCHBISHOP. That is true. But I should know. You short-lived people are so childish. If I met a man of my own age I should recognize him at once. I have never done so.

MRS LUTESTRING. Would you recognize a woman of your age, do you think?

THE ARCHBISHOP. I—[*He stops and turns upon her with a searching look, startled by the suggestion and the suspicion it rouses*].

MRS LUTESTRING. What is your age, Mr Archbishop?

BURGE-LUBIN. Two hundred and eighty-three, he says. That is his little joke. Do you know, Mrs Lutestring, he had almost talked us into believing him when you came in and cleared the air with your robust common sense.

MRS LUTESTRING. Do you really feel that, Mr President? I hear the note of breezy assertion in your voice. I miss the note of conviction.

BURGE-LUBIN [*jumping up*] Look here. Let us stop talking damned nonsense. I dont wish to be disagreeable; but it's getting on my nerves. The best joke wont bear being pushed beyond a certain point. That point has been reached. I—I'm rather busy this morning. We all have our hands pretty full. Confucius here will tell you that I have a heavy day before me.

BARNABAS. Have you anything more important than this thing, if it's true?

BURGE-LUBIN. Oh, if, if, if it's true! But it isn't true.

BARNABAS. Have you anything at all to do?

BURGE-LUBIN. Anything to do! Have you forgotten, Barnabas, that I happen to be President, and that the weight of the entire public business of this country is on my shoulders?

BARNABAS. Has he anything to do, Confucius?

CONFUCIUS. He has to be President.

BARNABAS. That means that he has nothing to do.

BURGE-LUBIN [*sulkily*] Very well, Barnabas. Go on making a fool of yourself. [*He sits down*]. Go on.

BARNABAS. I am not going to leave this room until we get to the bottom of this swindle.

MRS LUTESTRING [*turning with deadly gravity on the Accountant General*] This what, did you say?

CONFUCIUS. These expressions cannot be sustained. You obscure the discussion in using them.

BARNABAS [*glad to escape from her gaze by addressing Confucius*] Well, this unnatural horror. Will that satisfy you?

CONFUCIUS. That is in order. But we do not commit ourselves to the implications of the word horror.

THE ARCHBISHOP. By the word horror the Accountand General means only something unusual.

CONFUCIUS. I notice that the honorable Domestic Minister, on learning the advanced age of the venerable prelate, shews no sign of surprise or incredulity.

BURGE-LUBIN. She doesnt take it seriously. Who would? Eh, Mrs Lutestring?

MRS LUTESTRING. I take it very seriously indeed, Mr President. I see now that I was not mistaken at first. I have met the Archbishop before.

THE ARCHBISHOP. I felt sure of it. This vision of a door opening to me, and a woman's face welcoming me, must be a reminiscence of something that really happened; though I see it now as an angel opening the gate of heaven.

MRS LUTESTRING. Or a parlormaid opening the door of the house of the young woman you were in love with?

THE ARCHBISHOP [*making a wry face*] Is that the reality? How these things grow in our imagination! But may I say, Mrs Lutestring, that the transfiguration of a parlormaid to an angel is not more amazing than her transfiguration to the very dignified and able Domestic Minister I am addressing. I recognize the angel in you. Frankly, I do not recognize the parlormaid.

BURGE-LUBIN. Whats a parlormaid?

MRS LUTESTRING. An extinct species. A woman in a black dress and white apron, who opened the house door when people knocked or rang, and was either your tyrant or your slave. I was a parlormaid in the house of one of the Accountant General's remote ancestors. [*To Confucius*]. You asked me my age, Mr Chief Secretary. I am two hundred and seventy-four.

BURGE-LUBIN [*gallantly*] You dont look it. You really dont look it.

MRS LUTESTRING [*turning her face gravely towards him*] Look again, Mr President.

BURGE-LUBIN [*looking at her bravely until the smile fades from his face, and he suddenly covers his eyes with his hands*] Yes: you do look it. I am convinced. It's true. Now call up the Lunatic Asylum, Confucius; and tell them to send an ambulance for me.

MRS LUTESTRING [*to the Archbishop*] Why have you given away your secret? our secret?

THE ARCHBISHOP. They found it out. The cinema records betrayed me. But I never dreamt that there were others. Did you?

MRS LUTESTRING. I knew one other. She was a cook. She grew tired, and killed herself.

THE ARCHBISHOP. Dear me! However, her death simplifies the situation, as I have been able to convince these gentlemen that the matter had better go no further.

MRS LUTESTRING. What! When the President knows! It will be all over the place before the end of the week.

BURGE-LUBIN [*injured*] Really, Mrs Lutestring! You speak as if I were a notoriously indiscreet person. Barnabas: have I such a reputation?

BARNABAS [*resignedly*] It cant be helped. It's constitutional.

CONFUCIUS. It is utterly unconstitutional. But, as you say, it cannot be helped.

BURGE-LUBIN [*solemnly*] I deny that a secret of State has ever passed my lips—except perhaps to the Minister of Health, who is discretion personified. People think, because she is a negress—

MRS LUTESTRING. It does not matter much now. Once, it would have mattered a great deal. But my children are all dead.

THE ARCHBISHOP. Yes: the children must have been a terrible difficulty. Fortunately for me, I had none.

MRS LUTESTRING. There was one daughter who was the child of my very heart. Some years after my first drowning I learnt that she had lost her sight. I went to her. She was an old woman of ninety-six, blind. She asked me to sit and talk with her because my voice was like the voice of her dead mother.

BURGE-LUBIN. The complications must be frightful. Really I hardly know whether I do want to live much longer than other people.

MRS LUTESTRING. You can always kill yourself, as cook did; but that was influenza. Long life is complicated, and even terrible; but it is glorious all the same. I would no more change places with an ordinary woman than with a mayfly that lives only an hour.

THE ARCHBISHOP. What set you thinking of it first?

MRS LUTESTRING. Conrad Barnabas' book. Your wife told me it was more wonderful than Napoleon's Book of Fate and Old Moore's Almanac, which cook and I used to read. I was very ignorant: it did not seem so impossible to me as to an educated woman. Yet I forgot all about it, and married and drudged as a poor man's wife, and brought up children, and looked twenty years older than I really was, until one day, long after my husband died and my children were out in the world working for themselves, I noticed that I looked twenty years younger than I really was. The truth came to me in a flash.

BURGE-LUBIN. An amazing moment. Your feelings must have been beyond description. What was your first thought?

MRS LUTESTRING. Pure terror. I saw that the little money I had laid up would not last, and that I must go out and work again. They had things called Old Age Pensions then: miserable pittances for worn-out old laborers to die on. I thought I should be found out if I went on drawing it too long. The horror of facing another lifetime of drudgery, of missing my hard-earned rest and losing my poor little savings, drove everything else out of my mind. You people nowadays can have no conception of the dread of poverty that hung over us then, or of the utter tiredness of forty years' unending overwork and striving to make a shilling do the work of a pound.

THE ARCHBISHOP. I wonder you did not kill yourself. I often wonder why the poor in those evil old times did not kill themselves. They did not even kill other people.

MRS LUTESTRING. You never kill yourself, because you always may as well wait until tomorrow. And you have not energy or conviction enough to kill the others. Besides, how can you blame them when you would do as they do if you were in their place?

BURGE-LUBIN. Devilish poor consolation, that.

MRS LUTESTRING. There were other consolations in those days for people like me. We drank preparations of alcohol to relieve the strain of living and give us an artificial happiness.

BURGE-LUBIN ⎧[*all together,*] Alcohol!
CONFUCIUS   ⎨   *making*   ⎬ Pfff. . . .!
BARNABAS   ⎩ *wry faces*]   ⎭ Disgusting.

MRS LUTESTRING. A little alcohol would improve your temper and manners, and make you much easier to live with, Mr Accountant General.

BURGE-LUBIN [*laughing*] By George, I believe you! Try it, Barnabas.

CONFUCIUS. No. Try tea. It is the more civilized poison of the two.

MRS LUTESTRING. You, Mr President, were born intoxicated with your own well-fed natural exuberance. You cannot imagine what alcohol was to an underfed poor woman. I had carefully arranged my little savings so that I could get drunk, as we called it, once a week; and my only pleasure was looking forward to that poor little debauch. That is what saved me from suicide. I could not bear to miss my next carouse. But when I stopped working, and lived on my pension, the fatigue of my life's drudgery began to wear off, because, you see, I was not really old. I recuperated. I looked younger and younger. And at last I was rested enough to have courage and strength to begin life again. Besides, political changes were making it easier: life was a little better worth living for the nine-tenths of the people who used to be mere drudges. After that, I never turned back or faltered. My only regret now is that I shall die when I am three hundred or thereabouts. There was only one thing that made life hard; and that is gone now.

CONFUCIUS. May we ask what that was?

MRS LUTESTRING. Perhaps you will be offended if I tell you.

BURGE-LUBIN. Offended! My dear lady, do you suppose, after such a stupendous revelation, that anything short of a blow from a sledge-hammer could produce the smallest impression on any of us?

MRS LUTESTRING. Well, you see, it has been so hard on me never to meet a grown-up person. You are all such children. And I never was very fond of children, except that one girl who woke up the mother passion in me. I have been very lonely sometimes.

BURGE-LUBIN [*again gallant*] But surely, Mrs Lutestring, that has been your own fault. If I may say so, a lady of your attractions need never have been lonely.

MRS LUTESTRING. Why?

BURGE-LUBIN. Why! Well—. Well, er—. Well, er er—. Well! [*He gives it up*].

THE ARCHBISHOP. He means that you might have married. Curious, how little they understand our position.

MRS LUTESTRING. I did marry. I married again on my hundred and first birthday. But of course I had to marry an elderly man; a man over sixty. He was a great painter. On his deathbed he said to me "It has taken me fifty years to learn my trade, and to paint all the foolish pictures a man must paint and get rid of before he comes through them to the great things he ought to paint. And now that my foot is at last on the threshold of the temple I find that it is also the threshold of my tomb." That man would have been the greatest painter of all time if he could have lived as long as I. I saw him die of old age whilst he was still, as he said himself, a gentleman amateur, like all modern painters.

BURGE-LUBIN. But why had you to marry an elderly man? Why not marry a young one? or shall I say a middle-aged one? If my own affections were not already engaged; and if, to tell the truth, I were not a little afraid of you—for you are a very superior woman, as we all acknowledge—I should esteem myself happy in—er—er—

MRS LUTESTRING. Mr President: have you ever tried to take advantage of the innocence of a little child for the gratification of your senses?

BURGE-LUBIN. Good Heavens, madam, what do you take me for? What right have you to ask me such a question?

MRS LUTESTRING. I am at present in my two hundred and seventy-fifth year. You suggest that I should take advantage of the innocence of a child of thirty, and marry it.

THE ARCHBISHOP. Can you shortlived people not understand that as the confusion and immaturity and primitive animalism in which we live for the first hundred years of our life is worse in this matter of sex than in any other you are intolerable to us in that relation?

BURGE-LUBIN. Do you mean to say, Mrs Lutestring, that you regard me as a child?

MRS LUTESTRING. Do you expect me to regard you as a completed soul? Oh, you may well be afraid of me. There are moments when your levity, your ingratitude, your shallow jollity, make my gorge rise so against you that if I could not remind myself that you are a child I should be tempted to doubt your right to live at all.

CONFUCIUS. Do you grudge us the few years we have? you who have three hundred!

BURGE-LUBIN. You accuse me of levity! Must I remind you, madam, that I am the President, and that you are only the head of a department?

BARNABAS. Ingratitude too! You draw a pension for three hundred years when we owe you only seventy-eight; and you call us ungrateful!

MRS LUTESTRING. I do. When I think of the blessings that have been showered on you, and contrast them with the poverty! the humiliations! the anxieties! the heartbreak! the insolence and tyranny that were the daily lot of mankind when I was learning to suffer instead of learning to live! when I see how lightly you take it all! how you quarrel over the crumpled leaves in your beds of roses! how you are so dainty about your work that unless it is made either interesting or delightful to you you leave it to negresses and Chinamen, I ask myself whether even three hundred years of thought and experience can save you from being superseded by the Power that created you and put you on your trial.

BURGE-LUBIN. My dear lady: our Chinese and colored friends are perfectly happy. They are twenty times better off here than they would be in China or Liberia. They do their work admirably; and in doing it they set us free for higher employments.

THE ARCHBISHOP [*who has caught the infection of her indignation*] What higher employments are you capable of? you that are superannuated at seventy and dead at eighty!

MRS LUTESTRING. You are not really doing higher work. You are supposed to make the decisions and give the orders; but the negresses and the Chinese make up your minds for you and tell you what orders to give, just as my brother, who was a sergeant in the Guards, used to prompt his officers in the old days. When I want to get anything done at the Health Ministry I do not come to you: I go to the black lady who has been the real president during your present term of office, or to Confucius, who goes on for ever while presidents come and presidents go.

BURGE-LUBIN. This is outrageous. This is treason to the white race. And let me tell you, madam, that I have never in my life met the Minister of Health, and that I protest against the vulgar color prejudice which

What appals me is that their amusements should amuse
them.   They are the amusements of boys and girls.
They are pardonable up to the age of fifty or sixty:
after that they are ridiculous.   I tell you, what is wrong
with us is that we are a non-adult race; and the Irish
and the Scots, and the niggers and Chinks, as you call
them, though their lifetime is as short as ours, or
shorter, yet do somehow contrive to grow up a little
before they die.   We die in boyhood; the maturity that
should make us the greatest of all the nations lies beyond
the grave for us.   Either we shall go under as grey-
beards with golf clubs in our hands, or we must will to
live longer.

MRS LUTESTRING.   Yes: that is it.   I could not have
expressed it in words; but you have expressed it for me.
I felt, even when I was an ignorant domestic slave, that
we had the possibility of becoming a great nation within
us; but our faults and follies drove me to cynical hope-
lessness.   We all ended then like that.   It is the highest
creatures who take the longest to mature, and are the
most helpless during their immaturity.   I know now that
it took me a whole century to grow up.   I began my serious life when I was a hundred and twenty.   Asiatics cannot control me: I am not a child in their hands, as you
are, Mr President.   Neither, I am sure, is the Archbishop.   They respect me.   You are not grown up
enough even for that, though you were kind enough to
say that I frighten you.

BURGE-LUBIN.   Honestly, you do.   And will you think
me very rude if I say that if I must choose between a
white woman old enough to be my great-grandmother
and a black woman of my own age, I shall probably find
the black woman more sympathetic?

MRS LUTESTRING.   And more attractive in color, perhaps?

BURGE-LUBIN. Yes. Since you ask me, more—well, not more attractive: I do not deny that you have an excellent appearance—but I will say, richer. More Venetian. Tropical. "The shadowed livery of the burnished sun."

MRS LUTESTRING. Our women, and their favorite story writers, begin already to talk about men with golden complexions.

CONFUCIUS [*expanding into a smile all across both face and body*] A-a-a-a———h!

BURGE-LUBIN. Well, what of it, madam? Have you read a very interesting book by the librarian of the Biological Society suggesting that the future of the world lies with the Mulatto?

MRS LUTESTRING [*rising*] Mr Archbishop: if the white race is to be saved, our destiny is apparent.

THE ARCHBISHOP. Yes: our duty is pretty clear.

MRS LUTESTRING. Have you time to come home with me and discuss the matter?

THE ARCHBISHOP [*rising*] With pleasure.

BARNABAS [*rising also and rushing past Mrs Lutestring to the door, where he turns to bar her way*] No you dont. Burge: you understand, dont you?

BURGE-LUBIN. No. What is it?

BARNABAS. These two are going to marry.

BURGE-LUBIN. Why shouldnt they, if they want to?

BARNABAS. They dont want to. They will do it in cold blood because their children will live three hundred years. It mustnt be allowed.

CONFUCIUS. You cannot prevent it. There is no law that gives you power to interfere with them.

BARNABAS. If they force me to it I will obtain legislation against marriages above the age of seventy-eight.

THE ARCHBISHOP. There is not time for that before

we are married, Mr Accountant General. Be good enough to get out of the lady's way.

BARNABAS. There is time to send the lady to the lethal chamber before anything comes of your marriage. Dont forget that.

MRS LUTESTRING. What nonsense, Mr Accountant General! Good afternoon, Mr President. Good afternoon, Mr Chief Secretary. [*They rise and acknowledge her salutation with bows. She walks straight at the Accountant General, who instinctively shrinks out of her way as she leaves the room*].

THE ARCHBISHOP. I am surprised at you, Mr Barnabas. Your tone was like an echo from the Dark Ages. [*He follows the Domestic Minister*].

Confucius, shaking his head and clucking with his tongue in deprecation of this painful episode, moves to the chair just vacated by the Archbishop and stands behind it with folded palms, looking at the President. The Accountant General shakes his fist after the departed visitors, and bursts into savage abuse of them.

BARNABAS. Thieves! Cursed thieves! Vampires! What are you going to do, Burge?

BURGE-LUBIN. Do?

BARNABAS. Yes, do. There must be dozens of these people in existence. Are you going to let them do what the two who have just left us mean to do, and crowd us off the face of the earth?

BURGE-LUBIN [*sitting down*] Oh, come, Barnabas! What harm are they doing? Arnt you interested in them? Dont you like them?

BARNABAS. Like them! I hate them. They are monsters, unnatural monsters. They are poison to me.

BURGE-LUBIN. What possible objection can there be to their living as long as they can? It does not shorten our lives, does it?

BARNABAS. If I have to die when I am seventy-eight, I dont see why another man should be privileged to live to be two hundred and seventy-eight. It does shorten my life, relatively. It makes us ridiculous. If they grew to be twelve feet high they would make us all dwarfs. They talked to us as if we were children. There is no love lost between us: their hatred of us came out soon enough. You heard what the woman said, and how the Archbishop backed her up?

BURGE-LUBIN. But what can we do to them?

BARNABAS. Kill them.

BURGE-LUBIN. Nonsense!

BARNABAS. Lock them up. Sterilize them somehow, anyhow.

BURGE-LUBIN. But what reason could we give?

BARNABAS. What reason can you give for killing a snake? Nature tells you to do it.

BURGE-LUBIN. My dear Barnabas, you are out of your mind.

BARNABAS. Havnt you said that once too often already this morning?

BURGE-LUBIN. I dont believe you will carry a single soul with you.

BARNABAS. I understand. I know you. You think you are one of them.

CONFUCIUS. Mr Accountant General: you may be one of them.

BARNABAS. How dare you accuse me of such a thing? I am an honest man, not a monster. I won my place in public life by demonstrating that the true expectation of human life is seventy-eight point six. And I will resist any attempt to alter or upset it to the last drop of my blood if need be.

BURGE-LUBIN. Oh, tut tut! Come, come! Pull yourself together. How can you, a descendant of the great

Conrad Barnabas, the man who is still remembered by his masterly Biography of a Black Beetle, be so absurd?

BARNABAS. You had better go and write the autobiography of a jackass. I am going to raise the country against this horror, and against you, if you shew the slightest sign of weakness about it.

CONFUCIUS [*very impressively*] You will regret it if you do.

BARNABAS. What is to make me regret it?

CONFUCIUS. Every mortal man and woman in the community will begin to count on living for three centuries. Things will happen which you do not foresee: terrible things. The family will dissolve: parents and children will be no longer the old and the young: brothers and sisters will meet as strangers after a hundred years separation: the ties of blood will lose their innocence. The imaginations of men, let loose over the possibilities of three centuries of life, will drive them mad and wreck human society. This discovery must be kept a dead secret. [*He sits down.*]

BARNABAS. And if I refuse to keep the secret?

CONFUCIUS. I shall have you safe in a lunatic asylum the day after you blab.

BARNABAS. You forget that I can produce the Archbishop to prove my statement.

CONFUCIUS. So can I. Which of us do you think he will support when I explain to him that your object in revealing his age is to get him killed?

BARNABAS [*desperate*] Burge: are you going to back up this yellow abomination against me? Are we public men and members of the Government? or are we damned blackguards?

CONFUCIUS [*unmoved*] Have you ever known a public man who was not what vituperative people call a damned blackguard when some inconsiderate person wanted to tell the public more than was good for it?

BARNABAS. Hold your tongue, you insolent heathen. Burge: I spoke to you.

BURGE-LUBIN. Well, you know, my dear Barnabas, Confucius is a very long-headed chap. I see his point.

BARNABAS. Do you? Then let me tell you that, except officially, I will never speak to you again. Do you hear?

BURGE-LUBIN [*cheerfully*] You will. You will.

BARNABAS. And dont you ever dare speak to me again. Do you hear? [*He turns to the door.*]

BURGE-LUBIN. I will. I will. Good-bye, Barnabas. God bless you.

BARNABAS. May you live forever, and be the laughing-stock of the whole world! [*He dashes out in a fury*].

BURGE-LUBIN [*laughing indulgently*] He will keep the secret all right. I know Barnabas. You neednt worry.

CONFUCIUS [*troubled and grave*] There are no secrets except the secrets that keep themselves. Consider. There are those films at the Record Office. We have no power to prevent the Master of the Records from publishing this discovery made in his department. We cannot silence the American—who can silence an American? —nor the people who were there today to receive him. Fortunately, a film can prove nothing but a resemblance.

BURGE-LUBIN. Thats very true. After all, the whole thing is confounded nonsense, isnt it?

CONFUCIUS [*raising his head to look at him*] You have decided not to believe it now that you realize its inconveniences. That is the English method. It may not work in this case.

BURGE-LUBIN. English be hanged! It's common sense. You know, those two people got us hypnotized:

not a doubt of it.   They must have been kidding us.
They were, wernt they?

CONFUCIUS.   You looked into that woman's face; and
you believed.

BURGE-LUBIN.   Just so.   Thats where she had me.   I
shouldnt have believed her a bit if she'd turned her back
to me.

CONFUCIUS [*shakes his head slowly and repeatedly*] ? ? ?

BURGE-LUBIN.   You really think——?   [*He hesitates*].

CONFUCIUS.   The Archbishop has always been a puzzle
to me.   Ever since I learnt to distinguish between one
English face and another I have noticed what the woman
pointed out: that the English face is not an adult face,
just as the English mind is not an adult mind.

BURGE-LUBIN.   Stow it, John Chinaman.   If ever there
was a race divinely appointed to take charge of the non-
adult races and guide them and train them and keep
them out of mischief until they grow up to be capable
of adopting our institutions, that race is the English
race.   It is the only race in the world that has that characteristic.   Now!

CONFUCIUS.   That is the fancy of a child nursing a
doll.   But it is ten times more childish of you to dispute the highest compliment ever paid you.

BURGE-LUBIN.   You call it a compliment to class us
as grown-up chi'ren.

CONFUCIUS.   Not grown-up children, children at fifty,
sixty, seventy.   Your maturity is so late that you never
attain to it.   You have to be governed by races which
are mature at forty.   That means that you are poten-
tially the most highly developed race on earth, and
would be actually the greatest if you could live long
enough to attain to maturity.

BURGE-LUBIN [*grasping the idea at last*] By George!

Confucius, youre right! I never thought of that. That
explains everything. We are just a lot of schoolboys:
theres no denying it. Talk to an Englishman about
anything serious, and he listens to you curiously for a
moment just as he listens to a chap playing classical
music. Then he goes back to his marine golf, or motor-
ing, or flying, or women, just like a bit of stretched
elastic when you let it go. [*Soaring to the height of his
theme*]. Oh, youre quite right. We are only in our infancy. I ought to be in a perambulator, with a nurse
shoving me along. It's true: it's absolutely true. But
some day we'll grow up; and then, by Jingo, we'll
shew em.

CONFUCIUS. The Archbishop is an adult. When I
was a child I was dominated and intimidated by people
whom I now know to have been weaker and sillier than I,
because there was some mysterious quality in their mere
age that overawed me. I confess that, though I have
kept up appearances, I have always been afraid of the
Archbishop.

BURGE-LUBIN. Between ourselves, Confucius, so
have I.

CONFUCIUS. It is this that convinced me. It was this
in the woman's face that convinced you. Their new departure in the history of the race is no fraud. It does
not even surprise me.

BURGE-LUBIN. Oh, come! Not surprise you! It's
your pose never to be surprised at anything; but if you
are not surprised at this you are not human.

CONFUCIUS. I am staggered, just as a man may be
staggered by an explosion for which he has himself laid
the charge and lighted the fuse. But I am not surprised, because, as a philosopher and a student of evolutionary biology, I have come to regard some such development as this as inevitable. If I had not thus prepared

myself to be credulous, no mere evidence of films and well-told tales would have persuaded me to believe. As it is, I do believe.

BURGE-LUBIN. Well, that being settled, what the devil is to happen next? Whats the next move for us?

CONFUCIUS. We do not make the next move. The next move will be made by the Archbishop and the woman.

BARGE-LUBIN. Their marriage?

CONFUCIUS. More than that. They have made the momentous discovery that they are not alone in the world.

BURGE-LUBIN. You think there are others?

CONFUCIUS. There must be many others. Each of them believes that he or she is the only one to whom the miracle has happened. But the Archbishop knows better now. He will advertise in terms which only the longlived people will understand. He will bring them together and organize them. They will hasten from all parts of the earth. They will become a great Power.

BURGE-LUBIN [a little alarmed] I say, will they? I suppose they will. I wonder is Barnabas right after all? Ought we to allow it?

CONFUCIUS. Nothing that we can do will stop it. We cannot in our souls really want to stop it: the vital force that has produced this change would paralyze our opposition to it, if we were mad enough to oppose. But we will not oppose. You and I may be of the elect, too.

BURGE-LUBIN. Yes: thats what gets us every time. What the deuce ought we to do? Something must be done about it, you know.

CONFUCIUS. Let us sit still, and meditate in silence on the vistas before us.

BURGE-LUBIN. By George, I believe youre right. Let us.

They sit meditating, the Chinaman naturally, the President with visible effort and intensity. He is positively glaring into the future when the voice of the Negress is heard.

THE NEGRESS. Mr President.

BURGE-LUBIN [*joyfully*] Yes. [*Taking up a peg.*] Are you at home?

THE NEGRESS. No. Omega, zero, x squared.

The President rapidly puts the peg in the switchboard; works the dial; and presses the button. The screen becomes transparent; and the Negress, brilliantly dressed, appears on what looks like the bridge of a steam yacht in glorious sea weather. The installation with which she is communicating is beside the binnacle.

CONFUCIUS [*looking round, and recoiling with a shriek of disgust*] Ach! Avaunt! Avaunt! [*He rushes from the room*].

BURGE-LUBIN. What part of the coast is that?

THE NEGRESS. Fishguard Bay. Why not run over ʌnd join me for the afternoon? I am disposed to be approachable at last.

BURGE-LUBIN. But Fishguard! Two hundred and seventy miles!

THE NEGRESS. There is a lightning express on the Irish Air Service at half-past sixteen. They will drop you by a parachute in the bay. The dip will do you good. I will pick you up and dry you and give you a first-rate time.

BURGE-LUBIN. Delightful. But a little risky, isnt it?

THE NEGRESS. Risky! I thought you were afraid of nothing.

BURGE-LUBIN. I am not exactly afraid; but—

THE NEGRESS [*offended*] But you think it is not good

enough. Very well [*she raises her hand to take the peg out of her switchboard*].

BURGE-LUBIN [*imploringly*] No: stop: let me explain: hold the line just one moment. Oh, please.

THE NEGRESS [*waiting with her hand poised over the peg*] Well?

BURGE-LUBIN. The fact is, I have been behaving very recklessly for some time past under the impression that my life would be so short that it was not worth bothering about. But I have just learnt that I may live— well, much longer than I expected. I am sure your good sense will tell you that this alters the case. I—

THE NEGRESS [*with suppressed rage*] Oh, quite. Pray dont risk your precious life on my account. Sorry for troubling you. Good-bye. [*She snatches out her peg and vanishes*].

BURGE-LUBIN [*urgently*] No: please hold on. I can convince you— [*a loud buzz-uzz-uzz*]. Engaged! Who is she calling up now? [*He presses the button and calls*] The Chief Secretary. Say I want to see him again, just for a moment.

CONFUCIUS'S VOICE. Is the woman gone?

BURGE-LUBIN. Yes, yes: it's all right. Just a moment if—[*Confucius returns*] Confucius: I have some important business at Fishguard. The Irish Air Service can drop me in the bay by parachute. I suppose it's quite safe, isnt it?

CONFUCIUS. Nothing is quite safe. The air service is as safe as any other travelling service. The parachute is safe. But the water is not safe.

BURGE-LUBIN. Why? They will give me an unsinkable tunic, wont they?

CONFUCIUS. You will not sink; but the sea is very cold. You may get rheumatism for life.

BURGE-LUBIN. For life! That settles it: I wont risk it.

CONFUCIUS. Good. You have at last become prudent: you are no longer what you call a sportsman: you are a sensible coward, almost a grown-up man. I congratulate you.

BURGE-LUBIN [*resolutely*] Coward or no coward, I will not face an eternity of rheumatism for any woman that ever was born. [*He rises and goes to the rack for his fillet*]. I have changed my mind; I am going home. [*He cocks the fillet rakishly*]. Good evening.

CONFUCIUS. So early? If the Minister of Health rings you up, what shall I tell her?

BURGE-LUBIN. Tell her to go to the devil. [*He goes out*].

CONFUCIUS [*shaking his head, shocked at the President's impoliteness*] No. No, no, no, no, no. Oh, these English! these crude young civilizations! Their manners! Hogs. Hogs.

PART IV

TRAGEDY OF
AN ELDERLY GENTLEMAN

XXXV

TRAGEDY OF
AN ELDERLY GENTLEMAN

ACT I

Burrin pier on the south shore of Galway Bay in Ireland, a region of stone-capped hills and granite fields. It is a fine summer day in the year 3000 A.D. On an ancient stone stump, about three feet thick and three feet high, used for securing ships by ropes to the shore, and called a bollard or holdfast, an elderly gentleman sits facing the land, with his head bowed and his face in his hands, sobbing. His sunburnt skin contrasts with his white whiskers and eyebrows. He wears a black frock-coat, a white waistcoat, lavender trousers, a brilliant silk cravat with a jewelled pin stuck in it, a tall hat of grey felt, and patent leather boots with white spats. His starched linen cuffs protrude from his coat sleeves; and his collar, also of starched white linen, is Gladstonian. On his right, three or four full sacks, lying side by side on the flags, suggest that the pier, unlike many remote Irish piers, is occasionally useful as well as romantic. On his left, behind him, a flight of stone steps descends out of sight to the sea level.

A woman with a silk tunic and sandals, wearing little else except a cap with the number 2 on it in gold, comes up the steps from the sea, and stares in astonishment at the sobbing man. Her age cannot be guessed: her face is firm and chiselled like a young face; but her expression is unyouthful in its severity and determination.

THE WOMAN. What is the matter?

The elderly gentleman looks up; hastily pulls him-self together; takes out a silk handkerchief and dries his tears lightly with a brave attempt to smile through them; and tries to rise gallantly, but sinks back].

THE WOMAN. Do you need assistance?

THE ELDERLY GENTLEMAN. No. Thank you very much. No. Nothing. The heat. [*He punctuates with sniffs, and dabs with his handkerchief at his eyes and nose*]. Hay fever.

THE WOMAN. You are a foreigner, are you not?

THE ELDERLY GENTLEMAN. No. You must not re-gard me as a foreigner. I am a Briton.

THE WOMAN. You come from some part of the British Commonwealth?

THE ELDERLY GENTLEMAN [*amiably pompous*] From its capital, madam.

THE WOMAN. From Baghdad?

THE ELDERLY GENTLEMAN. Yes. You may not be aware, madam, that these islands were once the centre of the British Commonwealth, during a period now known as The Exile. They were its headquarters a thousand years ago. Few people know this interesting circumstance now; but I assure you it is true. I have come here on a pious pilgrimage to one of the numerous lands of my fathers. We are of the same stock, you and I. Blood is thicker than water. We are cousins.

THE WOMAN. I do not understand. You say you have come here on a pious pilgrimage. Is that some new means of transport?

THE ELDERLY GENTLEMAN [*again shewing signs of distress*] I find it very difficult to make myself under-stood here. I was not referring to a machine, but to a—a—a sentimental journey.

THE WOMAN. I am afraid I am as much in the dark

as before. You said also that blood is thicker than water. No doubt it is; but what of it?

THE ELDERLY GENTLEMAN. Its meaning is obvious.

THE WOMAN. Perfectly. But I assure you I am quite aware that blood is thicker than water.

THE ELDERLY GENTLEMAN [*sniffing: almost in tears again*] We will leave it at that, madam.

THE WOMAN [*going nearer to him and scrutinizing him with some concern*] I am afraid you are not well. Were you not warned that it is dangerous for shortlived people to come to this country? There is a deadly disease called discouragement, against which shortlived people have to take very strict precautions. Intercourse with us puts too great a strain on them.

THE ELDERLY GENTLEMAN [*pulling himself together huffily*] It has no effect on me, madam. I fear my conversation does not interest you. If not, the remedy is in your own hands.

THE WOMAN [*looking at her hands, and then looking inquiringly at him*] Where?

THE ELDERLY GENTLEMAN [*breaking down*] Oh, this is dreadful. No understanding, no intelligence, no sympathy—[*his sobs choke him*].

THE WOMAN. You see, you are ill.

THE ELDERLY GENTLEMAN [*nerved by indignation*] I am not ill. I have never had a day's illness in my life.

THE WOMAN. May I advise you?

THE ELDERLY GENTLEMAN. I have no need of a lady doctor, thank you, madam.

THE WOMAN [*shaking her head*] I am afraid I do not understand. I said nothing about a butterfly.

THE ELDERLY GENTLEMAN. Well, *I* said nothing about a butterfly.

THE WOMAN. You spoke of a lady doctor. The word is known here only as the name of a butterfly.

THE ELDERLY GENTLEMAN [*insanely*] I give up. I can bear this no longer. It is easier to go out of my mind at once. [*He rises and dances about, singing*].

> I'd be a butterfly, born in a bower,
> Making apple dumplings without any flour.

THE WOMAN [*smiling gravely*] It must be at least a hundred and fifty years since I last laughed. But if you do that any more I shall certainly break out like a primary of sixty. Your dress is so extraordinarily ridiculous.

THE ELDERLY GENTLEMAN [*halting abruptly in his antics*] My dress ridiculous! I may not be dressed like a Foreign Office clerk; but my clothes are perfectly in fashion in my native metropolis, where yours—pardon my saying so—would be considered extremely unusual and hardly decent.

THE WOMAN. Decent? There is no such word in our language. What does it mean?

THE ELDERLY GENTLEMAN. It would not be decent for me to explain. Decency cannot be discussed without indecency.

THE WOMAN. I cannot understand you at all. I fear you have not been observing the rules laid down for shortlived visitors.

THE ELDERLY GENTLEMAN. Surely, madam, they do not apply to persons of my age and standing. I am not a child, nor an agricultural laborer.

THE WOMAN [*severely*] They apply to you very strictly. You are expected to confine yourself to the society of children under sixty. You are absolutely forbidden to approach fully adult natives under any circumstances. You cannot converse with persons of my age for long without bringing on a dangerous attack of discouragement. Do you realize that you are already shewing grave symptoms of that very distressing and usually fatal complaint?

THE ELDERLY GENTLEMAN.   Certainly not, madam.   I am fortunately in no danger of contracting it.   I am quite accustomed to converse intimately and at the greatest length with the most distinguished persons.   If you cannot discriminate between hay fever and imbecility, I can only say that your advanced years carry with them the inevitable penalty of dotage.

THE WOMAN.   I am one of the guardians of this district; and I am responsible for your welfare—

THE ELDERLY GENTLEMAN.   The Guardians!   Do you take me for a pauper?

THE WOMAN.   I do not know what a pauper is.   You must tell me who you are, if it is possible for you to express yourself intelligibly—

THE ELDERLY GENTLEMAN [*snorts indignantly*]!

THE WOMAN [*continuing*]—and why are wandering here alone without a nurse.

THE ELDERLY GENTLEMAN [*outraged*] Nurse!

THE WOMAN.   Shortlived visitors are not allowed to go about here without nurses.   Do you not know that rules are meant to be kept?

THE ELDERLY GENTLEMAN.   By the lower classes, no doubt.   But to persons in my position there are certain courtesies which are never denied by well-bred people; and—

THE WOMAN.   There are only two human classes here: the shortlived and the normal.   The rules apply to the shortlived, and are for their own protection.   Now tell me at once who you are.

THE ELDERLY GENTLEMAN [*impressively*] Madam, I am a retired gentleman, formerly Chairman of the All-British Synthetic Egg and Vegetable Cheese Trust in Baghdad, and now President of the British Historical and Archæological Society, and a Vice-President of the Travellers' Club.

THE WOMAN. All that does not matter.

THE ELDERLY GENTLEMAN [*again snorting*] Hm! Indeed!

THE WOMAN. Have you been sent here to make your mind flexible?

THE ELDERLY GENTLEMAN. What an extraordinary question! Pray do you find my mind noticeably stiff?

THE WOMAN. Perhaps you do not know that you are on the west coast of Ireland, and that it is the practice among natives of the Eastern Island to spend some years here to acquire mental flexibility. The climate has that effect.

THE ELDERLY GENTLEMAN [*haughtily*] I was born, not in Eastern Island, but, thank God, in dear old British Baghdad; and I am not in need of a mental health resort.

THE WOMAN. Then why are you here?

THE ELDERLY GENTLEMAN. Am I trespassing? I was not aware of it.

THE WOMAN. Trespassing? I do not understand the word.

THE ELDERLY GENTLEMAN. Is this land private property. If so, I make no claim. I proffer a shilling in satisfaction of damage (if any), and am ready to withdraw if you will be good enough to shew me the nearest way. [*He offers her a shilling*].

THE WOMAN [*taking it and examining it without much interest*] I do not understand a single word of what you have just said.

THE ELDERLY GENTLEMAN. I am speaking the plainest English. Are you the landlord?

THE WOMAN [*shaking her head*] There is a tradition in this part of the country of an animal with a name like that. It used to be hunted and shot in the barbarous ages. It is quite extinct now.

THE ELDERLY GENTLEMAN [*breaking down again*] It is a dreadful thing to be in a country where nobody understands civilized institutions. [*He collapses on the bollard, struggling with his rising sobs*]. Excuse me. Hay fever.

THE WOMAN [*taking a tuning-fork from her girdle and holding it to her ear; then speaking into space on one note, like a chorister intoning a psalm*] Burrin Pier Galway please send someone to take charge of a discouraged shortliver who has escaped from his nurse male harmless babbles unintelligibly with moments of sense distressed hysterical foreign dress very funny has curious fringe of white sea-weed under his chin.

THE ELDERLY GENTLEMAN. This is a gross impertinence. An insult.

THE WOMAN [*replacing her tuning-fork and addressing the elderly gentleman*] These words mean nothing to me. In what capacity are you here? How did you obtain permission to visit us?

THE ELDERLY GENTLEMAN [*importantly*] Our Prime Minister, Mr Badger Bluebin, has come to consult the oracle. He is my son-in-law. We are accompanied by his wife and daughter: my daughter and granddaughter. I may mention that General Aufsteig, who is one of our party, is really the Emperor of Turania travelling incognito. I understand he has a question to put to the oracle informally. I have come solely to visit the country.

THE WOMAN. Why should you come to a place where you have no business?

THE ELDERLY GENTLEMAN. Great Heavens, madam, can anything be more natural? I shall be the only member of the Travellers' Club who has set foot on these shores. Think of that! My position will be unique.

THE WOMAN. Is that an advantage? We have a person here who has lost both legs in an accident. His position is unique. But he would much rather be like everyone else.

THE ELDERLY GENTLEMAN. This is maddening. There is no analogy whatever between the two cases.

THE WOMAN. They are both unique.

THE ELDERLY GENTLEMAN. Conversation in this place seems to consist of ridiculous quibbles. I am heartily tired of them.

THE WOMAN. I conclude that your Travellers' Club is an assembly of persons who wish to be able to say that they have been in some place where nobody else has been.

THE ELDERLY GENTLEMAN. Of course if you wish to sneer at us—

THE WOMAN. What is sneer?

THE ELDERLY GENTLEMAN [*with a wild sob*] I shall drown myself.

He makes desperately for the edge of the pier, but is confronted by a man with the number one on his cap, who comes up the steps and intercepts him. He is dressed like the woman; but a slight moustache proclaims his sex.

THE MAN [*to the elderly gentleman*] Ah, here you are. I shall really have to put a collar and lead on you if you persist in giving me the slip like this.

THE WOMAN. Are you this stranger's nurse?

THE MAN. Yes. I am very tired of him. If I take my eyes off him for a moment, he runs away and talks to everybody.

THE WOMAN [*after taking out her tuning-fork and sounding it, intones as before*] Burrin Pier. Wash out. [*She puts up the fork, and addresses the man*]. I sent a call for someone to take care of him. I have been trying to talk to him; but I can understand very little of what he says. You must take better care of him: he is badly discouraged already. If I can be of any further use, Fusima, Gort, will find me. [*She goes away*].

THE ELDERLY GENTLEMAN. Any further use! She has been of no use to me. She spoke to me without any introduction, like any improper female. And she has made off with my shilling.

THE MAN. Please speak slowly: I cannot follow. What is a shilling? What is an introduction? Improper female doesnt make sense.

THE ELDERLY GENTLEMAN. Nothing seems to make sense here. All I can tell you is that she was the most impenetrably stupid woman I have ever met in the whole course of my life.

THE MAN. That cannot be. She cannot appear stupid to you. She is a secondary, and getting on for a tertiary at that.

THE ELDERLY GENTLEMAN. What is a tertiary? Everybody here keeps talking to me about primaries and secondaries and tertiaries as if people were geological strata.

THE MAN. The primaries are in their first century. The secondaries are in their second century. I am still classed as a primary [*he points to his number*]; but I may almost call myself a secondary, and I shall be ninety-five next January. The tertiaries are in their third century. Did you not see the number two on her badge? She is an advanced secondary.

THE ELDERLY GENTLEMAN. That accounts for it. She is in her second childhood.

THE MAN. Her second childhood! She is in her fifth childhood.

THE ELDERLY GENTLEMAN [*again resorting to the*

bollard] Oh! I cannot bear these unnatural arrangements.

THE MAN [*impatient and helpless*] You shouldnt have come among us. This is no place for you.

THE ELDERLY GENTLEMAN [*nerved by indignation*] May I ask why? I am a Vice-President of the Travellers' Club. I have been everywhere: I hold the record in the Club for civilized countries.

THE MAN. What is a civilized country?

THE ELDERLY GENTLEMAN. It is—well, it is a civilized country. [*Desperately*] I dont know: I—I—I—I shall go mad if you keep on asking me to tell you these things that everybody knows. Countries where you can travel comfortably. Where there are good hotels. Excuse me; but, though you say you are ninety-four, you are worse company than a child of five with your eternal questions. Why not call me Daddy at once?

THE MAN. I did not know your name was Daddy.

THE ELDERLY GENTLEMAN. My name is Joseph Popham Bolge Bluebin Barlow, O.M.

THE MAN. That is five men's names. Daddy is shorter. And O.M. will not do here. It is our name for certain wild creatures, descendants of the aboriginal inhabitants of this coast. They used to be called the O'Mulligans. We will stick to Daddy.

THE ELDERLY GENTLEMAN. People will think I am your father.

THE MAN [*shocked*] Sh-sh! People here never allude to such relationships. It is not quite delicate, is it? What does it matter whether you are my father or not?

THE ELDERLY GENTLEMAN. My worthy nonagenarian friend: your faculties are totally decayed. Could you not find me a guide of my own age?

THE MAN. A young person?

THE ELDERLY GENTLEMAN. Certainly not. I cannot go about with a young person.

THE MAN. Why?

THE ELDERLY GENTLEMAN. Why! Why!! Why!!! Have you no moral sense?

THE MAN. I shall have to give you up. I cannot understand you.

THE ELDERLY GENTLEMAN. But you meant a young woman, didn't you?

THE MAN. I meant simply somebody of your own age. What difference does it make whether the person is a man or a woman?

THE ELDERLY GENTLEMAN. I could not have believed in the existence of such scandalous insensibility to the elementary decencies of human intercourse.

THE MAN. What are decencies?

THE ELDERLY GENTLEMAN [shrieking] Everyone asks me that.

THE MAN [taking out a tuning-fork and using it as the woman did] Zozim on Burrin Pier to Zoo Ennistymon I have found the discouraged shortliver he has been talking to a secondary and is much worse I am too old he is asking for someone of his own age or younger come if you can. [He puts up his fork and turns to the Elderly Gentleman]. Zoo is a girl of fifty, and rather childish at that. So perhaps she may make you happy.

THE ELDERLY GENTLEMAN. Make me happy! A bluestocking of fifty! Thank you.

THE MAN. Bluestocking? The effort to make out your meaning is fatiguing. Besides, you are talking too much to me: I am old enough to discourage you. Let us be silent until Zoo comes. [He turns his back on the Elderly Gentleman, and sits down on the edge of the pier, with his legs dangling over the water].

THE ELDERLY GENTLEMAN. Certainly. I have no

wish to force my conversation on any man who does not
desire it. Perhaps you would like to take a nap. If so,
pray do not stand on ceremony.

THE MAN. What is a nap?

THE ELDERLY GENTLEMAN [*exasperated, going to him
and speaking with great precision and distinctness*] A
nap, my friend, is a brief period of sleep which over-
takes superannuated persons when they endeavor to
entertain unwelcome visitors or to listen to scientific lectures. Sleep. Sleep. [*Bawling into his ear*] Sleep.

THE MAN. I tell you I am nearly a secondary. I
never sleep.

THE ELDERLY GENTLEMAN [*awestruck*] Good
Heavens!

*A young woman with the number one on her cap
arrives by land. She looks no older than Savvy Barnabas, whom she somewhat resembles, looked a thousand
years before. Younger, if anything.*

THE YOUNG WOMAN. Is this the patient?

THE MAN [*scrambling up*] This is Zoo. [*To Zoo*].
Call him Daddy.

THE ELDERLY GENTLEMAN [*vehemently*] No.

THE MAN [*ignoring the interruption*] Bless you for
taking him off my hands! I have had as much of him as
I can bear. [*He goes down the steps and disappears*].

THE ELDERLY GENTLEMAN [*ironically taking off his
hat and making a sweeping bow from the edge of the
pier in the direction of the Atlantic Ocean*] Good afternoon, sir; and thank you very much for your extraordinary politeness, your exquisite consideration for my
feelings, your courtly manners. Thank you from the
bottom of my heart. [*Clapping his hat on again*] Pig!
Ass!

ZOO [*laughs very heartily at him*] ! ! !

THE ELDERLY GENTLEMAN [*turning sharply on her*]

Good afternoon, madam. I am sorry to have had to put your friend in his place; but I find that here as elsewhere it is necessary to assert myself if I am to be treated with proper consideration. I had hoped that my position as a guest would protect me from insult.

zoo. Putting my friend in his place. That is some poetic expression, is it not? What does it mean?

THE ELDERLY GENTLEMAN. Pray, is there no one in these islands who understands plain English?

zoo. Well, nobody except the oracles. They have to make a special historical study of what we call the dead thought.

THE ELDERLY GENTLEMAN. Dead thought! I have heard of the dead languages, but never of the dead thought.

zoo. Well, thoughts die sooner than languages. I understand your language; but I do not always understand your thought. The oracles will understand you perfectly. Have you had your consultation yet?

THE ELDERLY GENTLEMAN. I did not come to consult the oracle, madam. I am here simply as a gentleman travelling for pleasure in the company of my daughter, who is the wife of the British Prime Minister, and of General Aufsteig, who, I may tell you in confidence, is really the Emperor of Turania, the greatest military genius of the age.

zoo. Why should you travel for pleasure! Can you not enjoy yourself at home?

THE ELDERLY GENTLEMAN. I wish to see the world.

zoo. It is too big. You can see a bit of it anywhere.

THE ELDERLY GENTLEMAN [*out of patience*] Damn it, madam, you dont want to spend your life looking at the same bit of it! [*Checking himself*] I beg your pardon for swearing in your presence.

zoo. Oh! That is swearing, is it? I have read

about that. It sounds quite pretty. Dammitmaddam, dammitmaddam, dammitmaddan, dammitmaddam. Say it as often as you please: I like it.

THE ELDERLY GENTLEMAN [*expanding with intense relief*] Bless you for those profane but familiar words! Thank you, thank you. For the first time since I landed in this terrible country I begin to feel at home. The strain which was driving me mad relaxes: I feel almost as if I were at the club. Excuse my taking the only available seat: I am not so young as I was. [*He sits on the bollard*]. Promise me that you will not hand me over to one of these dreadful tertiaries or secondaries or whatever you call them.

ZOO. Never fear. They had no business to give you in charge to Zozim. You see he is just on the verge of becoming a secondary; and these adolescents will give themselves the airs of tertiaries. You naturally feel more at home with a flapper like me. [*She makes herself comfortable on the sacks*].

THE ELDERLY GENTLEMAN. Flapper? What does that mean?

ZOO. It is an archaic word which we still use to describe a female who is no longer a girl and is not yet quite adult.

THE ELDERLY GENTLEMAN. A very agreeable age to associate with, I find. I am recovering rapidly. I have a sense of blossoming like a flower. May I ask your name?

ZOO. Zoo.

THE ELDERLY GENTLEMAN. Miss Zoo.

ZOO. Not Miss Zoo. Zoo.

THE ELDERLY GENTLEMAN. Precisely. Er—Zoo what?

ZOO. No. Not Zoo What. Zoo. Nothing but Zoo.

THE ELDERLY GENTLEMAN [*puzzled*] Mrs Zoo, perhaps.

zoo.   No.   Zoo.   Cant you catch it?   Zoo.

THE ELDERLY GENTLEMAN.   Of course.   Believe me, I did not really think you were married: you are obviously too young; but here it is so hard to feel sure—er—

zoo [*hopelessly puzzled*] What?

THE ELDERLY GENTLEMAN.   Marriage makes a difference, you know.   One can say things to a married lady that would perhaps be in questionable taste to anyone without that experience.

zoo.   You are getting out of my depth: I dont understand a word you are saying.   Married and questionable taste convey nothing to me.   Stop, though.   Is married an old form of the word mothered?

THE ELDERLY GENTLEMAN.   Very likely.   Let us drop the subject.   Pardon me for embarrassing you.   I should not have mentioned it.

zoo.   What does embarrassing mean?

THE ELDERLY GENTLEMAN.   Well, really!   I should have thought that so natural and common a condition would be understood as long as human nature lasted.   To embarrass is to bring a blush to the cheek.

zoo.   What is a blush?

THE ELDERLY GENTLEMAN [*amazed*] Dont you blush? ? ?

zoo.   Never heard of it.   We have a word flush, meaning a rush of blood to the skin.   I have noticed it in my babies, but not after the age of two.

THE ELDERLY GENTLEMAN.   Your babies! ! !   I fear I am treading on very delicate ground; but your appearance is extremely youthful; and if I may ask how many—?

zoo.   Only four as yet.   It is a long business with

us. I specialize in babies. My first was such a success
that they made me go on. I—

THE ELDERLY GENTLEMAN [*reeling on the bollard*]
Oh dear!

zoo. Whats the matter? Anything wrong?

THE ELDERLY GENTLEMAN. In Heaven's name,
madam, how old are you?

zoo. Fifty-six.

THE ELDERLY GENTLEMAN. My knees are trembling.
I fear I am really ill. Not so young as I was.

zoo. I noticed that you are not strong on your legs
yet. You have many of the ways and weaknesses of a
baby. No doubt that is why I feel called on to mother
you. You certainly are a very silly little Daddy.

THE ELDERLY GENTLEMAN [*stimulated by indignation*] My name, I repeat, is Joseph Popham Bolge Bluebin Barlow, O.M.

zoo. What a ridiculously long name! I cant call
you all that. What did your mother call you?

THE ELDERLY GENTLEMAN. You recall the bitterest
struggles of my childhood. I was sensitive on the point.
Children suffer greatly from absurd nicknames. My
mother thoughtlessly called me Iddy Toodles. I was
called Iddy until I went to school, when I made **my first**
stand for children's rights by insisting on being called
at least Joe. At fifteen I refused to answer to anything
shorter than Joseph. At eighteen I discovered that the
name Joseph was supposed to indicate an unmanly
prudery because of some old story about a Joseph who
rejected the advances of his employer's wife: very
properly in my opinion. I then became Popham to my
family and intimate friends, and Mister Barlow to the
rest of the world. My mother slipped back to Iddy
when her faculties began to fail her, poor woman; but I
could not resent that, at her age.

zoo. Do you mean to say that your mother bothered about you after you were ten?

THE ELDERLY GENTLEMAN. Naturally, madam. She was my mother. What would you have had her do?

zoo. Go on to the next, of course. After eight or nine children become quite uninteresting, except to themselves. I shouldnt know my two eldest if I met them.

THE ELDERLY GENTLEMEN [again drooping] I am dying. Let me die. I wish to die.

zoo [going to him quickly and supporting him] Hold up. Sit up straight. Whats the matter?

THE ELDERLY GENTLEMAN [faintly] My spine, I think. Shock. Concussion.

zoo [maternally] Pow wow wow! What is there to shock you? [Shaking him playfully]. There! Sit up; and be good.

THE ELDERLY GENTLEMAN [still feebly] Thank you. I am better now.

zoo [resuming her seat on the sacks] But what was all the rest of that long name for? There was a lot more of it. Blops Booby or something.

THE ELDERLY GENTLEMAN [impressively] Bolge Bluebin, madam: a historical name. Let me inform you that I can trace my family back for more than a thousand years, from the Eastern Empire to its ancient seat in these islands, to a time when two of my ancestors, Joyce Bolge and Hengist Horsa Bluebin, wrestled with one another for the prime ministership of the British Empire, and occupied that position successively with a glory of which we can in these degenerate days form but a faint conception. When I think of these mighty men, lions in war, sages in peace, not babblers and charlatans like the pigmies who now occupy their places in Baghdad, but strong silent men, ruling an empire on which the sun never set, my eyes fill with tears: my heart bursts with emotion: I feel that to have lived but to the dawn of manhood in their day, and then died for them, would have been a nobler and happier lot than the ignominious ease of my present longevity.

zoo. Longevity! [*She laughs*].

THE ELDERLY GENTLEMAN. Yes, madam, relative longevity. As it is, I have to be content and proud to know that I am descended from both those heroes.

zoo. You must be descended from every Briton who was alive in their time. Dont you know that?

THE ELDERLY GENTLEMAN. Do not quibble, madam. I bear their names, Bolge and Bluebin; and I hope I have inherited something of their majestic spirit. Well, they were born in these islands. I repeat, these islands were then, incredible as it now seems, the centre of the British Empire. When that centre shifted to Baghdad, and the Englishman at last returned to the true cradle of his race in Mesopotamia, the western islands were cast off, as they had been before by the Roman Empire. But it was to the British race, and in these islands, that the greatest miracle in history occurred.

zoo. Miracle?

THE ELDERLY GENTLEMAN. Yes: the first man to live three hundred years was an Englishman. The first, that is, since the contemporaries of Methuselah.

zoo. Oh, that!

THE ELDERLY GENTLEMAN. Yes, that, as you call it so flippantly. Are you aware, madam, that at that immortal moment the English race had lost intellectual credit to such an extent that they habitually spoke of one another as fatheads? Yet England is now a sacred grove to which statesmen from all over the earth come to consult English sages who speak with the experience of two and a half centuries of life. The land that once exported cotton shirts and hardware now exports nothing but wisdom. You see before you, madam, a man utterly weary of the week-end riverside hotels of the Euphrates, the minstrels and pierrots on the sands of the Persian Gulf, the toboggans and funiculars of the Hindoo Koosh. Can you wonder that I turn, with a hungry heart, to the mystery and beauty of these haunted islands, thronged with spectres from a magic past, made holy by the footsteps of the wise men of the West. Consider this island on which we stand, the last foothold of man on this side of the Atlantic: this Ireland, described by the earliest bards as an emerald gem set in a silver sea! Can I, a scion of the illustrious British race, ever forget that when the Empire transferred its seat to the East, and said to the turbulent Irish race which it had oppressed but never conquered, "At last we leave you to yourselves; and much good may it do you," the Irish as one man uttered the historic shout "No: we'll be damned if you do," and emigrated to the countries where there was still a Nationalist question, to India, Persia, and Corea, to Morocco, Tunis, and Tripoli. In these countries they were ever foremost in the struggle for national independence; and the world rang continually with the story of their sufferings and wrongs. And what poem can do justice to the end, when it came at last? Hardly two hundred years had elapsed when the claims of nationality were so universally conceded that there was no longer a single country on the face of the earth with a national grievance or a national movement. Think of the position of the Irish, who had lost all their political faculties by disuse except that of nationalist agitation, and who owed their position as the most interesting race on earth solely to their sufferings! The very countries they had helped to set free boycotted them as intolerable bores. The communities which had once idolized them as the incarnation of all that is adorable in the warm heart and witty brain, fled from them as from a pestilence. To regain their lost prestige, the Irish claimed the city of Jerusalem, on the ground that they were the lost tribes of Israel; but on their approach the Jews abandoned the city and redistributed themselves throughout Europe. It was then that these devoted Irishmen, not one of whom had ever seen Ireland, were counselled by an English Archbishop, the father of the oracles, to go back to their own country. This had never once occurred to them, because there was nothing to prevent them and nobody to forbid them. They jumped at the suggestion. They landed here: here in Galway Bay, on this very ground. When they reached the shore the older men and women flung themselves down and passionately kissed the soil of Ireland, calling on the young to embrace the earth that had borne their ancestors. But the young looked gloomily on, and said "There is no earth, only stone." You will see by looking round you why they said that: the fields here are of stone: the hills are capped with granite. They all left for England next day; and no Irishman ever again confessed of being Irish, even to his own children; so that when that generation passed away the Irish race vanished from human knowledge. And the dispersed Jews did the same lest they should be sent back to Palestine. Since then the world, bereft of its Jews and its Irish, has been a tame dull place. Is there no pathos for you in this story? Can you not understand now why I am come to visit the scene of this tragic effacement of a race of heroes and poets?

zoo. We still tell our little children stories like that, to help them to understand. But such things do not happen really. That scene of the Irish landing here and kissing the ground might have happened to a hundred people. It couldnt have happened to a hundred thousand: you know that as well as I do. And what a ridiculous thing to call people Irish because they live in Ireland! you might as well call them Airish because they live in air. They must be just the same as other people. Why do you shortlivers persist in making up silly stories about the world and trying to act as if they were true? Contact with truth hurts and frightens you: you escape from it into an imaginary vacuum in which you can indulge your desires and hopes and loves and hates without any obstruction from the solid facts of life. You love to throw dust in your own eyes.

THE ELDERLY GENTLEMAN. It is my turn now, madam, to inform you that I do not understand a single word you are saying. I should have thought that the use of a vacuum for removing dust was a mark of civilization rather than of savagery.

ZOO [*giving him up as hopeless*] Oh, Daddy, Daddy: I can hardly believe that you are human, you are so stupid. It was well said of your people in the olden days, "Dust thou art; and to dust thou shalt return."

THE ELDERLY GENTLEMAN [*nobly*] My body is dust, madam: not my soul. What does it matter what my body is made of? the dust of the ground, the particles of the air, or even the slime of the ditch? The important thing is that when my Creator took it, whatever it was, He breathed into its nostrils the breath of life; and Man became a living soul. Yes, madam, a living soul. I am not the dust of the ground: I am a living soul. That is an exalting, a magnificent thought. It is also a great scientific fact. I am not interested in the chemicals and the microbes: I leave them to the chumps and noodles, to the blockheads and the muckrakers who are incapable of their own glorious destiny, and unconscious of their own divinity. They tell me there are leucocytes in my blood, and sodium and carbon in my flesh. I thank them for the information, and tell them that there are blackbeetles in my kitchen, washing soda in my laundry, and coal in my cellar. I do not deny their existence; but I keep them in their proper place, which is not, if I may be allowed to use an antiquated form of expression, the temple of the Holy Ghost. No doubt you think me behind the times; but I rejoice in my enlightenment; and I recoil from your ignorance, your blindness, your imbecility. Humanly I pity you. Intellectually I despise you.

zoo. Bravo, Daddy! You have the root of the matter in you. You will not die of discouragement after all.

THE ELDERLY GENTLEMAN. I have not the smallest intention of doing so, madam. I am no longer young; and I have moments of weakness; but when I approach this subject the divine spark in me kindles and glows, the corruptible becomes incorruptible, and the mortal Bolge Bluebin Barlow puts on immortality. On this ground I am your equal, even if you survive me by ten thousand years.

zoo. Yes; but what do we know about this breath of life that puffs you up so exaltedly? Just nothing. So let us shake hands as cultivated Agnostics, and change the subject.

THE ELDERLY GENTLEMAN. Cultivated fiddlesticks, madam! You cannot change this subject until the heavens and the earth pass away. I am not an Agnostic: I am a gentleman. When I believe a thing I say I believe it: when I dont believe it I say I dont believe it. I do not shirk my responsibilities by pretending that I know nothing and therefore can believe nothing. We cannot disclaim knowledge and shirk responsibility. We must proceed on assumptions of some sort or we cannot form a human society.

zoo. The assumptions must be scientific, Daddy. We must live by science in the long run.

THE ELDERLY GENTLEMAN.   I have the utmost respect, madam, for the magnificent discoveries which we owe to science. But any fool can make a discovery. Every baby has to discover more in the first years of its life than Roger Bacon ever discovered in his laboratory. When I was seven years old I discovered the sting of the wasp. But I do not ask you to worship me on that account. I assure you, madam, the merest mediocrities can discover the most surprising facts about the physical universe as soon as they are civilized enough to have time to study these things, and to invent instruments and apparatus for research. But what is the consequence? Their discoveries discredit the simple stories of our religion. At first we had no idea of astronomical space. We believed the sky to be only the ceiling of a room as large as the earth, with another rocm on top of it. Death was to us a going upstairs into that room, or, if we did not obey the priests, going downstairs into the coal cellar. We founded our religion, our morality, our laws, our lessons, our poems, our prayers, on that simple belief. Well, the moment men became astronomers and made telescopes, their belief perished. When they could no longer believe in the sky, they found that they could no longer believe in their Deity, because they had always thought of him as living in the sky. When the priests themselves ceased to believe in their Deity and began to believe in astronomy, they changed their name and their dress, and called themselves doctors and men of science. They set up a new religion in which there was no Deity, but only wonders and miracles, with scientific instruments and apparatus as the wonder workers. Instead of worshipping the greatness and wisdom of the Deity, men gaped foolishly at the million billion miles of space and worshipped the astronomer as infallible and omniscient. They built temples for his telescopes. Then they looked into their own bodies with microscopes, and found there, not the soul they had formerly believed in, but millions of micro-organisms; so they gaped at these as foolishly as at the millions of miles, and built microscope temples in which horrible sacrifices were offered. They even gave their own bodies to be sacrificed by the microscope man, who was worshipped, like the astronomer, as infallible and omniscient. Thus our discoveries, instead of increasing our wisdom, only destroyed the little childish wisdom we had. All I can grant you is that they increased our knowledge.

zoo. Nonsense! Consciousness of a fact is not knowledge of it: if it were, the fish would know more of the sea than the geographers and the naturalists.

THE ELDERLY GENTLEMAN. That is an extremely acute remark, madam. The dullest fish could not possibly know less of the majesty of the ocean than many geographers and naturalists of my acquaintance.

zoo. Just so. And the greatest fool on earth, by merely looking at a mariners' compass, may become conscious of the fact that the needle turns always to the pole. Is he any the less a fool with the consciousness than he was without it?

THE ELDERLY GENTLEMAN. Only a more conceited one, madam, no doubt. Still, I do not quite see how you can be aware of the existence of a thing without knowing it.

zoo. Well, you can see a man without knowing him, can you not?

THE ELDERLY GENTLEMAN [*illuminated*] Oh how true! Of course, of course. There is a member of the Travellers' Club who has questioned the veracity of an experience of mine at the South Pole. I see that man almost every day when I am at home. But I refuse to know him.

zoo. If you could see him much more distinctly through a magnifying glass, or examine a drop of his blood through a microscope, or dissect out all the organs and analyze them chemically, would you know him then?

THE ELDERLY GENTLEMAN. Certainly not. Any such investigation could only increase the disgust with which he inspires me, and make me more determined than ever not to know him on any terms.

zoo. Yet you would be much more conscious of him, would you not?

THE ELDERLY GENTLEMAN. I should not allow that to commit me to any familiarity with the fellow. I have been twice at the Summer Sports at the South Pole; and this man pretended he had been to the North Pole, which can hardly be said to exist, as it is in the middle of the sea. He declared he had hung his hat on it.

zoo [*laughing*] He knew that travellers are amusing only when they are telling lies. Perhaps if you looked at that man through a microscope you would find some good in him.

THE ELDERLY GENTLEMAN. I do not want to find any good in him. Besides, madam, what you have just said encourages me to utter an opinion of mine which is so advanced! so intellectually daring! that I have never ventured to confess to it before, lest I should be imprisoned for blasphemy, or even burnt alive.

zoo. Indeed! What opinion is that?

THE ELDERLY GENTLEMAN [*after looking cautiously round*] I do not approve of microscopes. I never have.

zoo. You call that advanced! Oh, Daddy, that is pure obscurantism.

THE ELDERLY GENTLEMAN. Call it so if you will, madam; but I maintain that it is dangerous to shew too

much to people who do not know what they are looking
at. I think that a man who is sane as long as he looks
at the world through his own eyes is very likely to become a dangerous madman if he takes to looking at the
world through telescopes and microscopes. Even when
he is telling fairy stories about giants and dwarfs, the
giants had better not be too big nor the dwarfs too small
and too malicious. Before the microscope came, our
fairy stories only made the children's flesh creep pleasantly, and did not frighten grown-up persons at all.
But the microscope men terrified themselves and everyone else out of their wits with the invisible monsters
they saw: poor harmless little things that die at the
touch of a ray of sunshine, and are themselves the victims
of all the diseases they are supposed to produce! Whatever the scientific people may say, imagination without
microscopes was kindly and often courageous, because
it worked on things of which it had some real knowledge. But imagination with microscopes, working on a
terrifying spectacle of millions of grotesque creatures
of whose nature it had no knowledge, became a cruel,
terror-stricken, persecuting delirium. Are you aware,
madam, that a general massacre of men of science took
place in the twenty-first century of the pseudo-Christian
era, when all their laboratories were demolished, and all
their apparatus destroyed?

zoo. Yes: the shortlived are as savage in their advances as in their relapses. But when Science crept
back, it had been taught its place. The mere collectors
of anatomical or chemical facts were not supposed to
know more about Science than the collector of used post-
age stamps about international trade or literature. The
scientific terrorist who was afraid to use a spoon or a
tumbler until he had dipt it in some poisonous acid to
kill the microbes, was no longer given titles, pensions,

and monstrous powers over the bodies of other people: he was sent to an asylum, and treated there until his recovery.   But all that is an old story: the extension of life to three hundred years has provided the human race with capable leaders, and made short work of such childish stuff.

THE ELDERLY GENTLEMAN [*pettishly*] You seem to credit every advance in civilization to your inordinately long livers.   Do you not know that this question was familiar to men who died before they had reached my own age?

zoo.   Oh yes: one or two of them hinted at it in a feeble way.   An ancient writer whose name has come down to us in several forms, such as Shakespear, Shelley, Sheridan, and Shoddy, has a remarkable passage about your dispositions being horribly shaken by thoughts beyond the reaches of your souls.   That does not come to much, does it?

THE ELDERLY GENTLEMAN.   At all events, madam, I may remind you, if you come to capping ages, that whatever your secondaries and tertiaries may be, you are younger than I am.

zoo.   Yes, Daddy; but it is not the number of years we have behind us, but the number we have before us, that makes us careful and responsible and determined to find out the truth about everything.   What does it matter to you whether anything is true or not?   your flesh is as grass: you come up like a flower, and wither in your second childhood.   A lie will last your time: it will not last mine.   If I knew I had to die in twenty years it would not be worth my while to educate myself: I should not bother about anything but having a little pleasure while I lasted.

THE ELDERLY GENTLEMAN.   Young woman: you are mistaken.   Shortlived as we are, we—the best of us, I mean—regard civilization and learning, art and science, as an ever-burning torch, which passes from the hand of one generation to the hand of the next, each generation kindling it to a brighter, prouder flame. Thus each life-time, however short, contributes a brick to a vast and growing edifice, a page to a sacred volume, a chapter to a Bible, a Bible to a literature. We may be insects; but like the coral insect we build islands which become continents: like the bee we store sustenance for future communities. The individual perishes; but the race is immortal. The acorn of today is the oak of the next millennium. I throw my stone on the cairn and die; but later comers add another stone and yet another; and lo! a mountain. I—

ZOO [*interrupts him by laughing heartily at him*]! ! !

THE ELDERLY GENTLEMAN [*with offended dignity*] May I ask what I have said that calls for this merriment?

ZOO. Oh, Daddy, Daddy, Daddy, you are a funny little man, with your torches, and your flames, and your bricks and edifices and pages and volumes and chapters and coral and insects and bees and acorns and stones and mountains.

THE ELDERLY GENTLEMAN. Metaphors, madam. Metaphors merely.

ZOO. Images, images, images. I was talking about men, not about images.

THE ELDERLY GENTLEMAN. I was illustrating—not, I hope, quite infelicitously—the great march of Progress. I was shewing you how, shortlived as we orientals are, mankind gains in stature from generation to generation, from epoch to epoch, from barbarism to civilization, from civilization to perfection.

ZOO. I see. The father grows to be six feet high, and hands on his six feet to his son, who adds another six feet and becomes twelve feet high, and hands his twelve feet on to his son, who is full-grown at eighteen feet, and so on. In a thousand years you would all be three or four miles high. At that rate your ancestors Bilge and Bluebeard, whom you call giants, must have been about quarter of an inch high.

THE ELDERLY GENTLEMAN. I am not here to bandy quibbles and paradoxes with a girl who blunders over the greatest names in history. I am in earnest. I am treating a solemn theme seriously. I never said that the son of a man six feet high would be twelve feet high.

ZOO. You didnt mean that?

THE ELDERLY GENTLEMAN. Most certainly not.

ZOO. Then you didnt mean anything. Now listen to me, you little ephemeral thing. I knew quite well what you meant by your torch handed on from generation to generation. But every time that torch is handed on, it dies down to the tiniest spark; and the man who gets it can rekindle it only by his own light. You are no taller than Bilge or Bluebeard; and you are no wiser. Their wisdom, such as it was, perished with them: so did their strength, if their strength ever existed outside your imagination. I do not know how old you are: you look about five hundred—

THE ELDERLY GENTLEMAN. Five hundred! Really, madam—

ZOO [continuing]; but I know, of course, that you are an ordinary shortliver. Well, your wisdom is only such wisdom as a man can have before he has had experience enough to distinguish his wisdom from his folly, his destiny from his delusions, his—

THE ELDERLY GENTLEMAN. In short, such wisdoms as your own.

ZOO. No, no, no, no. How often must I tell you that we are made wise not by the recollections of our past, but

by the responsibilities of our future. I shall be more
reckless when I am a tertiary than I am today. If you
cannot understand that, at least you must admit that I
have learnt from tertiaries. I have seen their work and
lived under their institutions. Like all young things
I rebelled against them; and in their hunger for new
lights and new ideas they listened to me and encouraged
me to rebel. But my ways did not work; and theirs did;
and they were able to tell me why. They have no power
over me except that power: they refuse all other power;
and the consequence is that there are no limits to their
power except the limits they set themselves. You are
a child governed by children, who make so many mistakes and are so naughty that you are in continual re-
bellion against them; and as they can never convince you
that they are right: they can govern you only by beating
you, imprisoning you, torturing you, killing you if you
disobey them without being strong enough to kill or
torture them.

THE ELDERLY GENTLEMAN. That may be an unfortunate fact. I condemn it and deplore it. But our minds
are greater than the facts. We know better. The
greatest ancient teachers, followed by the galaxy of
Christs who arose in the twentieth century, not to mention such comparatively modern spiritual leaders as
Blitherinjam, Tosh, and Spiffkins, all taught that pun-
ishment and revenge, coercion and militarism, are mistakes, and that the golden rule—

ZOO [interrupting] Yes, yes, yes, Daddy: we longlived
people know that quite well. But did any of their disciples ever succeed in governing you for a single day on
their Christlike principles? It is not enough to know
what is good: you must be able to do it. They couldnt
do it because they did not live long enough to find out
how to do it, or to outlive the childish passions that pre-

vented them from really wanting to do it. You know very well that they could only keep order—such as it was—by the very coercion and militarism they were denouncing and deploring. They had actually to kill one another for preaching their own gospel, or be killed themselves.

THE ELDERLY GENTLEMAN. The blood of the martyrs, madam, is the seed of the Church.

ZOO. More images, Daddy! The blood of the short-lived falls on stony ground.

THE ELDERLY GENTLEMAN [*rising, very testy*] You are simply mad on the subject of longevity. I wish you would change it. It is rather personal and in bad taste. Human nature is human nature, longlived or shortlived, and always will be.

ZOO. Then you give up the idea of progress? You cry off the torch, and the brick, and the acorn, and all the rest of it?

THE ELDERLY GENTLEMAN. I do nothing of the sort. I stand for progress and for freedom broadening down from precedent to precedent.

ZOO. You are certainly a true Briton.

THE ELDERLY GENTLEMAN. I am proud of it. But in your mouth I feel that the compliment hides some insult; so I do not thank you for it.

ZOO. All I meant was that though Britons sometimes say quite clever things and deep things as well as silly and shallow things, they always forget them ten minutes after they have uttered them.

THE ELDERLY GENTLEMAN. Leave it at that, madam: leave it at that. [*He sits down again*]. Even a Pope is not expected to be continually pontificating. Our flashes of inspiration shew that our hearts are in the right place.

zoo. Of course. You cannot keep your heart in any place but the right place.

THE ELDERLY GENTLEMAN. Tcha!

zoo. But you can keep your hands in the wrong place. In your neighbors' pockets, for example. So, you see, it is your hands that really matter.

THE ELDERLY GENTLEMAN [*exhausted*] Well, a woman must have the last word. I will not dispute it with you.

zoo. Good. Now let us go back to the really interesting subject of our discussion. You remember? The slavery of the shortlived to images and metaphors.

THE ELDERLY GENTLEMAN [*aghast*] Do you mean to say, madam, that after having talked my head off, and reduced me to despair and silence by your intolerable loquacity, you actually propose to begin all over again? I shall leave you at once.

zoo. You must not. I am your nurse; and you must stay with me.

THE ELDERLY GENTLEMAN. I absolutely decline to do anything of the sort [*he rises and walks away with marked dignity*].

zoo [*using her tuning-fork*] Zoo on Burrin Pier to Oracle Police at Ennistymon have you got me? . . . What? . . . I am picking you up now but you are flat to my pitch. . . . Just a shade sharper. . . . Thats better: still a little more. . . . Got you: right. Isolate Burrin Pier quick.

THE ELDERLY GENTLEMAN [*is heard to yell*] Oh!

zoo [*still intoning*] Thanks. . . . Oh nothing serious I am nursing a shortliver and the silly creature has run away he has discouraged himself very badly by gadding about and talking to secondaries and I must keep him strictly to heel.

The Elderly Gentleman returns, indignant.

zoo.   Here he is you can release the Pier thanks. Good-bye. [*She puts up her tuning-fork*].

THE ELDERLY GENTLEMAN.   This is outrageous. When I tried to step off the pier on to the road, I received a shock, followed by an attack of pins and needles which ceased only when I stepped back on to the stones.

zoo.   Yes: there is an electric hedge there. It is a very old and very crude method of keeping animals from straying.

THE ELDERLY GENTLEMAN.   We are perfectly familiar with it in Baghdad, madam; but I little thought I should live to have it ignominiously applied to myself. You have actually Kiplingized me.

zoo.   Kiplingized! What is that?

THE ELDERLY GENTLEMAN.   About a thousand years ago there were two authors named Kipling. One was an eastern and a writer of merit: the other, being a western, was of course only an amusing barbarian. He is said to have invented the electric hedge. I consider that in using it on me you have taken a very great liberty.

zoo.   What is a liberty?

THE ELDERLY GENTLEMAN [*exasperated*] I shall not explain, madam. I believe you know as well as I do. [*He sits down on the bollard in dudgeon*].

zoo.   No: even you can tell me things I do not know. Havnt you noticed that all the time you have been here we have been asking you questions?

THE ELDERLY GENTLEMAN.   Noticed it! It has almost driven me mad. Do you see my white hair? It was hardly grey when I landed: there were patches of its original auburn still distinctly discernible.

zoo.   That is one of the symptoms of discouragement. But have you noticed something much more important to yourself: that is, that you have never asked us any questions, although we know so much more than you do?

THE ELDERLY GENTLEMAN. I am not a child, madam. I believe I have had occasion to say that before. And I am an experienced traveller. I know that what the traveller observes must really exist, or he could not observe it. But what the natives tell him is invariably pure fiction.

ZOO. Not here, Daddy. With us life is too long for telling lies. They all get found out. Youd better ask me questions while you have the chance.

THE ELDERLY GENTLEMAN. If I have occasion to consult the oracle I shall address myself to a proper one: to a tertiary: not to a primary flapper playing at being an oracle. If you are a nurserymaid, attend to your duties; and do not presume to ape your elders.

ZOO [rising ominously and reddening] You silly—

THE ELDERLY GENTLEMAN [thundering] Silence! Do you hear! Hold your tongue.

ZOO. Something very disagreeable is happening to me. I feel hot all over. I have a horrible impulse to injure you. What have you done to me?

THE ELDERLY GENTLEMAN [triumphant] Aha! I have made you blush. Now you know what blushing means. Blushing with shame!

ZOO. Whatever you are doing, it is something so utterly evil that if you do not stop I will kill you.

THE ELDERLY GENTLEMAN [apprehending his danger] Doubtless you think it safe to threaten an old man—

ZOO [fiercely] Old! You are a child: an evil child. We kill evil children here. We do it even against our own wills by instinct. Take care.

THE ELDERLY GENTLEMAN [rising with crestfallen courtesy] I did not mean to hurt your feelings. I— [swallowing the apology with an effort] I beg your pardon. [*He takes off his hat, and bows*].

zoo. What does that mean?

THE ELDERLY GENTLEMAN. I withdraw what I said.

zoo. How can you withdraw what you said?

THE ELDERLY GENTLEMAN. I can say no more than ·
that I am sorry.

zoo. You have reason to be. That hideous sensation
you gave me is subsiding; but you have had a very
narrow escape. Do not attempt to kill me again; for at
the first sign in your voice or face I shall strike you
dead.

THE ELDERLN GENTLEMAN. *I* attempt to kill you!
What a monstrous accusation!

zoo [*frowns*]!

THE ELDERLY GENTLEMAN [*prudently correcting himself*] I mean misunderstanding. I never dreamt of such
a thing. Surely you cannot believe that I am a murderer.

zoo. I know you are a murderer. It is not merely
that you threw words at me as if they were stones, meaning to hurt me. It was the instinct to kill that you
roused in me. I did not know it was in my nature:
never before has it wakened and sprung out at me, warning me to kill or be killed. I must now reconsider my
whole political position. I am no longer a Conservative.

THE ELDERLY GENTLEMAN [*dropping his hat*] Gracious Heavens! you have lost your senses. I am at the
mercy of a madwoman: I might have known it from
the beginning. I can bear no more of this. [*Offering
his chest for the sacrifice*] Kill me at once: and much
good may my death do you!

zoo. It would be useless unless all the other shortlivers were killed at the same time. Besides, it is a
measure which should be taken politically and constitu-

tionally, not privately. However, I am prepared to discuss it with you.

THE ELDERLY GENTLEMAN. No, no, no. I had much rather discuss your intention of withdrawing from the Conservative party. How the Conservatives have tolerated your opinions so far is more than I can imagine: I can only conjecture that you have contributed very liberally to the party funds. [*He picks up his hat, and sits down again*].

zoo. Do not babble so senselessly: our chief political controversy is the most momentous in the world for you and your like.

THE ELDERLY GENTLEMAN [*interested*] Indeed? Pray, may I ask what it is? I am a keen politician, and may perhaps be of some use. [*He puts on his hat, cocking it slightly*].

zoo. We have two great parties: the Conservative party and the Colonization party. The Colonizers are of opinion that we should increase our numbers and colonize. The Conservatives hold that we should stay as we are, confined to these islands, a race apart, wrapped up in the majesty of our wisdom on a soil held as holy ground for us by an adoring world, with our sacred frontier traced beyond dispute by the sea. They contend that it is our destiny to rule the world, and that even when we were shortlived we did so. They say that our power and our peace depend on our remoteness, our exclusiveness, our separation, and the restriction of our numbers. Five minutes ago that was my political faith. Now I do not think there should be any shortlived people at all. [*She throws herself again carelessly on the sacks*].

THE ELDERLY GENTLEMAN. Am I to infer that you deny my right to live because I allowed myself—perhaps injudiciously—to give you a slight scolding?

zoo. Is it worth living for so short a time? Are you any good to yourself?

THE ELDERLY GENTLEMAN [*stupent*] Well, upon my soul!

zoo. It is a very little soul. You only encourage the sin of pride in us, and keep us looking down at you instead of up to something higher than ourselves.

THE ELDERLY GENTLEMAN. Is not that a selfish view, madam? Think of the good you do us by your oracular counsels!

zoo. What good have our counsels ever done you? You come to us for advice when you know you are in difficulties. But you never know you are in difficulties until twenty years after you have made the mistakes that led to them; and then it is too late. You cannot understand our advice: you often do more mischief by trying to act on it than if you had been left to your own childish devices. If you were not childish you would not come to us at all: you would learn from experience that your consultations of the oracle are never of any real help to you. You draw wonderful imaginary pictures of us, and write fictitious tales and poems about our beneficent operations in the past, our wisdom, our justice, our mercy: stories in which we often appear as sentimental dupes of your prayers and sacrifices; but you do it only to conceal from yourselves the truth that you are incapable of being helped by us. Your Prime Minister pretends that he has come to be guided by the oracle; but we are not deceived: we know quite well that he has come here so that when he goes back he may have the authority and dignity of one who has visited the holy islands and spoken face to face with the ineffable ones. He will pretend that all the measures he wishes to take for his own purposes have been enjoined on him by the oracle.

THE ELDERLY GENTLEMAN. But you forget that the answers of the oracle cannot be kept secret or misrepresented. They are written and promulgated. The Leader of the Opposition can obtain copies. All the nations know them. Secret diplomacy has been totally abolished.

ZOO. Yes: you publish documents; but they are garbled or forged. And even if you published our real answers it would make no difference, because the shortlived cannot interpret the plainest writings. Your scriptures command you in the plainest terms to do exactly the contrary of everything your own laws and chosen rulers command and execute. You cannot defy Nature. It is a law of Nature that there is a fixed relation between conduct and length of life.

THE ELDERLY GENTLEMAN. I have never heard of any such law, madam.

ZOO. Well, you are hearing of it now.

THE ELDERLY GENTLEMAN. Let me tell you that we shortlivers, as you call us, have lengthened our lives very considerably.

ZOO. How?

THE ELDERLY GENTLEMAN. By saving time. By enabling men to cross the ocean in an afternoon, and to see and to speak to one another when they are thousands of miles apart. We hope shortly to orgaize their labor, and press natural forces into their service, so scientifically that the burden of labor will cease to be perceptible, leaving common men more leisure than they will know what to do with.

ZOO. Daddy: the man whose life is lengthened in this way may be busier than a savage; but the difference between such men living seventy years and those living three hundred would be all the greater; for to a shortliver increase of years is only increase of sorrow; but to

a longliver every extra year is a prospect which forces
him to stretch his faculties to the utmost to face it.
Therefore I say that we who live three hundred years
can be of no use to you who live less than a hundred,
and that our true destiny is not to advise and govern
you, but to supplant and supersede you. In that faith
I now declare myself a Colonizer and an Exterminator.

THE ELDERLY GENTLEMAN. Oh, steady! steady!
Pray! pray! Reflect, I implore you. It is possible to
colonize without exterminating the natives. Would
you treat us less mercifully than our barbarous forefathers treated the Redskin and the Negro? Are we
not, as Britons, entitled at least to some reservations?

ZOO. What is the use of prolonging the agony? You
would perish slowly in our presence, no matter what we
did to preserve you. You were almost dead when I took
charge of you today, merely because you had talked for
a few minutes to a secondary. Besides, we have our own
experience to go upon. Have you never heard that our
children occasionally revert to the ancestral type, and
are born shortlived?

THE ELDERLY GENTLEMAN [*eagerly*] Never. I hope
you will not be offended if I say that it would be a great
comfort to me if I could be placed in charge of one of
those normal individuals.

ZOO. Abnormal, you mean. What you ask is impossible: we weed them all out.

THE ELDERLY GENTLEMAN. When you say that you
weed them out, you send a cold shiver down my spine. I
hope you dont mean that you—that you—that you as-
sist Nature in any way?

ZOO. Why not? Have you not heard the saying of
the Chinese sage Dee Ning, that a good garden needs
weeding? But it is not necessary for us to interfere.
We are naturally rather particular as to the conditions

on which we consent to live. One does not mind the accidental loss of an arm or a leg or an eye: after all, no one with two legs is unhappy because he has not three; so why should a man with one be unhappy because he has not two? But infirmities of mind and temper are quite another matter. If one of us has no self-control, or is too weak to bear the strain of our truthful life without wincing, or is tormented by depraved appetites and superstitions, or is unable to keep free from pain and depression, he naturally becomes discouraged, and refuses to live.

THE ELDERLY GENTLEMAN. Good Lord! Cuts his throat, do you mean?

ZOO. No: why should he cut his throat? He simply dies. He wants to. He is out of countenance, as we call it.

THE ELDERLY GENTLEMAN. Well!!! But suppose he is depraved enough not to want to die, and to settle the difficulty by killing all the rest of you?

ZOO. Oh, he is one of the thoroughly degenerate shortlivers whom we occasionally produce. He emigrates.

THE ELDERLY GENTLEMAN. And what becomes of him then?

ZOO. You shortlived people always think very highly of him. You accept him as what you call a great man.

THE ELDERLY GENTLEMAN. You astonish me; and yet I must admit that what you tell me accounts for a great deal of the little I know of the private life of our great men. We must be very convenient to you as a dumping place for your failures.

ZOO. I admit that.

THE ELDERLY GENTLEMAN. Good. Then if you carry out your plan of colonization, and leave no shortlived countries in the world, what will you do with your undesirables?

zoo. Kill them. Our tertiaries are not at all squeamish about killing.

THE ELDERLY GENTLEMAN. Gracious Powers!

zoo [*glancing up at the sun*] Come. It is just sixteen o'clock; and you have to join your party at half-past in the temple in Galway.

THE ELDERLY GENTLEMAN [*rising*] Galway! Shall I at last be able to boast of having seen that magnificent city?

zoo. You will be disappointed: we have no cities. There is a temple of the oracle: that is all.

THE ELDERLY GENTLEMAN. Alas! and I came here to fulfil two long-cherished dreams. One was to see Galway. It has been said, "See Galway and die." The other was to contemplate the ruins of London.

zoo. Ruins! We do not tolerate ruins. Was London a place of any importance?

THE ELDERLY GENTLEMAN [*amazed*] What! London! It was the mightiest city of antiquity. [*Rhetorically*] Situate just where the Dover Road crosses the Thames, it—

zoo [*curtly interrupting*] There is nothing there now. Why should anybody pitch on such a spot to live? The nearest houses are at a place called Strand-on-the-Green: it is very old. Come. We shall go across the water. [*She goes down the steps*].

THE ELDERLY GENTLEMAN. Sic transit gloria mundi!

zoo [*from below*] What did you say?

THE ELDERLY GENTLEMAN [*despairingly*] Nothing. You would not understand. [*He goes down the steps*].

ACT II

A courtyard before the columned portico of a temple. The temple door is in the middle of the portico. A veiled and robed woman of majestic carriage passes along behind the columns towards the entrance. From the opposite direction a man of compact figure, clean-shaven, saturnine, and self-centered, in short, very like Napoleon I, and wearing a military uniform of Napoleonic cut, marches with measured steps; places his hand in his lapel in the traditional manner; and fixes the woman with his eye. She stops, her attitude expressing haughty amazement at his audacity. He is on her right: she on his left.

NAPOLEON [*impressively*] I am the Man of Destiny.

THE VEILED WOMAN [*unimpressed*] How did you get in here?

NAPOLEON. I walked in. I go on until I am stopped. I never am stopped. I tell you I am the Man of Destiny.

THE VEILED WOMAN. You will be a man of very short destiny if you wander about here without one of our children to guide you. I suppose you belong to the Baghdad envoy.

NAPOLEON. I came with him; but I do not belong to

him. I belong to myself. Direct me to the oracle if you can. If not, do not waste my time.

THE VEILED WOMAN. Your time, poor creature, is short. I will not waste it. Your envoy and his party will be here presently. The consultation of the oracle is arranged for them, and will take place according to the prescribed ritual. You can wait here until they come [*she turns to go into the temple*].

NAPOLEON. I never wait. [*She stops*]. The prescribed ritual is, I believe, the classical one of the pythoness on her tripod, the intoxicating fumes arising from the abyss, the convulsions of the priestess as she delivers the message of the God, and so on. That sort of thing does not impose on me: I use it myself to impose on simpletons. I believe that what is, is. I know that what is not, is not. The antics of a woman sitting on a tripod and pretending to be drunk do not interest me. Her words are put into her mouth, not by a god, but by a man three hundred years old, who has had the capacity to profit by his experience. I wish to speak to that man face to face, without mummery or imposture.

THE VEILED WOMAN. You seem to be an unusually sensible person. But there is no old man. I am the oracle on duty today. I am on my way now to take my place on the tripod, and go through the usual mummery, as you rightly call it, to impress your friend the envoy. As you are superior to that kind of thing, you may consult me now. [*She leads the way into the middle of the courtyard*]. What do you want to know?

NAPOLEON [*following her*] Madam: I have not come all this way to discuss matters of State with a woman. I must ask you to direct me to one of your oldest and ablest men.

THE ORACLE. None of our oldest and ablest men or women would dream of wasting their time on you. You would die of discouragement in their presence in less than three hours.

NAPOLEON. You can keep this idle fable of discouragement for people credulous enough to be intimidated by it, madam. I do not believe in metaphysical forces.

THE ORACLE. No one asks you to. A field is something physical, is it not. Well, I have a field.

NAPOLEON. I have several million fields. I am Emperor of Turania.

THE ORACLE. You do not understand. I am not speaking of an agricultural field. Do you not know that every mass of matter in motion carries with it an invisible gravitational field, every magnet an invisible magnetic field, and every living organism a mesmeric field? Even you have a perceptible mesmeric field. Feeble as it is, it is the strongest I have yet observed in a shortliver.

NAPOLEON. By no means feeble, madam. I understand you now; and I may tell you that the strongest characters blench in my presence, and submit to my domination. But I do not call that a physical force.

THE ORACLE. What else do you call it, pray? Our physicists deal with it. Our mathematicians express its measurements in algebraic equations.

NAPOLEON. Do you mean that they could measure mine?

THE ORACLE. Yes: by a figure infinitely near to zero. Even in us the force is negligible during our first century of life. In our second century it develops quickly, and becomes dangerous to shortlivers who venture into its field. If I were not veiled and robed in insulating material you could not endure my presence; and I am still a young woman: one hundred and seventy if you wish to know exactly.

NAPOLEON [*folding his arms*] I am not intimidated: no woman alive, old or young, can put me out of countenance. Unveil, madam. Disrobe. You will move this temple as easily as shake me.

THE ORACLE. Very well [*she throws back her veil*].

NAPOLEON [*shrieking, staggering, and covering his eyes*] No. Stop. Hide your face again. [*Shutting his eyes and distractedly clutching at his throat and heart*] Let me go. Help! I am dying.

THE ORACLE. Do you still wish to consult an older person?

NAPOLEON. No, no. The veil, the veil, I beg you.

THE ORACLE [*replacing the veil*] So.

NAPOLEON. Ouf! One cannot always be at one's best. Twice before in my life I have lost my nerve and behaved like a poltroon. But I warn you not to judge my quality by these involuntary moments.

THE ORACLE. I have no occasion to judge of your quality. You want my advice. Speak quickly; or I shall go about my business.

NAPOLEON [*after a moment's hesitation, sinks respectfully on one knee*] I—

THP ORACLE. Oh, rise, rise. Are you so foolish as to offer me this mummery which even you despise?

NAPOLEON [*rising*] I knelt in spite of myself. I compliment you on your impressiveness, madam.

THE ORACLE [*impatiently*] Time! time! time! time!

NAPOLEON. You will not grudge me the necessary time, madam, when you know my case. I am a man gifted with a certain specific talent in a degree altogether extraordinary. I am not otherwise a very extraordinary person: my family is not influential; and without this talent I should cut no particular figure in the world.

THE ORACLE. Why cut a figure in the world?

NAPOLEON. Superiority will make itself felt, madam. But when I say I possess this talent I do not express myself accurately. The truth is that my talent possesses me. It is genius. It drives me to exercise it. I must exercise it. I am great when I exercise it. At other moments I am nobody.

THE ORACLE. Well, exercise it. Do you need an oracle to tell you that?

NAPOLEON. Wait. This talent involves the shedding of human blood.

THP ORACLE. Are you a surgeon, or a dentist?

NAPOLEON. Psha! You do not appreciate me, madam. I mean the shedding of oceans of blood, the death of millions of men.

THE ORACLE. They object, I suppose.

NAPOLEON. Not at all. They adore me.

THE ORACLE. Indeed!

NAPOLEON. I have never shed blood with my own hand. They kill each other: they die with shouts of triumph on their lips. Those who die cursing do not curse me. My talent is to organize this slaughter; to give mankind this terrible joy which they call glory; to let loose the devil in them that peace has bound in chains.

THE ORACLE. And you? Do you share their joy?

NAPOLEON. Not at all. What satisfaction is it to me to see one fool pierce the entrails of another with a bayonet? I am a man of princely character, but of simple personal tastes and habits. I have the virtues of a laborer: industry and indifference to personal comfort. But I must rule, because I am so superior to other men that it is intolerable to me to be misruled by them. Yet only as a slayer can I become a ruler. I cannot be great as a writer: I have tried and failed. I have no talent as a sculptor or painter; and as lawyer, preacher, doctor, or actor, scores of second-rate men can do as well as I, or better. I am not even a diplomatist: I can only play my trump card of force. What I can do is to organize war. Look at me! I seem a man like other men, because nine-tenths of me is common humanity. But the other tenth is a faculty for seeing things as they are that no other man possesses.

THE ORACLE. You mean that you have no imagination?

NAPOLEON [*forcibly*] I mean that I have the only imagination worth having: the power of imagining things as they are, even when I cannot see them. You feel yourself my superior, I know: nay, you are my superior: have I not bowed my knee to you by instinct? Yet I challenge you to a test of our respective powers. Can you calculate what the mathematicians call vectors, without putting a single algebraic symbol on paper? Can you launch ten thousand men across a frontier and a chain of mountains and know to a mile exactly where they will be at the end of seven weeks? The rest is nothing: I got it all from the books at my military school. Now this great game of war, this playing with armies as other men play with bowls and skittles, is one which I must go on playing, partly because a man must do what he can and not what he would like to do, and partly because, if I stop, I immediately lose my power and become a beggar in the land where I now make men drunk with glory.

THE ORACLE. No doubt then you wish to know how to extricate yourself from this unfortunate position?

NAPOLEON. It is not generally considered unfortunate, madam. Supremely fortunate rather.

THE ORACLE. If you think so, go on making them drunk with glory. Why trouble me with their folly and your vectors?

NAPOLEON. Unluckily, madam, men are not only

heroes: they are also cowards. They desire glory; but they dread death.

THE ORACLE. Why should they? Their lives are too short to be worth living. That is why they think your game of war worth playing.

NAPOLEON. They do not look at it quite in that way. The most worthless soldier wants to live for ever. To make him risk being killed by the enemy I have to convince him that if he hesitates he will inevitably be shot at dawn by his own comrades for cowardice.

THE ORACLE. And if his comrades refuse to shoot him?

NAPOLEON. They will be shot too, of course.

THE ORACLE. By whom?

NAPOLEON. By their comrades.

THE ORACLE. And if they refuse?

NAPOLEON. Up to a certain point they do not refuse.

THE ORACLE. But when that point is reached, you have to do the shooting yourself, eh?

NAPOLEON. Unfortunately, madam, when that point is reached, they shoot me.

THE ORACLE. Mf! It seems to me they might as well shoot you first as last. Why dont they?

NAPOLEON. Because their love of fighting, their desire for glory, their shame of being branded as dastards, their instinct to test themselves in terrible trials, their fear of being killed or enslaved by the enemy, their belief that they are defending their hearths and homes, overcome their natural cowardice, and make them willing not only to risk their own lives but to kill everyone who refuses to take that risk. But if war continues too long, there comes a time when the soldiers, and also the tax-payers who are supporting and munitioning them, reach a condition which they describe as being fed up. The troops have proved their courage, and want to go home and enjoy in peace the glory it has earned them. Besides, the risk of death for each soldier becomes a certainty if the fighting goes on for ever: he hopes to escape for six months, but knows he cannot escape for six years. The risk of bankruptcy for the citizen becomes a certainty in the same way. Now what does this mean for me?

THE ORACLE. Does that matter in the midst of such calamity?

NAPOLEON. Psha! madam: it is the only thing that matters: the value of human life is the value of the greatest living man. Cut off that infinitesimal layer of grey matter which distinguishes my brain from that of the common man, and you cut down the stature of humanity from that of a giant to that of a nobody. I matter supremely: my soldiers do not matter at all: there are plenty more where they came from. If you kill me, or put a stop to my activity (it is the same thing), the nobler part of human life perishes. You must save the world from that catastrophe, madam. War has made me popular, powerful, famous, historically immortal. But I foresee that if I go on to the end it will leave me execrated, dethroned, imprisoned, perhaps executed. Yet if I stop fighting I commit suicide as a great man and become a common one. How am I to escape the horns of this tragic dilemma? Victory I can guarantee: I am invincible. But the cost of victory is the demoralization, the depopulation, the ruin of the victors no less than of the vanquished. How am I to satisfy my genius by fighting until I die? that is my question to you.

THE ORACLE. Were you not rash to venture into these sacred islands with such a question on your lips? Warriors are not popular here, my friend.

NAPOLEON. If a soldier were restrained by such a

consideration, madam, he would no longer be a soldier. Besides, [*he produces a pistol*] I have not come unarmed.

THE ORACLE.   What is that thing?

NAPOLEON.   It is an instrument of my profession, madam. I raise this hammer; I point the barrel at you; I pull this trigger that is against my forefinger; and you fall dead.

THE ORACLE.   Shew it to me [*she puts out her hand to take it from him*].

NAPOLEON [*retreating a step*] Pardon me, madam. I never trust my life in the hands of a person over whom I have no control.

THE ORACLE [*sternly*] Give it to me [*she raises her hand to her veil*].

NAPOLEON [*dropping the pistol and covering his eyes*] Quarter! Kamerad! Take it, madam [*he kicks it towards her*]: I surrender.

THE ORACLE.   Give me that thing. Do you expect me to stoop for it?

NAPOLEON [*taking his hands from his eyes with an effort*] A poor victory, madam [*he picks up the pistol and hands it to her*]: there was no vector strategy needed to win it. [*Making a **pose** of his humiliation*] But enjoy your triumph: you have made me—ME! Cain Adamson Charles Napoleon! Emperor of Turania! cry for quarter.

THE ORACLE.   The way out of your difficulty, Cain Adamson, is very simple.

NAPOLEON [*eagerly*] Good. What is it?

THE ORACLE.   To die before the tide of glory turns. Allow me [*she shoots him*].

He falls with a shriek. She throws the pistol away and goes haughtily into the temple.

NAPOLEON [*scrambling to his feet*] Murderess! Monster! She-devil! Unnatural, inhuman wretch! You deserve to be hanged, guillotined, broken on the wheel, burnt alive. No sense of the sacredness of human life! No thought for my wife and children! Bitch! Sow! Wanton! [*He picks up the pistol*]. And missed me at five yards! Thats a woman all over.

He is going away whence he came when Zoo arrives and confronts him at the head of a party consisting of the British Envoy, the Elderly Gentleman, the Envoy's wife, and her daughter, aged about eighteen. The Envoy, a typical politician, looks like an imperfectly reformed criminal disguised by a good tailor. The dress of the ladies is coeval with that of the Elderly Gentleman, and suitable for public official ceremonies in western capitals at the XVIII-XIX fin de siècle.

They file in under the portico. Zoo immediately comes out imperiously to Napoleon's right, whilst the Envoy's wife hurries effusively to his left. The Envoy meanwhile passes along behind the columns to the door, followed by his daughter. The Elderly Gentleman stops just where he entered, to see why Zoo has swooped so abruptly on the Emperor of Turania.

zoo [*to Napoleon, severely*] What are you doing here by yourself? You have no business to go about here alone. What was that noise just now? What is that in your hand?

Napoleon glares at her in speechless fury; pockets the pistol; and produces a whistle.

THE ENVOY'S WIFE. Arnt you coming with us to the oracle, sire?

NAPOLEON. To hell with the oracle, and with you too [*he turns to go*]!

THE ENVOY'S WIFE   ⎫ [*together*] ⎬ Oh, sire!!
zoo   ⎭   Where are you go-
                               ing?

NAPOLEON. To fetch the police. [*He goes out past

Zoo, almost jostling her, and blowing piercing blasts on his whistle].

ZOO [*whipping out her tuning-fork and intoning*] Hallo Galway Central.   [*The whistling continues*]. Stand by to isolate.   [*To the Elderly Gentleman, who is staring after the whistling Emperor*] How far has he gone?

THE ELDERLY GENTLEMAN.   To that curious statue of a fat old man.

ZOO [*quickly, intoning*] Isolate the Falstaff monument isolate hard.   Paralyze—[*the whistling stops*]. Thank you.   [*She puts up her tuning fork*].   He shall not move a muscle until I come to fetch him.

THE ENVOY'S WIFE.   Oh! he will be frightfully angry! Did you hear what he said to me?

ZOO.   Much we care for his anger!

THE DAUGHTER [*coming forward between her mother and Zoo*].   Please, madam, whose statue is it? and where can I buy a picture postcard of it?   It is so funny.   I will take a snapshot when we are coming back; but they come out so badly sometimes.

ZOO.   They will give you pictures and toys in the temple to take away with you.   The story of the statue is too long.   It would bore you [*she goes past them across the courtyard to get rid of them*].

THE WIFE [*gushing*] Oh no, I assure you.

THE DAUGHTER [*copying her mother*] We should be so interested.

ZOO.   Nonsense!   All I can tell you about it is that a thousand years ago, when the whole world was given over to you shortlived people, there was a war called the War to End War.   In the war which followed it about ten years later, none of the soldiers were killed; but seven of the capital cities of Europe were wiped out of existence.   It seems to have been a great joke: for the

statesmen who thought they had sent ten million common men to their deaths were themselves blown into
fragments with their houses and families, while the ten
million men lay snugly in the caves they had dug for
themselves. Later on even the houses escaped; but their
inhabitants were poisoned by gas that spared no living
soul. Of course the soldiers starved and ran wild; and
that was the end of pseudo-Christian civilization. The
last civilized thing that happened was that the statesmen discovered that cowardice was a great patriotic
virtue; and a public monument was erected to its first
preacher, an ancient and very fat sage called Sir John
Falstaff. Well [*pointing*], thats Falstaff.

THE ELDERLY GENTLEMAN [*coming from the portico
to his granddaughter's right*] Great Heavens! And at
the base of this monstrous poltroon's statue the War
God of Turania is now gibbering impotently.

ZOO. Serve him right! War God indeed!

THE ENVOY [*coming between his wife and Zoo*] I dont
know any history: a modern Prime Minister has something better to do than sit reading books; but—

THE ELDERLY GENTLEMAN [*interrupting him encouragingly*] You make history, Ambrose.

THE ENVOY. Well, perhaps I do; and perhaps history makes me. I hardly recognize myself in the newspapers sometimes, though I suppose leading articles are
the materials of history, as you might say. But what
I want to know is, how did war come back again? and
how did they make those poisonous gases you speak of?
We should be glad to know; for they might come in very
handy if we have to fight Turania. Of course I am all
for peace, and dont hold with the race of armaments in
principle; still, we must keep ahead or be wiped out.

ZOO You can make the gases for yourselves when
your chemists find out how. Then you will do as you

did before: poison each other until there are no chemists left, and no civilization.   You will then begin all over again as half-starved ignorant savages, and fight with boomerangs and poisoned arrows until you work up to the poison gases and high explosives once more, with the same result.   That is, unless we have sense enough to make an end of this ridiculous game by destroying you.

THE ENVOY [*aghast*] Destroying us!

THE ELDERLY GENTLEMAN.   I told you, Ambrose.   I warned you.

THE ENVOY.   But—

ZOO [*impatiently*] I wonder what Zozim is doing.   He ought to be here to receive you.

THE ELDERLY GENTLEMAN.   Do you mean that rather insufferable young man whom you found boring me on the pier?

ZOO.   Yes.   He has to dress-up in a Druids' robe, and put on a wig and a long false beard, to impress you silly people.   *I* have to put on a purple mantle.   I have no patience with such mummery; but you expect it from us; so I suppose it must be kept up.   Will you wait here until Zozim comes, please [*she turns to enter the temple*].

THE ENVOY.   My good lady, is it worth while dressing-up and putting on false beards for us if you tell us beforehand that it is all humbug?

ZOO.   One would not think so; but if you wont believe in anyone who is not dressed-up, why, we must dress-up for you.   It was you who invented all this nonsense, not we.

THE ELDERLY GENTLEMAN.   But do you expect us to be impressed, after this?

ZOO.   I dont expect anything.   I know, as a matter of experience, that you will be impressed.   The oracle will frighten you out of your wits. [*She goes into the temple*].

THE WIFE. These people treat us as if we were dirt beneath their feet. I wonder at you putting up with it, Amby. It would serve them right if we went home at once: wouldnt it, Eth?

THE DAUGHTER. Yes, mamma. But perhaps they wouldnt mind.

THE ENVOY. No use talking like that, Molly. Ive got to see this oracle. The folks at home wont know how we have been treated: all theyll know is that Ive stood face to face with the oracle and had the straight tip from her. I hope this Zozim chap is not going to keep us waiting much longer; for I feel far from comfortable about the approaching interview; and thats the honest truth.

THE ELDERLY GENTLEMAN. I never thought I should want to see that man again; but now I wish he would take charge of us instead of Zoo. She was charming at first: quite charming; but she turned into a fiend because I had a few words with her. You would not believe: she very nearly killed me. You heard what she said just now. She belongs to a party here which wants to have us all killed.

THE WIFE [*terrified*] Us! But we have done nothing: we have been as nice to them as nice could be. Oh, Amby, come away, come away: there is something dreadful about this place and these people.

THE ENVOY. There is, and no mistake. But youre safe with me: you ought to have sense enough to know that.

THE ELDERLY GENTLEMAN. I am sorry to say, Molly, that it is not merely us four poor weak creatures they want to kill, but the entire race of Man, except themselves.

THE ENVOY.   Not so poor, neither, Poppa.   Nor so
weak, if you are going to take in all the Powers.   If it
comes to killing, two can play at that game, longlived
or shortlived.

THE ELDERLY GENTLEMAN.   No, Ambrose: we should
have no chance.   We are worms beside these fearful
people: mere worms.

*Zozim comes from the temple, robed majestically,
and wearing a wreath of mistletoe in his flowing white
wig.   His false beard reaches almost to his waist.   He
carries a staff with a curiously carved top.*

ZOZIM [*in the doorway, impressively*] Hail, strangers!

ALL [*reverently*] Hail!

ZOZIM.   Are ye prepared?

THE ENVOY.   We are.

ZOZIM [*unexpectedly becoming conversational, and
strolling down carelessly to the middle of the group between the two ladies*] Well, I'm sorry to say the oracle
is not.   She was delayed by some member of your party
who got loose; and as the show takes a bit of arranging,
you will have to wait a few minutes.   The ladies can go
inside and look round the entrance hall and get pictures
and things if you want them.

THE WIFE   ⎱   ⎰Thank you.   ⎱ [*They go
                    ⎰[*together*]⎰I should like to,⎰ *into the
THE DAUGHTER ⎰   ⎱ very much.   ⎰ temple*].

THE ELDERLY GENTLEMAN [*in dignified rebuke of
Zozim's levity*] Taken in this spirit, sir, the show, as
you call it, becomes almost an insult to our common
sense.

ZOZIM.   Quite, I should say.   You need not keep it up
with me.

THE ENVOY [*suddenly making himself very agreeable*] Just so: just so.   We can wait as long as you

please. And now, if I may be allowed to seize the oppor-
tunity of a few minutes' friendly chat——?

ZOZIM. By all means, if only you will talk about
things I can understand.

THE ENVOY. Well, about this colonizing plan of
yours. My father-in-law here has been telling me something about it; and he has just now let out that you
want not only to colonize us, but to——to——to——well,
shall we say to supersede us? Now why supersede us?
Why not live and let live? Theres not a scrap of ill-
feeling on our side. We should welcome a colony of
immortals—we may almost call you that—in the British
Middle East. No doubt the Turanian Empire, with its
Mahometan traditions, overshadows us now. We have
had to bring the Emperor with us on this expedition,
though of course you know as well as I do that he has
imposed himself on my party just to spy on me. I dont
deny that he has the whip hand of us to some extent,
because if it came to a war none of our generals could
stand up against him. I give him best at that game: he
is the finest soldier in the world. Besides, he is an emperor and an autocrat; and I am only an elected representative of the British democracy. Not that our
British democrats wont fight: they will fight the heads
off all the Turanians that ever walked; but then it takes
so long to work them up to it, while he has only to say
the word and march. But you people would never get
on with him. Believe me, you would not be as comfortable in Turania as you would be with us. We understand you. We like you. We are easy-going people;
and we are rich people. That will appeal to you.
Turania is a poor place when all is said. Five-eighths
of it is desert. They dont irrigate as we do. Besides—
now I am sure this will appeal to you and to all right-
minded men—we are Christians.

zozim.   The old uns prefer Mahometans.

the envoy [*shocked*] What!

zozim [*distinctly*] They prefer Mahometans. Whats wrong with that?

the envoy.   Well, of all the disgraceful—

the elderly gentleman [*diplomatically interrupting his scandalized son-in-law*] There can be no doubt, I am afraid, that by clinging too long to the obsolete features of the old pseudo-Christian Churches we allowed the Mahometans to get ahead of us at a very critical period of the development of the Eastern world. When the Mahometan Reformation took place, it left its followers with the enormous advantage of having the only established religion in the world in whose articles of faith any intelligent and educated person could believe.

the envoy.   But what about our Reformation? Dont give the show away, Poppa. We followed suit, didnt we?

the elderly gentleman.   Unfortunately, Ambrose, we could not follow suit very rapidly. We had not only a religion to deal with, but a Church.

zozim.   What is a Church?

the envoy.   Not know what a Church is! Well!

the elderly gentleman.   You must excuse me; but if I attempted to explain you would only ask me what a bishop is; and that is a question that no mortal man can answer. All I can tell you is that Mahomet was a truly wise man; for he founded a religion without a Church; consequently when the time came for a Reformation of the mosques there were no bishops and priests to obstruct it. Our bishops and priests prevented us for two hundred years from following suit; and we have never recovered the start we lost then. I can only plead that we did reform our Church at last. No doubt we had to make a few compromises as a matter of good taste; but there is now very little in our Articles of Religion that is not accepted as at least allegorically true by our Higher Criticism.

THE ENVOY [*encouragingly*] Besides, does it matter? Why, *I* have never read the Articles in my life; and I am Prime Minister! Come! if my services in arranging for the reception of a colonizing party would be acceptable, they are at your disposal. And when I say a reception I mean a reception. Royal honors, mind you! A salute of a hundred and one guns! The streets lined with troops! The Guards turned out at the Palace! Dinner at Guildhall!

ZOZIM. Discourage me if I know what youre talking about! I wish Zoo would come: she understands these things. All I can tell you is that the general opinion among the Colonizers is in favor of beginning in a country where the people are of a different color from us; so that we can make short work without any risk of mistakes.

THE ENVOY. What do you mean by short work? I hope—

ZOZIM [*with obviously feigned geniality*] Oh, nothing, nothing, nothing. We are thinking of trying North America: thats all. You see, the Red Men of that country used to be white. They passed through a period of sallow complexions, followed by a period of no complexions at all, into the red characteristic of their climate. Besides, several cases of long life have occurred in North America. They joined us here; and their stock soon reverted to the original white of these islands.

THE ELDERLY GENTLEMAN. But have you considered the possibility of your colony turning red?

ZOZIM. That wont matter. We are not particular about our pigmentation. The old books mention red-faced Englishmen: they appear to have been common objects at one time.

THE ELDERLY GENTLEMAN [*very persuasively*] But do you think you would be popular in North America? It seems to me, if I may say so, that on your own shewing you need a country in which society is organized in a series of highly exclusive circles, in which the privacy of private life is very jealously guarded, and in which no one presumes to speak to anyone else without an introduction following a strict examination of social credentials. It is only in such a country that persons of special tastes and attainments can form a little world of their own, and protect themselves absolutely from intrusion by common persons. I think I may claim that our British society has developed this exclusiveness to perfection. If you would pay us a visit and see the working of our caste system, our club system, our guild system, you would admit that nowhere else in the world, least of all, perhaps, in North America, which has a regrettable tradition of social promiscuity, could you keep yourselves so entirely to yourselves.

ZOZIM [*good-naturedly embarrassed*] Look here. There is no good discussing this. I had rather not explain; but it wont make any difference to our Colonizers what sort of shortlivers they come across. We shall arrange all that. Never mind how. Let us join the ladies.

THE ELDERLY GENTLEMAN [*throwing off his diplomatic attitude and abandoning himself to despair*] We understand you only too well, sir. Well, kill us. End the lives you have made miserably unhappy by opening up to us the possibility that any of us may live three hundred years. I solemnly curse that possibility. To you it may be a blessing, because you do live three hundred years. To us, who live less than a hundred, whose flesh is as grass, it is the most unbearable burden our poor tortured humanity has ever groaned under.

THE ENVOY. Hullo, Poppa! Steady! How do you make that out?

ZOZIM. What is three hundred years? Short enough, if you ask me. Why, in the old days you people lived on the assumption that you were going to last out for ever and ever and ever. Immortal, you thought yourselves. Were you any happier then?

THE ELDERLY GENTLEMAN. As President of the Baghdad Historical Society I am in a position to inform you that the communities which took this monstrous pretension seriously were the most wretched of which we have any record. My Society has printed an editio princeps of the works of the father of history, Thucyderodotus Macollybuckle. Have you read his account of what was blasphemously called the Perfect City of God, and the attempt made to reproduce it in the northern part of these islands by Jonhobsnoxius, called the Lebiathan? Those misguided people sacrificed the fragment of life that was granted to them in an imaginary immortality. They crucified the prophet who told them to take no thought for the morrow, and that here and now was their Australia: Australia being a term signifying paradise, or an eternity of bliss. They tried to produce a condition of death in life: to mortify the flesh, as they called it.

ZOZIM. Well, you are not suffering from that, are you? You have not a mortified air.

THE ELDERLY GENTLEMAN. Naturally we are not absolutely insane and suicidal. Nevertheless we impose on ourselves abstinences and disciplines and studies that are meant to prepare us for living three centuries. And we seldom live one. My childhood was made unnecessarily painful, my boyhood unnecessarily laborious, by

riciculous preparations for a length of days which the
chances were fifty thousand to one against my ever
attaining. I have been cheated out of the natural joys
and freedoms of my life by this dream to which the
existence of these islands and their oracles gives a
delusive possibility of realization. I curse the day when
long life was invented, just as the victims of Jonhobsnoxius cursed the day when eternal life was invented.

ZOZIM. Pooh! You could live three centuries if you
choose.

THE ELDERLY GENTLEMAN. That is what the fortunate always say to the unfortunate. Well, I do not
choose. I accept my three score and ten years. If they
are filled with usefulness, with justice, with mercy, with
good-will: if they are the lifetime of a soul that never
loses its honor and a brain that never loses its eagerness,
they are enough for me, because these things are infinite
and eternal, and can make ten of my years as long as
thirty of yours. I shall not conclude by saying live as
long as you like and be damned to you, because I have
risen for the moment far above any ill-will to you or to
any fellow-creature; but I am your equal before that
eternity in which the difference between your lifetime
and mine is as the difference between one drop of water
and three in the eyes of the Almighty Power from which
we have both proceeded.

ZOZIM [*impressed*] You spoke that piece very well,
Daddy. I couldnt talk like that if I tried. It sounded
fine. Ah! here come the ladies.

*To his relief, they have just appeared on the
threshold of the temple.*

THE ELDERLY GENTLEMAN [*passing from exaltation
to distress*] It means nothing to him: in this land of discouragement the sublime has become the ridiculous.
[*Turning on the hopelessly puzzled Zozim*] "Behold,

thou hast made my days as it were a span long; and mine age is even as nothing in respect of thee."

THE DAUGHTER
THE WIFE
[*running to him*]

Poppa, Poppa: dont look like that.

Oh, grandpa, whats the matter?

ZOZIM [*with a shrug*] Discouragement!

THE ELDERLY GENTLEMAN [*throwing off the women with a superb gesture*] Liar! [*Recollecting himself, he adds, with noble courtesy, raising his hat and bowing*] I beg your pardon, sir; but I am NOT discouraged.

A burst of orchestral music, through which a powerful gong sounds, is heard from the temple. Zoo, in a purple robe, appears in the doorway.

ZOO. Come. The oracle is ready.

Zozim motions them to the threshold with a wave of his staff. The Envoy and the Elderly Gentleman take off their hats and go into the temple on tiptoe, Zoo leading the way. The Wife and Daughter, frightened as they are, raise their heads uppishly and follow flat-footed, sustained by a sense of their Sunday clothes and social consequence. Zozim remains in the portico, alone.

ZOZIM [*taking off his wig, beard, and robe, and bundling them under his arm*] Ouf! [*He goes home*].

ACT III

Inside the temple. A gallery overhanging an abyss. Dead silence. The gallery is brightly lighted; but beyond is a vast gloom, continually changing in intensity. A shaft of violet light shoots upward; and a very harmonious and silvery carillon chimes. When it ceases the violet ray vanishes.

Zoo comes along the gallery followed by the Envoy's daughter, his wife, the Envoy himself, and the Elderly Gentleman. The two men are holding their hats with the brims near their noses, as if prepared to pray into them at a moment's notice. Zoo halts: they all follow her example. They contemplate the void with awe. Organ music of the kind called sacred in the nineteenth century begins. Their awe deepens. The violet ray, now a diffused mist, rises again from the abyss.

THE WIFE [*to Zoo, in a reverent whisper*] Shall we kneel?

ZOO [*loudly*] Yes, if you want to. You can stand on your head if you like. [*She sits down carelessly on the gallery railing, with her back to the abyss*].

THE ELDERLY GENTLEMAN [*jarred by her callousness*] We desire to behave in a becoming manner.

ZOO. Very well. Behave just as you feel. It doesnt matter how you behave. But keep your wits about you when the pythoness ascends, or you will forget the questions you have come to ask her.

221

THE ENVOY }
THE DAUGHTER } [*simultaneously*] { [*very nervous, takes out a paper to refresh his memory*] Ahem! [*alarmed*] The pythoness. Is she a snake?

THE ELDERLY GENTLEMAN. Tch-ch! The priestess of the oracle. A sybil. A prophetess. Not a snake.

THE WIFE. How awful!

ZOO. I'm glad you think so.

THE WIFE. Oh dear! Dont you think so?

ZOO. No. This sort of thing is got up to impress you, not to impress me.

THE ELDERLY GENTLEMAN. I wish you would let it impress us, then, madam. I am deeply impressed; but you are spoiling the effect.

ZOO. You just wait. All this business with colored lights and chords on that old organ is only tomfoolery. Wait till you see the pythoness.

The Envoy's wife falls on her knees, and takes refuge in prayer.

THE DAUGHTER [*trembling*] Are you really going to see a woman who has lived three hundred years?

ZOO. Stuff! Youd drop dead if a tertiary as much as looked at you. The oracle is only a hundred and seventy; and youll find it hard enough to stand her.

THE DAUGHTER [*piteously*] Oh! [*she falls on her knees*].

THE ENVOY. Whew! Stand by me, Poppa. This is a little more than I bargained for. Are you going to kneel; or how?

THE ELDERLY GENTLEMAN. Perhaps it would be in better taste.

The two men kneel.

The vapor of the abyss thickens; and a distant roll of thunder seems to come from its depths. The python-

*ess, seated on her tripod, rises slowly from it. She has
discarded the insulating robe and veil in which she con-
versed with Napoleon, and is now draped and hooded in
voluminous folds of a single piece of grey-white stuff.
Something supernatural about her terrifies the be-
holders, who throw themselves on their faces. Her out-
line flows and waves: she is almost distinct at moments,
and again vague and shadowy: above all, she is larger
than life-size, not enough to be measured by the flustered
congregation, but enough to affect them with a dreadful
sense of her supernaturalness.*

zoo. Get up, get up. Do pull yourselves together,
you people.

*The Envoy and his family, by shuddering negatively,
intimate that it is impossible. The Elderly Gentleman
manages to get on his hands and knees.*

zoo. Come on, Daddy: you are not afraid. Speak to
her. She wont wait here all day for you, you know.

THE ELDERLY GENTLEMAN [*rising very deferentially
to his feet*] Madam: you will excuse my very natural
nervousness in addressing, for the first time in my life,
a—a—a—a goddess. My friend and relative the Envoy
is unhinged. I throw myself upon your indulgence—

zoo [*interrupting him intolerantly*] Dont throw yourself on anything belonging to her or you will go right
through her and break your neck. She isnt solid, like
you.

THE ELDERLY GENTLEMAN. I was speaking fig-
uratively—

zoo. You have been told not to do it. Ask her what
you want to know; and be quick about it.

THE ELDERLY GENTLEMAN [*stooping and taking the
prostrate Envoy by the shoulders*] Ambrose: you must
make an effort. You cannot go back to Baghdad without the answers to your questions.

THE ENVOY [*rising to his knees*] I shall be only too
glad to go back alive on any terms. If my legs would
support me I'd just do a bunk straight for the ship.

THE ELDERLY GENTLEMAN. No, no. Remember:
your dignity—

THE ENVOY. Dignity be damned! I'm terrified.
Take me away, for God's sake.

THE ELDERLY GENTLEMAN [*producing a brandy flask
and taking the cap off*] Try some of this. It is still
nearly full, thank goodness!

THE ENVOY [*clutching it and drinking eagerly*] Ah!
thats better. [*He tries to drink again. Finding that
he has emptied it, he hands it back to his father-in-law
upside down*].

THE ELDERLY GENTLEMAN [*taking it*] Great heavens!
He has swallowed half-a-pint of neat brandy. [*Much
perturbed, he screws the cap on again, and pockets the
flask*].

THE ENVOY [*staggering to his feet; pulling a paper
from his pocket; and speaking with boisterous confidence*] Get up, Molly. Up with you, Eth.

The two women rise to their knees.

THE ENVOY. What I want to ask is this. [*He refers
to the paper*]. Ahem! Civilization has reached a crisis.
We are at the parting of the ways. We stand on the
brink of the Rubicon. Shall we take the plunge? Already a leaf has been torn out of the book of the Sybil.
Shall we wait until the whole volume is consumed? On
our right is the crater of the volcano: on our left the
precipice. One false step, and we go down to annihila-
tion dragging the whole human race with us. [*He
pauses for breath*].

THE ELDERLY GENTLEMAN [*recovering his spirits under the familiar stimulus of political oratory*] Hear,
hear!

zoo. What are you raving about? Ask your question while you have the chance? What is it you want to know?

THE ENVOY [*patronizing her in the manner of a Premier debating with a very young member of the Opposition*] A young woman asks me a question. I am always glad to see the young taking an interest in politics. It is an impatient question; but it is a practical question, an intelligent question. She asks why we seek to lift a corner of the veil that shrouds the future from our feeble vision.

zoo. I dont. I ask you to tell the oracle what you want, and not keep her sitting there all day.

THE ELDERLY GENTLEMAN [*warmly*] Order, order!

zoo. What does "Order, order!" mean?

THE ENVOY. I ask the august oracle to listen to my voice—

zoo. You people seem never to tire of listening to your voices; but it doesnt amuse us. What do you want?

THE ENVOY. I want, young woman, to be allowed to proceed without unseemly interruptions.

A low roll of thunder comes from the abyss.

THE ELDERLY GENTLEMAN. There! Even the oracle is indignant. [*To the Envoy*] Do not allow yourself to be put down by this lady's rude clamor, Ambrose. Take no notice. Proceed.

THE ENVOY'S WIFE. I can't bear this much longer, Amby. Remember: *I* havnt had any brandy.

HIS DAUGHTER [*trembling*] There are serpents curling in the vapor. I am afraid of the lightning. Finish it, Papa; or I shall die.

THE ENVOY [*sternly*] Silence. The destiny of British civilization is at stake. Trust me. I am not afraid. As I was saying—where was I?

zoo. I dont know. Does anybody?

THE ELDERLY GENTLEMAN [*tactfully*]You were just coming to the election, I think.

THE ENVOY [*reassured*] Just so. The election. Now what we want to know is this: ought we to dissolve in August, or put it off until next spring?

zoo. Dissolve? In what? [*Thunder*]. Oh! I beg your pardon. That means that the oracle understands you, and desires me to hold my tongue.

THE ENVOY [*fervently*] I thank the oracle.

THE WIFE [*to Zoo*] Serve you right!

THE ELDERLY GENTLEMAN. Before the oracle replies, I should like to be allowed to state a few of the reasons why, in my opinion, the Government should hold on until the spring. In the first—

Terrific lighting and thunder. The Elderly Gentleman is knocked flat; but as he immediately sits up again dazedly it is clear that he is none the worse for the shock. The ladies cower in terror. The Envoy's hat is blown off; but he seizes it just as it quits his temples, and holds it on with both hands. He is recklessly drunk, but quite articulate, as he seldom speaks in public without taking stimulants before hand.

THE ENVOY [*taking one hand from his hat to make a gesture of stilling the tempest*] Thats enough. We know how to take a hint. I'll put the case in three words. I am the leader of the Potterbill party. My party is in power. I am Prime Minister. The Opposition—the Rotterjacks—have won every bye-election for the last six months. They—

THE ELDERLY GENTLEMAN [*scrambling heatedly to his feet*] Not by fair means. By bribery, by misrepresentation, by pandering to the vilest prejudices [*muttered thunder*]—I beg your pardon. [*He is silent*].

THE ENVOY. Never mind the bribery and lies. The

oracle knows all about that. The point is that though
our five years will not expire until the year after next,
our majority will be eaten away at the bye-elections by
about Easter. We cant wait: we must start some question that will excite the public, and go to the country
on it. But some of us say do it now. Others say wait
til the spring. We cant make up our minds one way or
the other. Which would you advise?

ZOO. But what is the question that is to excite your
public?

THE ENVOY. That doesnt matter. I dont know yet.
We will find a question all right enough. The oracle
can foresee the future; we cannot. [*Thunder*]. What
does that mean? What have I done now?

ZOO [*severely*] How often must you be told that we
cannot foresee the future? There is no such thing as
the future until it is the present.

THE ELDERLY GENTLEMAN. Allow me to point out,
madam, that when the Potterbill party sent to consult
the oracle fifteen years ago, the oracle prophesied that
the Potterbills would be victorious at the General Election; and they were. ' So it is evident that the oracle
can forsee the future, and is sometimes willing to reveal it.

THE ENVOY. Quite true. Thank you, Poppa. I appeal now, over your head, young woman, direct to the
August Oracle, to repeat the signal favor conferred on
my illustrious predecessor, Sir Fuller Eastwind, and to
answer me exactly as he was answered.

The oracle raises her hand to command silence.

ALL. Sh-sh-sh!

*Invisible trombones utter three solemn blasts in the
manner of Die Zauberflöte.*

THE ELDERLY GENTLEMAN. May I—

zoo [*quickly*] Hush. The oracle is going to speak.

THE ORACLE. Go home, poor fool.

She vanishes; and the atmosphere changes to prosaic daylight. Zoo comes off the railing; throws off her robe; makes a bundle of it; and tucks it under her arm. The magic and mystery are gone. The women rise to their feet. The Envoy's party stare at one another helplessly.

zoo. The same reply, word for word, that your illustrious predecessor, as you call him, got fifteen years ago. You asked for it; and you got it. And just think of all the important questions you might have asked. She would have answered them, you know. It is always like that. I will go and arrange to have you sent home: you can wait for me in the entrance hall. [*She goes out*].

THE ENVOY. What possessed me to ask for the same answer old Eastwind got?

THE ELDERLY GENTLEMAN. But it was not the same answer. The answer to Eastwind was an inspiration to our party for years. It won us the election.

THE ENVOY'S DAUGHTER. I learnt it at school, granpa. It wasnt the same at all. I can repeat it. [*She quotes*] "When Britain was cradled in the west, the east wind hardened her and made her great. Whilst the east wind prevails Britain shall prosper. The east wind shall wither Britain's enemies in the day of contest. Let the Rotterjacks look to it."

THE ENVOY. The old man invented that. I see it all. He was a doddering old ass when he came to consult the oracle. The oracle naturally said "Go home, poor fool." There was no sense in saying that to me; but as that girl said, I asked for it. What else could the poor old chap do but fake up an answer fit for publication?

There were whispers about it; but nobody believed them. I believe them now.

THE ELDERLY GENTLEMAN. Oh, I cannot admit that Sir Fuller Eastwind was capable of such a fraud.

THE ENVOY. He was capable of anything: I knew his private secretary. And now what are we going to say? You dont suppose I am going back to Baghdad to tell the British Empire that the oracle called me a fool, do you?

THE ELDERLY GENTLEMAN. Surely we must tell the truth, however painful it may be to our feelings.

THE ENVOY. I am not thinking of my feelings: I am not so selfish as that, thank God. I am thinking of the country: of our party. The truth, as you call it, would put the Rotterjacks in for the next twenty years. It would be the end of me politically. Not that I care for that: I am only too willing to retire if you can find a better man. Dont hesitate on my account.

THE ELDERLY GENTLEMAN. No, Ambrose: you are indispensable. There is no one else.

THE ENVOY. Very well, then. What are you going to do?

THE ELDERLY GENTLEMAN. My dear Ambrose, you are the leader of the party, not I. What are you going to do?

THE ENVOY. I am going to tell the exact truth: thats what I'm going to do. Do you take me for a liar?

THE ELDERLY GENTLEMAN [*puzzled*] Oh, I beg your pardon. I understood you to say—

THE ENVOY [*cutting him short*] You understood me to say that I am going back to Baghdad to tell the British electorate that the oracle repeated to me, word for word, what it said to Sir Fuller Eastwind fifteen years ago. Molly and Ethel can bear me out. So must you, if you are an honest man. Come on.

He goes out, followed by his wife and daughter.

THE ELDERLY GENTLEMAN [*left alone and shrinking into an old and desolate figure*] What am I to do? I am a most perplexed and wretched man. [*He falls on his knees, and stretches his hands in entreaty over the abyss*]. I invoke the oracle. I cannot go back and connive at a blasphemous lie. I implore guidance.

The Pythoness walks in on the gallery behind him, and touches him on the shoulder. Her size is now natural. Her face is hidden by her hood. He flinches as if from an electric shock; turns to her; and cowers, covering his eyes in terror.

THE ELDERLY GENTLEMAN. No: not close to me. I'm afraid I cant bear it.

THE ORACLE [*with grave pity*] Come: look at me. I am my natural size now: what you saw there was only a foolish picture of me thrown on a cloud by a lantern. How can I help you?

THE ELDERLY GENTLEMAN. They have gone back to lie about your answer. I cannot go with them. I cannot live among people to whom nothing is real. I have become incapable of it through my stay here. I implore to be allowed to stay.

THE ORACLE. My friend: if you stay with us you will die of discouragement.

THE ELDERLY GENTLEMAN. If I go back I shall die of disgust and despair. I take the nobler risk. I beg you, do not cast me out.

He catches her robe and holds her.

THE ORACLE. Take care. I have been here one hundred and seventy years. Your death does not mean to me what it means to you.

THE ELDERLY GENTLEMAN. It is the meaning of life, not of death, that makes banishment so terrible to me.

THE ORACLE. Be it so, then. You may stay.

She offers him her hands. He grasps them and raises himself a little by clinging to her. She looks steadily into its face. He stiffens; a little convulsion shakes him; his grasp releases; and he falls dead.

THE ORACLE [*looking down at the body*] Poor short-lived thing! What else could I do for you?

PART V
AS FAR AS THOUGHT CAN REACH
XXXVI

AS FAR AS THOUGHT CAN REACH

Summer afternoon in the year 31,920 A.D. A sunlit glade at the southern foot of a thickly wooded hill. On the west side of it, the steps and columned porch of a dainty little classic temple. Between it and the hill, a rising path to the wooded heights begins with rough steps of stones in the moss. On the opposite side, a grove. In the middle of the glade, an altar in the form of a low marble table as long as a man, set parallel to the temple steps and pointing to the hill. Curved marble benches radiate from it into the foreground; but they are not joined to it: there is plenty of space to pass between the altar and the benches.

A dance of youths and maidens is in progress. The music is provided by a few fluteplayers seated carelessly on the steps of the temple. There are no children; and none of the dancers seems younger than eighteen. Some of the youths have beards. Their dress, like the architecture of the theatre and the design of the altar and curved seats, resembles Grecian of the fourth century B.C., freely handled. They move with perfect balance and remarkable grace, racing through a figure like a farandole. They neither romp nor hug in our manner.

At the first full close they clap their hands to stop the musicians, who recommence with a saraband, during which a strange figure appears on the path beyond the temple. He is deep in thought, with his eyes closed and his feet feeling automatically for the rough irregular steps as he slowly descends them. Except for a sort of linen kilt consisting mainly of a girdle carrying a sporran and a few minor pockets, he is naked. In physical hardihood and uprightness he seems to be in the prime of life; and his eyes and mouth show no sign of age; but his face, though fully and firmly fleshed, bears a network of lines, varying from furrows to hairbreadth reticulations, as if Time had worked over every inch of it incessantly through whole geologic periods. His head is finely domed and utterly bald. Except for his eyelashes he is quite hairless. He is unconscious of his surroundings, and walks right into one of the dancing couples, separating them. He wakes up and stares about him. The couple stop indignantly. The rest stop. The music stops. The youth whom he has jostled accosts him without malice, but without anything that we should call manners.

THE YOUTH.   Now, then, ancient sleepwalker, why dont you keep your eyes open and mind where you are going?

THE ANCIENT [*mild, bland and indulgent*] I did not know there was a nursery here, or I should not have turned my face in this direction. Such accidents cannot always be avoided. Go on with your play: I will turn back.

THE YOUTH.   Why not stay with us and enjoy life for once in a way? We will teach you to dance.

THE ANCIENT.   No, thank you. I danced when I was a child like you. Dancing is a very crude attempt to get into the rhythm of life. It would be painful to me to go back from that rhythm to your babyish gambols: in fact I could not do it if I tried. But at your age it is pleasant; and I am sorry I disturbed you.

THE YOUTH.   Come! own up: arnt you very unhappy?

It's dreadful to see you ancients going about by yourselves, never noticing anything, never dancing, never
laughing, never singing, never getting anything out of
life.   None of us are going to be like that when we grow
up.   It's a dog's life.

THE ANCIENT.   Not at all.   You repeat that old
phrase without knowing that there was once a creature
on earth called a dog.   Those who are interested in extinct forms of life will tell you that it loved the sound
of its own voice and bounded about when it was happy,
just as you are doing here.   It is you, my children, who
are living the dog's life.

THE YOUTH.   The dog must have been a good sensible
creature: it set you a very wise example.   You should
let yourself go occasionally and have a good time.

THE ANCIENT.   My children: be content to let us ancients go our ways and enjoy ourselves in our own
fashion.

He turns to go.

THE MAIDEN.   But wait a moment.   Why will you not
tell us how you enjoy yourself?   You must have secret
pleasures that you hide from us, and that you never get
tired of.   I get tired of all our dances and all our tunes.
I get tired of all my partners.

THE YOUTH [*suspiciously*] Do you?   I shall bear that
in mind.

*They all look at one another as if there were some
sinister significance in what she has said.*

THE MAIDEN.   We all do: what is the use of pretending we dont?   It is natural.

SEVERAL YOUNG PEOPLE.   No, no.   We dont.   It is
not natural.

THE ANCIENT.   You are older than he is, I see.   You
are growing up.

THE MAIDEN. How do you know? I do not look so much older, do I?

THE ANCIENT. Oh, I was not looking at you. Your looks do not interest me.

THE MAIDEN. Thank you.

They all laugh.

THE YOUTH. You old fish! I believe you dont know the difference between a man and a woman.

THE ANCIENT. It has long ceased to interest me in the way it interests you. And when anything no longer interests us we no longer know it.

THE MAIDEN. You havnt told me how I shew my age. That is what I want to know. As a matter of fact I am older than this boy here: older than he thinks. How did you find that out?

THE ANCIENT. Easily enough. You are ceasing to pretend that these childish games—this dancing and singing and mating—do not become tiresome and unsatisfying after a while. And you no longer care to pretend that you are younger than you are. These are the signs of adolescence. And then, see these fantastic rags with which you have draped yourself. [*He takes up a piece of her draperies in his hand*]. It is rather badly worn here. Why do you not get a new one?

THE MAIDEN. Oh, I did not notice it. Besides, it is too much trouble. Clothes are a nuisance. I think I shall do without them some day, as you ancients do.

THE ANCIENT. Signs of maturity. Soon you will give up all these toys and games and sweets.

THE YOUTH. What! And be as miserable as you!

THE ANCIENT. Infant: one moment of the ecstasy of life as we live it would strike you dead. [*He stalks gravely out through the grove*].

They stare after him, much damped.

THE YOUTH [*to the musicians*] Let us have another dance.

The musicians shake their heads; get up from their seats on the steps; and troop away into the temple. The others follow them, except the Maiden, who sits down on the altar.

THE YOUTH [*turning on the steps*] Arnt you coming, Chloe?

THE MAIDEN [*shakes her head*]!

THE YOUTH [*hurrying back to her*] What is the matter?

THE MAIDEN [*tragically pensive*] I dont know.

THE YOUTH. Then there is something the matter. Is that what you mean?

THE MAIDEN. Yes. Something is happening to me. I dont know what.

THE YOUTH. You no longer love me. I have seen it for a month past.

THE MAIDEN. Dont you think all that is rather silly? We cannot go on as if this kind of thing, this dancing and sweethearting, were everything.

THE YOUTH. What is there better? What else is there worth living for?

THE MAIDEN. Oh, stuff! Dont be frivolous.

THE YOUTH. Something horrible is happening to you. You are losing all heart, all feeling. [*He sits on the altar beside her and buries his face in his hands*]. I am bitterly unhappy.

THE MAIDEN. Unhappy! Really, you must have a very empty head if there is nothing in it but a dance with one girl who is no better than any of the other girls.

THE YOUTH. You did not always think so. You used to be vexed if I as much as looked at another girl.

THE MAIDEN. What does it matter what I did when

I was a baby? Nothing existed for me then except what
I tasted and touched and saw; and I wanted all that for
myself, just as I wanted the moon to play with. Now
the world is opening out for me. More than the world:
the universe. Even little things are turning out to be
great things, and becoming intensely interesting. Have
you ever thought about the properties of numbers?

THE YOUTH [*sitting up, markedly disenchanted*] Numbers! ! ! I cannot imagine anything drier or more re-
pulsive.

THE MAIDEN. They are fascinating, just fascinating.
I want to get away from our eternal dancing and music,
and just sit down by myself and think about numbers.

THE YOUTH [*rising indignantly*] Oh, this is too much.
I have suspected you for some time past. We have all
suspected you. All the girls say that you have deceived
us as to your age: that you are getting flat-chested;
that you are bored with us; that you talk to the ancients
when you get the chance. Tell me the truth: how old
are you?

THE MAIDEN. Just twice your age, my poor boy.

THE YOUTH. Twice my age! Do you mean to say
you are four?

THE MAIDEN. Very nearly four.

THE YOUTH [*collapsing on the altar with a groan*]
Oh!

THE MAIDEN. My poor Strephon: I pretended I was
only two for your sake. I was two when you were born.
I saw you break from your shell; and you were such a
charming child! You ran round and talked to us all so
prettily, and were so handsome and well grown, that I
lost my heart to you at once. But now I seem to have
lost it altogether; bigger things are taking possession
of me. Still, we were very happy in our childish way
for the first year, wernt we?

STREPHON. I was happy until you began cooling towards me.

THE MAIDEN. Not towards you, but towards all the trivialities of our life here. Just think. I have hundreds of years to live: perhaps thousands. Do you suppose I can spend centuries dancing; listening to flutes ringing changes on a few tunes and a few notes; raving about the beauty of a few pillars and arches; making jingles with words; lying about with your arms round me, which is really neither comfortable nor convenient; everlastingly choosing colors for dresses, and putting them on, and washing; making a business of sitting together at fixed hours to absorb our nourishment; taking little poisons with it to make us delirious enough to imagine we are enjoying ourselves; and then having to pass the nights in shelters lying in cots and losing half our lives in a state of unconsciousness. Sleep is a shameful thing: I have not slept at all for weeks past. I have stolen out at night when you were all lying insensible—quite disgusting, I call it—and wandered about the woods, thinking, thinking, thinking; grasping the world; taking it to pieces; building it up again; devising methods; planning experiments to test the methods; and having a glorious time. Every morning I have come back here with greater and greater reluctance; and I know that the time will soon come—perhaps it has come already—when I shall not come back at all.

STREPHON. How horribly cold and uncomfortable!

THE MAIDEN. Oh, dont talk to me of comfort! Life is not worth living if you have to bother about comfort. Comfort makes winter a torture, spring an illness, summer an oppression, and autumn only a respite. The ancients could make life one long frowsty comfort if they chose. But they never lift a finger to make them-

selves comfortable. They will not sleep under a roof.
They will not clothe themselves: a girdle with a few
pockets hanging to it to carry things about in is all
they wear: they will sit down on the wet moss or in a
gorse bush when there is dry heather within two yards
of them. Two years ago, when you were born, I did not
understand this. Now I feel that I would not put myself to the trouble of walking two paces for all the comfort in the world.

STREPHON. But you dont know what this means to
me. It means that you are dying to me: yes, just dying.
Listen to me. [*He puts his arm around her*].

THE MAIDEN [*extricating herself*] Dont. We can talk
quite as well without touching one another.

STREPHON [*horrified*] Chloe! Oh, this is the worst
symptom of all! The ancients never touch one another.

THE MAIDEN. Why should they?

STREPHON. Oh, I dont know. But dont you want to
touch me? You used to.

THE MAIDEN. Yes: that is true: I used to. We used
to think it would be nice to sleep in one another's arms;
but we never could go to sleep because our weight
stopped our circulations just above the elbows. Then
somehow my feeling began to change bit by bit. I kept
a sort of interest in your head and arms long after I
lost interest in your whole body. And now that has
gone.

STREPHON. You no longer care for me at all, then?

THE MAIDEN. Nonsense! I care for you much more
seriously than before; though perhaps not so much for
you in particular. I mean I care more for everybody.
But I dont want to touch you unnecessarily; and I certainly dont want you to touch me.

STREPHON [*rising decisively*] That finishes it. You
dislike me.

THE MAIDEN [*impatiently*] I tell you again, I do not dislike you; but you bore me when you cannot understand; and I think I shall be happier by myself in future. You had better get a new companion. What about the girl who is to be born today?

STREPHON. I do not want the girl who is to be born today. How do I know what she will be like? I want you.

THE MAIDEN. You cannot have me. You must recognize facts and face them. It is no use running after a woman twice your age. I cannot make my childhood last to please you. The age of love is sweet; but it is short; and I must pay nature's debt. You no longer attract me; and I no longer care to attract you. Growth is too rapid at my age: I am maturing from week to week.

STREPHON. You are maturing, as you call it—I call it ageing—from minute to minute. You are going much further than you did when we began this conversation.

THE MAIDEN. It is not the ageing that is so rapid. It is the realization of it when it has actually happened. Now that I have made up my mind to the fact that I have left childhood behind me, it comes home to me in leaps and bounds with every word you say.

STREPHON. But your vow. Have you forgotten that? We all swore together in that temple; the temple of love. You were more earnest than any of us.

THE MAIDEN [*with a grim smile*] Never to let our hearts grow cold! Never to become as the ancients! Never to let the sacred lamp be extinguished! Never to change or forget! To be remembered for ever as the first company of true lovers faithful to this vow so often made and broken by past generations! Ha! ha! Oh, dear!

STREPHON. Well, you need not laugh. It is a beautiful and holy compact; and I will keep it whilst I live. Are you going to break it?

THE MAIDEN. Dear child: it has broken itself. The change has come in spite of my childish vow. [*She rises*]. Do you mind if I go into the woods for a walk by myself? This chat of ours seems to me an unbearable waste of time. I have so much to think of.

STREPHON [*again collapsing on the altar and covering his eyes with his hands*] My heart is broken. [*He weeps*].

THE MAIDEN [*with a shrug*] I have luckily got through my childhood without that experience. It shows how wise I was to choose a lover half my age. [*She goes towards the grove, and is disappearing among the trees, when another youth, older and manlier than Strephon, with crisp hair and firm arms, comes from the temple, and calls to her from the threshold*].

THE TEMPLE YOUTH. I say, Chloe. Is there any sign of the Ancient yet? The hour of birth is overdue. The baby is kicking like mad. She will break her shell prematurely.

THE MAIDEN [*looks across to the hill path; then points up it, and says*] She is coming, Acis.

The Maiden turns away through the grove and is lost to sight among the trees.

ACIS [*coming to Strephon*] Whats the matter? Has Chloe been unkind?

STREPHON. She has grown up in spite of all her promises. She deceived us about her age. She is four.

ACIS. Four! I am sorry, Strephon. I am getting on for three myself; and I know what old age is. I hate to say "I told you so"; but she was getting a little hard set and flat-chested and thin on the top, wasnt she?

STREPHON [*breaking down*] Dont.

ACIS. You must pull yourself together. This is going to be a busy day. First the birth. Then the Festival of the Artists.

STREPHON [*rising*] What is the use of being born if we have to decay into unnatural, heartless, loveless, joyless monsters in four short years? What use are the artists if they cannot bring their beautiful creations to life? I have a great mind to die and have done with it all. [*He moves away to the corner of the curved seat farthest from the theatre, and throws himself moodily into it*].

An Ancient Woman has descended the hill path during Stephen's lament, and has heard most of it. She is like the He-Ancient, equally bald, and equally without sexual charm, but intensely interesting and rather terrifying. Her sex is discoverable only by her voice, as her breasts are manly, and her figure otherwise not very different. She wears no clothes, but has draped herself rather perfunctorily with a ceremonial robe, and carries two implements like long slender saws. She comes to the altar between the two young men.

THE SHE-ANCIENT [*to Strephon*] Infant: you are only at the beginning of it all. [*To Acis*] Is the child ready to be born?

ACIS. More than ready, Ancient. Shouting and kicking and cursing. We have called to her to be quiet and wait until you come; but of course she only half understands, and is very impatient.

THE SHE-ANCIENT. Very well. Bring her out into the sun.

ACIS [*going quickly into the temple*] All ready. Come along.

Joyous processional music strikes up in the temple.

THE SHE-ANCIENT [*going close to Strephon*] Look at me.

STREPHON [*sulkily keeping his face averted*] Thank

you; but I dont want to be cured. I had rather be miserable in my own way than callous in yours.

THE SHE-ANCIENT. You like being miserable? You will soon grow out of that. [*She returns to the altar*].

The procession, headed by Acis, emerges from the temple. Six youths carry on their shoulders a burden covered with a gorgeous but light pall. Before them certain official maidens carry a new tunic, ewers of water, silver dishes pierced with holes, cloths, and immense sponges. The rest carry wands with ribbons, and strew flowers. The burden is deposited on the altar, and the pall removed. It is a huge egg.

THE SHE-ANCIENT [*freeing her arms from her robe, and placing her saws on the altar ready to her hand in a businesslike manner*] A girl, I think you said?

ACIS. Yes.

THE TUNIC BEARER. It is a shame. Why cant we have more boys?

SEVERAL YOUTHS [*protesting*] Not at all. More girls. We want new girls.

A GIRL'S VOICE FROM THE EGG. Let me out. Let me out. I want to be born. I want to be born. [*The egg rocks*].

ACIS [*snatching a wand from one of the others and whacking the egg with it*] Be quiet, I tell you. Wait. You will be born presently.

THE EGG. No, no: at once, at once. I want to be born: I want to be born. [*Violent kicking within the egg, which rocks so hard that it has to be held on the altar by the bearers*].

THE SHE-ANCIENT. Silence. [*The music stops; and the egg behaves itself*].

The She-Ancient takes her two saws, and with a couple of strokes rips the egg open. The Newly Born, a pretty girl who would have been guessed as seventeen

*in our day, sits up in the broken shell, exquisitely fresh
and rosy, but with filaments of spare albumen clinging
to her here and there. Immediately the maidens set to
work, some to shower water on her from the ewers
through the pierced dishes, others to rub her dry
with cloths. Meanwhile the youths beat the shell to
little pieces with their wands, all laughing at the Newly
Born who laughs imitatively. The Tunic Bearer clothes
her; and then they lift her to her feet and dance for-
wards, she dancing with them as best she can. Acis and
the She-Ancient come forward with them, he still on the
baby's right, she on her left].*

THE SHE-ANCIENT. What name have you chosen for
her?

ACIS. Amaryllis.

THE SHE-ANCIENT [*to the Newly Born*] Your name is
Amaryllis.

THE NEWLY BORN. What does it mean?

A YOUTH. Love.

A MAIDEN. Mother.

ANOTHER YOUTH. Lilies.

THE NEWLY BORN [*to Acis*] What is your name?

ACIS. Acis.

THE NEWLY BORN. I love you, Acis. I must have
you all to myself. Take me in your arms.

ACIS. Steady, young one. I am three years old.

THE NEWLY BORN. What has that to do with it? I
love you; and I must have you or I will go back into
my shell again.

ACIS. You cant. It's broken. Look here [*pointing
to Strephon, who has remained in his seat without looking round at the birth, wrapped up in his sorrow*]!
Look at this poor fellow!

THE NEWLY BORN. What is the matter with him?

ACIS. When he was born he chose a girl two years

old for his sweetheart. He is two years old now himself; and already his heart is broken because she is four. That means that she has grown up like this Ancient here, and has left him. If you choose me, we shall have only a year's happiness before I break your heart by growing up. Better choose the youngest you can find.

THE NEWLY BORN. I will not choose anyone but you. You must not grow up. We will love one another for ever. [*They all laugh*]. What are you laughing at?

THE SHE-ANCIENT. Listen, child—

THE NEWLY BORN. Do not come near me, you dreadful old creature. You frighten me.

ACIS. Just give her another moment. She is not quite reasonable yet. What can you expect from a child less than five minutes old?

THE NEWLY BORN. I think I feel a little more reasonable now. Of course I was rather young when I said that; but the inside of my head is changing very rapidly. I should like to have things explained to me.

ACIS [*to the She-Ancient*] Is she all right, do you think?

The She-Ancient looks at the Newly Born critically; feels her bumps like a phrenologist; grips her muscles and shakes her limbs; examines her teeth; looks into her eyes for a moment; and finally relinquishes her with an air of having finished her job.

THE SHE-ANCIENT. She will do. She may live.

They all wave their wands and shout for joy.

THE NEWLY BORN [*indignant*] I may live! Suppose there had been anything wrong with me?

THE SHE-ANCIENT. Children with anything wrong do not live here, my child. Life is not cheap with us. But you would not have felt anything.

THE NEWLY BORN. You mean that you would have murdered me!

THE SHE-ANCIENT. That is one of the funny words the newly born bring with them out of the past. You will forget it tomorrow. Now listen. You have four years of childhood before you. You will not be very happy; but you will be interested and amused by the novelty of the world; and your companions here will teach you how to keep up an imitation of happiness during your four years by what they call arts and sports and pleasures. The worst of your troubles is already over.

THE NEWLY BORN. What! In five minutes?

THE SHE-ANCIENT. No: you have been growing for two years in the egg. You began by being several sorts of creatures that no longer exist, though we have fossils of them. Then you became human; and you passed in fifteen months through a development that once cost human beings twenty years of awkward stumbling immaturity after they were born. They had to spend fifty years more in the sort of childhood you will complete in four years. And then they died of decay. But you need not die until your accident comes.

THE NEWLY BORN. What is my accident?

THE SHE-ANCIENT. Sooner or later you will fall and break your neck; or a tree will fall on you; or you will be struck by lightning. Something or other must make an end of you someday.

THE NEWLY BORN. But why should any of these things happen to me?

THE SHE-ANCIENT. There is no why. They do. Everything happens to everybody sooner or later if there is time enough. And with us there is eternity.

THE NEWLY BORN. Nothing need happen. I never heard such nonsense in all my life. I should know how to take care of myself.

THE SHE-ANCIENT. So you think.

THE NEWLY BORN. I dont think: I know. I shall enjoy life for ever and ever.

THE SHE-ANCIENT. If you should turn out to be a person of infinite capacity, you will no doubt find life infinitely interesting. However, all you have to do now is to play with your companions. They have many pretty toys, as you see: a playhouse, pictures, images, flowers, bright fabrics, music: above all, themselves; for the most amusing child's toy is another child. At the end of four years, your mind will change: you will become wise; and then you will be entrusted with power.

THE NEWLY BORN. But I want power now.

THE SHE-ANCIENT. No doubt you do; so that you could play with the world by tearing it to pieces.

THE NEWLY BORN. Only to see how it is made. I should put it all together again much better than before.

THE SHE-ANCIENT. There was a time when children were given the world to play with because they promised to improve it. They did not improve it; and they would have wrecked it had their power been as great as that which you will wield when you are no longer a child. Until your young companions will instruct you in whatever is necessary. You are not forbidden to speak to the ancients; but you had better not do so, as most of them have long ago exhausted all the interest there is in observing children and conversing with them. [*She turns to go*].

THE NEWLY BORN. Wait. Tell me some things that I ought to do and ought not to do. I feel the need of education.

They all laugh at her, except the She-Ancient.

THE SHE-ANCIENT. You will have grown out of that by tomorrow. Do what you please. [*She goes away up the hill path*].

The officials take their paraphernalia and the frag-ments of the egg back into the temple.

ACIS.   Just fancy: that old girl has been going for seven hundred years and hasnt had her fatal accident yet; and she is not a bit tired of it all.

THE NEWLY BORN.   How could anyone ever get tired of life?

ACIS.   They do.   That is, of the same life.   They manage to change themselves in a wonderful way.   You meet them sometimes with a lot of extra heads and arms and legs: they make you split laughing at them.   Most of them have forgotten how to speak: the ones that attend to us have to brush up their knowledge of the language once a year or so.   Nothing makes any dif-ference to them that I can see.   They never enjoy them-selves.   I dont know how they can stand it.   They dont even come to our festivals of the arts.   That old one who saw you out of your shell has gone off to moodle about doing nothing; though she knows that this is Festival Day.

THE NEWLY BORN.   What is Festival Day?

ACIS.   Two of our greatest sculptors are bringing us their latest masterpieces; and we are going to crown them with flowers and sing dithyrambs to them and dance round them.

THE NEWLY BORN.   How jolly!   What is a sculptor?

ACIS.   Listen here, young one.   You must find out things for yourself, and not ask questions.   For the first day or two you must keep your eyes and ears open and your mouth shut.   Children should be seen and not heard.

THE NEWLY BORN.   Who are you calling a child?   I am fully quarter of an hour old.   [*She sits down on the curved bench near Strephon with her maturest air*].

VOICES IN THE TEMPLE [*all expressing protest, disap-pointment, disgust*] Oh! Oh! Scandalous. Shameful.

Disgraceful. What filth! Is this a joke? Why, theyre ancients! Ss-s-s-sss! Are you mad, Arjillax? This is an outrage. An insult. Yah! etc. etc. etc. [*The malcontents appear on the steps, grumbling*].

ACIS. Hullo: whats the matter? [*He goes to the steps of the temple*].

The two sculptors issue from the temple. One has a beard two feet long: the other is beardless. Between them comes a handsome nymph with marked features, dark hair richly waved, and authoritative bearing.

THE AUTHORATATIVE NYMPH [*swooping down to the centre of the glade with the sculptors, between Acis and the Newly Born*] Do not try to browbeat me, Arjillax, merely because you are clever with your hands. Can you play the flute?

ARJILLAX [*the bearded sculptor on her right*] No, Ecrasia: I cannot. What has that to do with it? [*He is half derisive, half impatient, wholly resolved not to take her seriously in spite of her beauty and imposing tone*].

ECRASIA. Well, have you ever hesitated to criticize our best flute players, and to declare whether their music is good or bad? Pray have I not the same right to criticize your busts, though I cannot make images any more than you can play?

ARJILLAX. Any fool can play the flute, or play anything else, if he practises enough; but sculpture is a creative art, not a mere business of whistling into a pipe. The sculptor must have something of the god in him. From his hand comes a form which reflects a spirit. He does not make it to please you, nor even to please himself, but because he must. You must take what he gives you, or leave it if you are not worthy of it.

ECRASIA [*scornfully*] Not worthy of it! Ho! May I not leave it because it is not worthy of me?

ARJILLAX.   Of you! Hold your silly tongue, you conceited humbug. What do you know about it?

ECRASIA.   I know what every person of culture knows: that the business of the artist is to create beauty. Until today your works have been full of beauty; and I have been the first to point that out.

ARJILLAX.   Thank you for nothing. People have eyes, havnt they, to see what is as plain as the sun in the heavens without your pointing it out?

ECRASIA.   You were very glad to have it pointed out. You did not call me a conceited humbug then. You stifled me with caresses. You modelled me as the genius of art presiding over the infancy of your master here [*indicating the other sculptor*], Martellus.

MARTELLUS [*a silent and meditative listener, shudders and shakes his head, but says nothing*].

ARJILLAX [*quarrelsomely*] I was taken in by your talk.

ECRASIA.   I discovered your genius before anyone else did. Is that true, or is it not?

ARJILLAX.   Everybody knew I was an extraordinary person. When I was born my beard was three feet long.

ECRASIA.   Yes; and it has shrunk from three feet to two. Your genius seems to have been in the last foot of your beard; for you have lost both.

MARTELLUS [*with a short sardonic cachinnation*] He! My beard was three and a half feet long when I was born; and a flash of lightning burnt it off and killed the ancient who was delivering me. Without a hair on my chin I became the greatest sculptor in ten generations.

ECRASIA.   And yet you come to us today with empty hands. We shall actually have to crown Arjillax here because no other sculptor is exhibiting.

ACIS [*returning from the temple steps to behind the curved seat on the right of the three*] Whats the row,

Ecrasia? Why have you fallen out with Arjillax?

ECRASIA.   He has insulted me! outraged us! profaned
his art! You know how much we hoped from the twelve
busts he placed in the temple to be unveiled today. Well,
go in and look at them. That is all I have to say.
[*She sweeps to the curved seat, and sits down where Acis
is leaning over it*].

ACIS.   I am no great judge of sculpture. Art is not
my line. What is wrong with the busts?

ECRASIA.   Wrong with them! Instead of being ideally
beautiful nymphs and youths, they are horribly realistic
studies of—but I really cannot bring my lips to utter it.

*The Newly Born, full of curiosity, runs to the temple,
and peeps in.*

ACIS.   Oh, stow it, Ecrasia. Your lips are not so
squeamish as all that. Studies of what?

THE NEWLY BORN [*from the temple steps*] Ancients.

ACIS [*surprised but not scandalized*] Ancients!

ECRASIA.   Yes, ancients. The one subject that is by
the universal consent of all our connoisseurs absolutely
excluded from the fine arts. [*To Arjillax*] How can
you defend such a proceeding?

ARJILLAX.   If you come to that, what interest can
you find in the statues of smirking nymphs and postur-
ing youths you stick up all over the place?

ECRASIA.   You did not ask that when your hand was
still skilful enough to model them.

ARJILLAX.   Skilful! You high-nosed idiot, I could
turn such things out by the score with my eyes bandaged
and one hand tied behind me. But what use would they
be? They would bore me; and they would bore you if
you had any sense. Go in and look at my busts. Look
at them again and yet again until you receive the full
impression of the intensity of mind that is stamped on
them; and then go back to the pretty-pretty confec-

tionery you call sculpture, and see whether you can
endure its vapid emptiness. [*He mounts the altar impetuously*] Listen to me, all of you; and do you,
Ecrasia, be silent if you are capable of silence.

ECRASIA.   Silence is the most perfect expression of
scorn. Scorn! That is what I feel for your revolting
busts.

ARJILLAX. Fool: the busts are only the beginning of
a mighty design. Listen.

ACIS. Go ahead, old sport. We are listening.

*Martellus stretches himself on the sward beside the
altar. The Newly Born sits on the temple steps with her
chin on her hands, ready to devour the first oration she
has ever heard. The rest sit or stand at ease.*

ARJILLAX. In the records which generations of children have rescued from the stupid neglect of the
ancients, there has come down to us a fable which, like
many fables, is not a thing that was done in the past, but
a thing that is to be done in the future. It is a legend
of a supernatural being called the Archangel Michael.

THE NEWLY BORN. Is this a story? I want to hear a
story. [*She runs down the steps and sits on the altar at
Arjillax's feet*].

ARJILLAX. The Archangel Michael was a mighty
sculptor and painter. He found in the centre of the
world a temple erected to the goddess of the centre,
called Mediterranea. This temple was full of silly pictures of pretty children, such as Ecrasia approves.

ACIS. Fair play, Arjillax! If she is to keep silent,
let her alone.

ECRASIA. I shall not interrupt, Acis. Why should I
not prefer youth and beauty to age and ugliness?

ARJILLAX. Just so. Well, the Archangel Michael
was of my opinion, not yours. He began by painting
on the ceiling the newly born in all their childish beauty.

But when he had done this he was not satisfied; for the temple was no more impressive than it had been before, except that there was a strength and promise of greater things about his newly born ones than any other artist had attained to. So he painted all round these newly born a company of ancients, who were in those days called prophets and sybils, whose majesty was that of the mind alone at its intensest. And this painting was acknowledged through ages and ages to be the summit and masterpiece of art. Of course we cannot believe such a tale literally. It is only a legend. We do not believe in archangels; and the notion that thirty thousand years ago sculpture and painting existed, and had even reached the glorious perfection they have reached with us, is absurd. But what men cannot realize they can at least aspire to. They please themselves by pretending that it was realized in a golden age of the past. This splendid legend endured because it lived as a desire in the hearts of the greatest artists. The temple of Mediterranea never was built in the past, nor did Michael the Archangel exist. But today the temple is here [*he points to the porch*]; and the man is here [*he slaps himself on the chest*]. I, Arjillax, am the man. I will place in your theatre such images of the newly born as must satisfy even Ecrasia's appetite for beauty; and I will surround them with ancients more august than any who walk through our woods.

MARTELLUS [*as before*] Ha!

ARJILLAX [*stung*] Why do you laugh, you who have come empty-handed, and, it seems, empty-headed?

ECRASIA [*rising indignantly*] Oh, shame! You dare disparage Martellus, twenty times your master.

ACIS. Be quiet, will you [*he seizes her shoulders and thrusts her back into her seat*].

MARTELLUS. Let him disparage his fill, Ecrasia.

[*Sitting up*] My poor Arjillax, I too had this dream. I too found one day that my images of loveliness had become vapid, uninteresting, tedious, a waste of time and material. I too lost my desire to model limbs, and retained only my interest in heads and faces. I, too, made busts of ancients; but I had not your courage: I made them in secret, and hid them from you all.

ARJILLAX [*jumping down from the altar behind Martellus in his surprise and excitement*] You made busts of ancients! Where are they, man? Will you be talked out of your inspiration by Ecrasia and the fools who imagine she speaks with authority? Let us have them all set up beside mine in the theatre. I have opened the way for you; and you see I am none the worse.

MARTELLUS. Impossible. They are all smashed. [*He rises, laughing*].

ALL. Smashed!

ARJILLAX. Who smashed them?

MARTELLUS. I did. That is why I laughed at you just now. You will smash yours before you have completed a dozen of them. [*He goes to the end of the altar and sits down beside the Newly Born*].

ARJILLAX. But why?

MARTELLUS. Because you cannot give them life. A live ancient is better than a dead statue. [*He takes the Newly Born on his knee: she is flattered and voluptuously responsive*]. Anything alive is better than anything that is only pretending to be alive. [*To Arjillax*] Your disillusion with your works of beauty is only the beginning of your disillusion with images of all sorts. As your hand became more skilful and your chisel cut deeper, you strove to get nearer and nearer to truth and reality, discarding the fleeting fleshly lure, and making images of the mind that fascinates to the end. But how can so noble an inspiration be satisfied with any image, even an image of the truth? In the end the intellectual conscience that tore you away from the fleeting in art to the eternal must tear you away from art altogether, because art is false and life alone is true.

THE NEWLY BORN [*flings her arms round his neck and kisses him enthusiastically*].

MARTELLUS [*rises; carries her to the curved bench on his left; deposits her beside Strephon as if she were his overcoat; and continues without the least change of tone*] Shape it as you will, marble remains marble, and the graven image an idol. As I have broken my idols, and cast away my chisel and modelling tools, so will you too break these busts of yours.

ARJILLAX.   Never.

MARTELLUS.   Wait, my friend. I do not come empty-handed today, as you imagined. On the contrary, I bring with me such a work of art as you have never seen, and an artist who has surpassed both you and me further than we have surpassed all our competitors.

ECRASIA.   Impossible. The greatest things in art can never be surpassed.

ARJILLAX.   Who is this paragon whom you declare greater than I?

MARTELLUS.   I declare him greater than myself, Arjillax.

ARJILLAX [*frowning*] I understand. Sooner than not drown me, you are willing to clasp me round the waist and jump overboard with me.

ACIS.   Oh, stop squabbling. That is the worst of you artists. You are always in little squabbling cliques; and the worst cliques are those which consist of one man. Who is this new fellow you are throwing in one another's teeth?

ARJILLAX.   Ask Martellus: do not ask me. I know

nothing of him. [*He leaves Martellus, and sits down beside Ecrasia, on her left*].

MARTELLUS. You know him quite well. Pygmalion.

ECRASIA [*indignantly*] Pygmalion! That soulless creature! A scientist! A laboratory person!

ARJILLAX. Pygmalion produce a work of art! You have lost your artistic senses. The man is utterly incapable of modelling a thumb nail, let alone a human figure.

MARTELLUS. That does not matter: I have done the modelling for him.

ARJILLAX. What on earth do you mean?

MARTELLUS [*calling*] Pygmalion: come forth.

Pygmalion, a square-fingered youth with his face laid out in horizontal blocks, and a perpetual smile of eager benevolent interest in everything, and expectation of equal interest from everybody else, comes from the temple to the centre of the group, who regard him for the most part with dismay, as dreading that he will bore them. Ecrasia is openly contemptuous.

MARTELLUS. Friends: it is unfortunate that Pygmalion is constitutionally incapable of exhibiting anything without first giving a lecture about it to explain it; but I promise you that if you will be patient he will shew you the two most wonderful works of art in the world, and that they will contain some of my own very best workmanship. Let me add that they will inspire a loathing that will cure you of the lunacy of art for ever. [*He sits down next the Newly Born, who pouts and turns a very cold right shoulder to him, a demonstration utterly lost to him*].

Pygmalion, with the smile of a simpleton, and the eager confidence of a fanatical scientist, climbs awkwardly on to the altar. They prepare for the worst.

PYGMALION.   My friends: I will omit the algebra—

ACIS.   Thank God!

PYGMALION   [*continuing*]—because Martellus has made me promise to do so. To come to the point, I have succeeded in making artificial human beings. Real live ones, I mean.

INCREDULOUS VOICES.   Oh, come! Tell us another. Really, Pyg! Get out. You havnt. What a lie!

PYGMALION.   I tell you I have. I will shew them to you. It has been done before. One of the very oldest documents we possess mentions a tradition of a biologist who extracted certain unspecified minerals from the earth and, as it quaintly expresses it, "breathed into their nostrils the breath of life." This is the only tradition from the primitive ages which we can regard as really scientific. There are later documents which specify the minerals with great precision, even to their atomic weights; but they are utterly unscientific, because they overlook the element of life which makes all the difference between a mere mixture of salts and gases and a living organism. These mixtures were made over and over again in the crude laboratories of the Silly-Clever Ages; but nothing came of them until the ingredient which the old chronicler called the breath of life was added by this very remarkable early experimenter. In my view he was the founder of biological science.

ARJILLAX.   Is that all we know about him? It doesnt amount to very much, does it?

PYGMALION.   There are some fragments of pictures and documents which represent him as walking in a garden and advising people to cultivate their gardens. His name has come down to us in several forms. One of them is Jove. Another is Voltaire.

ECRASIA.   You are boring us to distraction with your Voltaire. What about your human beings?

ARJILLAX.   Aye: come to them.

PYGMALION.   I assure you that these details are intensely interesting.   [*Cries of* No!   They are not! Come to the human beings!   Conspuez Voltaire!   Cut it short, Pyg! *interrupt him from all sides*].   You will see their bearing presently.   I promise you I will not detain you long.   We know, we children of science, that the universe is full of forces and powers and energies of one kind and another.   The sap rising in a tree, the stone holding together in a definite crystalline structure, the thought of a philosopher holding his brain in form and operation with an inconceivably powerful grip, the urge of evolution: all these forces can be used by us.   For instance, I use the force of gravitation when I put a stone on my tunic to prevent it being blown away when I am bathing.   By substituting appropriate machines for the stone we have made not only gravitation our slave, but also electricity and magnetism, atomic attraction, repulsion, polarization, and so forth.   But hitherto the vital force has eluded us; so it has had to create machinery for itself.   It has created and developed bony structures of the requisite strength, and clothed them with cellular tissue of such amazing sensitiveness that the organs it forms will adapt their action to all the normal variations in the air they breathe, the food they digest, and the circumstances about which they have to think.   Yet, as these live bodies, as we call them, are only machines after all, it must be possible to construct them mechanically.

ARJILLAX.   Everything is possible.   Have you done it? that is the question.

PYGMALION.   Yes.   But that is a mere fact.   What is interesting is the explanation of the fact.   Forgive my saying so; but it is such a pity that you artists have no intellect.

ECRASIA [*sententiously*] I do not admit that. The artist divines by inspiration all the truths that the so-called scientist grubs up in his laboratory slowly and stupidly long afterwards.

ARJILLAX [*to Ecrasia, quarrelsomely*] What do you know about it? You are not an artist.

ACIS. Shut your heads, both of you. Let us have the artificial men. Trot them out, Pygmalion.

PYGMALION. It is a man and a woman. But I really must explain first.

ALL [*groaning*] ! ! !

PYGMALION. Yes: I—

ACIS. We want results, not explanations.

PYGMALION [*hurt*] I see I am boring you. Not one of you takes the least interest in science. Good-bye. [*He descends from the altar and makes for the temple*].

SEVERAL YOUTHS AND MAIDENS [*rising and rushing to him*] No, no. Dont go. Dont be offended. We want to see the artificial pair. We will listen. We are tremendously interested. Tell us all about it.

PYGMALION [*relenting*] I shall not detain you two minutes.

ALL. Half an hour if you like. Please go on, Pygmalion. [*They rush him back to the altar, and hoist him up on to it*]. Up you go.

They return to their former places.

PYGMALION. As I told you, lots of attempts were made to produce protoplasm in the laboratory. Why were these synthetic plasms, as they called them, no use?

ECRASIA. We are waiting for you to tell us.

THE NEWLY BORN [*modelling herself on Ecrasia, and trying to outdo her intellectually*] Clearly because they were dead.

PYGMALION. Not bad for a baby, my pet. But dead and alive are very loose terms. You are not half as much alive as you will be in another month or so. What was wrong with the synthetic protoplasm was that it could not fix and conduct the Life Force. It was like a wooden magnet or a lightning conductor made of silk: it would not take the current.

ACIS. Nobody but a fool would make a wooden magnet, and expect it to attract anything.

PYGMALION. He might if he were so ignorant as not to be able to distinguish between wood and soft iron. In those days they were very ignorant of the differences between things, because their methods of analysis were crude. They mixed up messes that were so like protoplasm that they could not tell the difference. But the difference was there, though their analysis was too superficial and incomplete to detect it. You must remember that these poor devils were very little better than our idiots: we should never dream of letting one of them survive the day of its birth. Why, the Newly Born there already knows by instinct many things that their greatest physicists could hardly arrive at by forty years of strenuous study. Her simple direct sense of space-time and quantity unconsciously solves problems which cost their most famous mathematicians years of prolonged and laborious calculations requiring such intense mental application that they frequently forgot to breathe when engaged in them, and almost suffocated themselves in consequence.

ECRASIA. Leave these obscure prehistoric abortions; and come back to your synthetic man and woman.

PYGMALION. When I undertook the task of making synthetic men, I did not waste my time on protoplasm. It was evident to me that if it were possible to make protoplasm in the laboratory, it must be equally possible to begin higher up and make fully evolved muscular and nervous tissues, bone, and so forth. Why make the seed when the making of the flower would be no greater miracle? I tried thousands of combinations before I succeeded in producing anything that would fix high-potential Life Force.

ARJILLAX. High what?

PYGMALION. High-po-tential. The Life Force is not so simple as you think. A high-potential current of it will turn a bit of dead tissue into a philosopher's brain. A low-potential current will reduce the same bit of tissue to a mass of corruption. Will you believe me when I tell you that, even in man himself, the Life Force used to slip suddenly down from its human level to that of a fungus, so that men found their flesh no longer growing as flesh, but proliferating horribly in a lower form which was called cancer, until the lower form of life killed the higher, and both perished together miserably?

MARTELLUS. Keep off the primitive tribes, Pygmalion. They interest you; but they bore these young things.

PYGMALION. I am only trying to make you understand. There was the Life Force raging all round me: there was I, trying to make organs that would capture it as a battery captures electricity, and tissues that would conduct it and operate it. It was easy enough to make eyes more perfect than our own, and ears with a larger range of sound; but they could neither see nor hear, because they were not susceptible to the Life Force. But it was far worse when I discovered how to make them susceptible; for the first thing that happened was that they ceased to be eyes and ears and turned into heaps of maggots.

ECRASIA. Disgusting! Please stop.

ACIS. If you dont want to hear, go away. You go ahead, Pyg.

PYGMALION. I went ahead. You see, the lower

potentials of the Life Force could make maggots, but not human eyes or ears. I improved the tissue until it was susceptible to a higher potential.

ARJILLAX [*intensely interested*] Yes; and then?

PYGMALION. Then the eyes and ears turned into cancers.

ECRASIA. Oh, hideous!

PYGMALION. Not at all. That was a great advance. It encouraged me so much that I put aside the eyes and ears, and made a brain. It wouldnt take the Life Force at all until I had altered its constitution a dozen times; but when it did, it took a much higher potential, and did not dissolve; and neither did the eyes and ears when I connected them up with the brain. I was able to make a sort of monster: a thing without arms or legs; and it really and truly lived for half-an-hour.

THE NEWLY BORN. Half-an-hour! What good was that? Why did it die?

PYGMALION. Its blood went wrong. But I got that right; and then I went ahead with a complete human body: arms and legs and all. He was my first man.

ARJILLAX. Who modelled him?

PYGMALION. I did.

MARTELLUS. Do you mean to say you tried your own hand before you sent for me?

PYGMALION. Bless you, yes, several times. My first man was the ghastliest creature: a more dreadful mixture of horror and absurdity than you who have not seen him can conceive.

ARJILLAX. If you modelled him, he must indeed have been a spectacle.

PYGMALION. Oh, it was not his shape. You see I did not invent that. I took actual measurements, and moulds from my own body. Sculptors do that sometimes, you know; though they pretend they dont.

MARTELLUS. Hm.

ARJILLAX. Hah!

PYGMALION. He was all right to look at, at first, or nearly so. But he behaved in the most appalling manner; and the subsequent developments were so disgusting that I really cannot describe them to you. He seized all sorts of things and swallowed them. He drank every fluid in the laboratory. I tried to explain to him that he must take nothing that he could not digest and assimilate completely; but of course he could not understand me. He assimilated a little of what he swallowed; but the process left horrible residues which he had no means of getting rid of. His blood turned to poison; and he perished in torments, howling. I then perceived that I had produced a prehistoric man; for there are certain traces in our own bodies of arrangements which enabled the earlier forms of mankind to renew their bodies by swallowing flesh and grains and vegetables and all sorts of unnatural and hideous foods, and getting rid of what they could not digest.

ECRASIA. But what a pity he died! What a glimpse of the past we have lost! He could have told us stories of the Golden Age.

PYGMALION. Not he. He was a most dangerous beast. He was afraid of me, and actually tried to kill me by snatching up things and striking at me with them. I had to give him two or three pretty severe shocks before I convinced him that he was at my mercy.

THE NEWLY BORN. Why did you not make a woman instead of a man? She would have known how to behave herself.

MARTELLUS. Why did you not make a man and a woman? Their children would have been interesting.

PYGMALION. I intended to make a woman; but after

my experience with the man it was out of the question.

ECRASIA.   Pray why?

PYGMALION.   Well, it is difficult to explain if you have not studied prehistoric methods of reproduction. You see the only sort of men and women I could make were men and women just like us as far as their bodies were concerned. That was how I killed the poor beast of a man. I hadnt provided for his horrible prehistoric methods of feeding himself. Suppose the woman had reproduced in some prehistoric way instead of being oviparous as we are? She couldnt have done it with a modern female body. Besides, the experiment might have been painful.

ECRASIA.   Then you have nothing to shew us at all?

PYGMALION.   Oh yes I have. I am not so easily beaten as that. I set to work again for months to find out how to make a digestive system that would deal with waste products and a reproductive system capable of internal nourishment and incubation.

ECRASIA.   Why did you not find out how to make them like us?

STREPHON [*crying out in his grief for the first time*] Why did you not make a woman whom you could love? That was the secret you needed.

THE NEWLY BORN.   Oh yes. How true! How great of you, darling Strephon! [*She kisses him impulsively*].

STREPHON [*passionately*] Let me alone.

MARTELLUS.   Control your reflexes, child.

THE NEWLY BORN.   My what!

MARTELLUS.   Your reflexes. The things you do without thinking. Pygmalion is going to shew you a pair of human creatures who are all reflexes and nothing else. Take warning by them.

THE NEWLY BORN.   But wont they be alive, like us?

PYGMALION.   That is a very difficult question to

answer, my dear. I confess I thought at first I had
created living creatures; but Martellus declares they are
only automata. But then Martellus is a mystic: *I* am a
man of science. He draws a line between an automaton
and a living organism. I cannot draw that line to my
own satisfaction.

MARTELLUS. Your artificial men have no self-control. They only respond to stimuli from without.

PYGMALION. But they are conscious. I have taught
them to talk and read; and now they tell lies. That is
so very lifelike.

MARTELLUS. Not at all. If they were alive they
would tell the truth. You can provoke them to tell any
silly lie; and you can foresee exactly the sort of lie they
will tell. Give them a clip below the knee, and they will
jerk their foot forward. Give them a clip in their
appetites or vanities or any of their lusts and greeds,
and they will boast and lie, and affirm and deny, and hate
and love without the slightest regard to the facts that
are staring them in the face, or to their own obvious
limitations. That proves that they are automata.

PYGMALION [*unconvinced*] I know, dear old chap; but
there really is some evidence that we are descended from
creatures quite as limited and absurd as these. After all,
the baby there is three-quarters an automaton. Look
at the way she has been going on!

THE NEWLY BORN [*indignantly*] What do you mean?
How have I been going on?

ECRASIA. If they have no regard for truth, they can
have no real vitality.

PYGMALION. Truth is sometimes so artificial: so
relative, as we say in the scientific world, that it is very
hard to feel quite sure that what is false and even
ridiculous to us may not be true to them.

ECRASIA. I ask you again, why did you not make

them like us? Would any true artist be content with less than the best?

PYGMALION. I couldnt. I tried. I failed. I am convinced that what I am about to shew you is the very highest living organism that can be produced in the laboratory. The best tissues we can manufacture will not take as high potentials as the natural product: that is where Nature beats us. You dont seem to understand, any of you, what an enormous triumph it was to produce consciousness at all.

ACIS. Cut the cackle; and come to the synthetic couple.

SEVERAL YOUTHS AND MAIDENS. Yes, yes. No more talking. Let us have them. Dry up, Pyg; and fetch them along. Come on: out with them! The synthetic couple: the synthetic couple.

PYGMALION [*waving his hands to appease them*] Very well, very well. Will you please whistle for them? They respond to the stimulus of a whistle.

All who can, whistle like streetboys.

ECRASIA [*makes a wry face and puts her fingers in her ears*]!

PYGMALION. Sh-sh-sh! Thats enough: thats enough: thats enough. [*Silence*]. Now let us have some music. A dance tune. Not too fast.

The flutists play a quiet dance.

MARTELLUS. Prepare yourselves for something ghastly.

Two figures, a man and woman of noble appearance, beautifully modelled and splendidly attired, emerge hand in hand from the temple. Seeing that all eyes are fixed on them, they halt on the steps, smiling with gratified vanity. The woman is on the man's left.

PYGMALION [*rubbing his hands with the purring satisfaction of a creator*] This way, please.

*The Figures advance condescendingly and pose them-
selves centrally between the curved seats.*

PYGMALION. Now if you will be so good as to oblige
us with a little something. You dance so beautifully,
you know. [*He sits down next Martellus, and whispers
to him*] It is extraordinary how sensitive they are to
the stimulus of flattery.

*The Figures, with a gracious air, dance pompously,
but very passably. At the close they bow to one another.*

ON ALL HANDS [*clapping*] Bravo! Thank you. Wonderful! Splendid. Perfect.

*The Figures acknowledge the applause in an obvious
condition of swelled head.*

THE NEWLY BORN. Can they make love?

PYGMALION. Yes: they can respond to every stimulus.
They have all the reflexes. Put your arm round the
man's neck, and he will put his arm round your body.
He cannot help it.

THE FEMALE FIGURE [*frowning*] Round mine, you
mean.

PYGMALION. Yours, too, of course, if the stimulus
comes from you.

ECRASIA. Cannot he do anything original?

PYGMALION. No. But then, you know, I do not admit
that any of us can do anything really original, though
Martellus thinks we can.

ACIS. Can he answer a question?

PYGMALION. Oh yes. A question is a stimulus, you
know. Ask him one.

ACIS [*to the Male Figure*] What do you think of what
you see around you? Of us, for instance, and our ways
and doings?

THE MALE FIGURE. I have not seen the newspaper today.

THE FEMALE FIGURE. How can you expect my husband to know what to think of you if you give him his breakfast without his paper?

MARTELLUS. You see. He is a mere automaton.

THE NEWLY BORN. I dont think I should like him to put his arm round my neck. I dont like them. [*The Male Figure looks offended, and the Female jealous*]. Oh, I thought they couldnt understand. Have they feelings?

PYGMALION. Of course they have. I tell you they have all the reflexes.

THE NEWLY BORN. But feelings are not reflexes.

PYGMALION. They are sensations. When the rays of light enter their eyes and make a picture on their retinas, their brains become conscious of the picture and they act accordingly. When the waves of sound started by your speaking enter their ears and record a disparaging remark on their keyboards, their brains become conscious of the disparagement and resent it accordingly. If you did not disparage them they would not resent it. They are merely responding to a stimulus.

THE MALE FIGURE. We are part of a cosmic system. Free will is an illusion. We are the children of Cause and Effect. We are the Unalterable, the Irresistible, the Irresponsible, the Inevitable.

My name is Ozymandias, king of kings:
Look on my works, ye mighty, and despair.

There is a general stir of curiosity at this.

ACIS. What the dickens does he mean?

THE MALE FIGURE. Silence, base accident of Nature. This [*taking the hand of the Female Figure and introducing her*] is Cleopatra-Semiramis, consort of the king of kings, and therefore queen of queens. Ye are things hatched from eggs by the brainless sun and the

blind fire; but the king of kings and queen of queens
are not accidents of the egg: they are thought-out and
hand-made to receive the sacred Life Force.   There is
one person of the king and one of the queen; but the
Life Force of the king and queen is all one: the glory
equal, the majesty co-eternal.   Such as the king is so is
the queen, the king thought-out and hand-made, the
queen thought-out and hand-made.   The actions of the
king are caused, and therefore determined, from the beginning of the world to the end; and the actions of the
queen are likewise.   The king logical and predetermined
and inevitable, and the queen logical and predetermined
and inevitable.   And yet they are not two logical and
predetermined and inevitable, but one logical and predetermined and inevitable.   Therefore confound not the
persons, nor divide the substance; but worship us twain
as one throne, two in one and one in two, lest by error ye
fall into irretrievable damnation.

THE FEMALE FIGURE.   And if any say unto you
"Which one?" remember that though there is one person
of the king and one of the queen, yet these two persons
are not alike, but are woman and man, and that as
woman was created after man, the skill and practice
gained in making him were added to her, wherefore she
is to be exalted above him in all personal respects, and—

THE MALE FIGURE.   Peace, woman; for this is a
damnable heresy.   Both Man and Woman are what they
are and must do what they must according to the eternal
laws of Cause and Effect.   Look to your words; for if
they enter my ear and jar too repugnantly on my sen-
sorium, who knows that the inevitable response to that
stimulus may not be a message to my muscles to snatch
up some heavy object and break you in pieces.

*The Female Figure picks up a stone and is about to
throw it at her consort.*

.

ARJILLAX [*springing up and shouting to Pygmalion, who is fondly watching the Male Figure*] Look out, Pygmalion! Look at the woman!

Pygmalion, seeing what is happening, hurls himself on the Female Figure and wrenches the stone out of her hand.

All spring up in consternation.

ARJILLAX. She meant to kill him.

STREPHON. This is horrible.

THE FEMALE FIGURE [*wrestling with Pygmalion*] Let me go. Let me go, will you. [*She bites his hand*].

PYGMALION [*releasing her and staggering*] Oh!

A general shriek of horror echoes his exclamation. He turns deadly pale, and supports himself against the end of the curved seat.

THE FEMALE FIGURE [*to her consort*] You would stand there and let me be treated like this, you unmanly coward.

Pygmalion falls dead.

THE NEWLY BORN. Oh! Whats the matter? Why did he fall? What has happened to him?

They look on anxiously as Martellus kneels down and examines the body of Pygmalion.

MARTELLUS. She has bitten a piece out of his hand nearly as large as a finger nail; enough to kill ten men. There is no pulse, no breath.

ECRASIA. But his thumb is clinched.

MARTELLUS. No: it has just straightened out. See! He has gone. Poor Pygmalion!

THE NEWLY BORN. Oh! [*She weeps*].

STREPHON. Hush, dear: thats childish.

THE NEWLY BORN [*subsiding with a sniff*] ! !

MARTELLUS [*rising*] Dead in his third year. What a loss to Science!

ARJILLAX. Who cares about Science? Serve him

right for making that pair of horrors!

THE MALE FIGURE [*glaring*] Ha!

THE FEMALE FIGURE.   Keep a civil tongue in your head, you.

THE NEWLY BORN.   Oh, do not be so unkind, Arjillax. You will make water come out of my eyes again.

MARTELLUS [*contemplating the Figures*] Just look at these two devils.   I modelled them out of the stuff Pygmalion made for them.   They are masterpieces of art.   And see what they have done!   Does that convince you of the value of art, Arjillax?

STREPHON.   They look dangerous.   Keep away from them.

ECRASIA.   No need to tell us that, Strephon.   Pf! They poison the air.

THE MALE FIGURE.   Beware, woman.   The wrath of Ozymandias strikes like the lightning.

THE FEMALE FIGURE.   You just say that again if you dare, you filthy creature.

ACIS.   What are you going to do with them, Martellus? You are responsible for them, now that Pygmalion has gone.

MARTELLUS.   If they were marble it would be simple enough: I could smash them.   As it is, how am I to kill them without making a horrible mess?

THE MALE FIGURE [*posing heroically*] Ha!   [*He declaims*].

> Come one: come all: this rock shall fly
> From its firm base as soon as I.

THE FEMALE FIGURE [*fondly*] My man!   My hero husband!   I am proud of you.   I love you.

MARTELLUS.   We must send out a message for an ancient.

ACIS.   Need we bother an ancient about such a trifle?

It will take less than half a second to reduce our poor
Pygmalion to a pinch of dust. Why not calcine the
two along with him?

MARTELLUS.   No: the two automata are trifles; but
the use of our powers of destruction is never a trifle. I
had rather have the case judged.

*The He-Ancient emerges from the grove. The Fig-
ures are panic-stricken.*

THE HE-ANCIENT [*mildly*] Am I wanted? I feel as if
I was. [*Seeing the body of Pygmalion, and immediately taking a sterner tone*] What! A child lost! A
life wasted! How has this happened?

THE FEMALE FIGURE [*frantically*] I didnt do it. It
was not me. May I be struck dead if I touched him.
It was he [*pointing to the Male Figure*].

ALL [*amazed at the lie*] Oh!

THE MALE FIGURE.   Liar. You bit him. Everyone
here saw you do it.

THE HE-ANCIENT.   Silence. [*Going between the Figures*] Who made these two loathsome dolls?

THE MALE FIGURE [*trying to assert himself with his
knees knocking*] My name is Ozymandias, king of—

THE HE-ANCIENT [*with a contemptuous gesture*]
Pooh!

THE MALE FIGURE [*falling on his knees*] Oh dont, sir.
Dont. She did it, sir: indeed she did.

THE FEMALE FIGURE [*howling lamentably*] Boohoo!
oo! ooh!

THE HE-ANCIENT.   Silence, I say.

*He knocks the Male Automaton upright by a very
light flip under the chin. The Female Automaton hardly
dares to sob. The immortals contemplate them with
shame and loathing. The She-Ancient comes from the
trees opposite the temple.*

THE SHE-ANCIENT.   Somebody wants me. What is the

matter? [*She comes to the left hand of the Female Figure, not seeing the body of Pygmalion*]. Pf! [*Severely*] You have been making dolls. You must not: they are not only disgusting: they are dangerous.

THE FEMALE FIGURE [*snivelling piteously*] I'm not a doll, mam. I'm only poor Cleopatra-Semiramis, queen of queens. [*Covering her face with her hands*] Oh, don't look at me like that, mam. I meant no harm. He hurt me: indeed he did.

THE HE-ANCIENT. The creature has killed that poor youth.

THE SHE-ANCIENT [*seeing the body of Pygmalion*] What! This clever child, who promised so well!

THE FEMALE FIGURE. He made me. I had as much right to kill him as he had to make me. And how was I to know that a little thing like that would kill him? I shouldnt die if he cut off my arm or leg.

ECRASIA. What nonsense!

MARTELLUS. It may not be nonsense. I daresay if you cut off her leg she would grow another, like the lobsters and the little lizards.

THE HE-ANCIENT. Did this dead boy make these two things?

MARTELLUS. He made them in his laboratory. I moulded their limbs. I am sorry. I was thoughtless: I did not foresee that they would kill and pretend to be persons they were not, and declare things that were false, and wish evil. I thought they would be merely mechanical fools.

THE MALE FIGURE. Do you blame us for our human nature?

THP FEMALE FIGURE. We are flesh and blood and not angels.

THE MALE FIGURE. Have you no hearts?

ARJILLAX.   They are mad as well as mischievous.
May we not destroy them?

STREPHON.   We abhor them.

THE NEWLY BORN.   We loathe them.

ECRASIA.   They are noisome.

ACIS.   I dont want to be hard on the poor devils;
but they are making me feel uneasy in my inside.   I
never had such a sensation before.

MARTELLUS.   I took a lot of trouble with them.   But
as far as I am concerned, destroy them by all means.
I loathed them from the beginning.

ALL.   Yes, yes: we all loathe them.   Let us calcine
them.

THE FEMALE FIGURE.   Oh, dont be so cruel.   I'm not
fit to die.   I will never bite anyone again.   I will tell
the truth.   I will do good.   Is it my fault if I was not
made properly?   Kill him; but spare me.

THE MALE FIGURE.   No!   I have done no harm: she
has.   Kill her if you like: you have no right to kill me.

THE NEWLY BORN.   Do you hear that?   They want to
have one another killed.

ARJILLAX.   Monstrous!   Kill them both.

THE HE-ANCIENT.   Silence.   These things are mere
automata: they cannot help shrinking from death at any
cost.   You see that they have no self-control, and are
merely shuddering through a series of reflexes.   Let us
see whether we cannot put a little more life into them.
[*He takes the Male Figure by the hand, and places his
disengaged hand on its head*].   Now listen.   One of you
two is to be destroyed.   Which of you shall it be?

THE MALE FIGURE [*after a slight convulsion during
which his eyes are fixed on the He-Ancient*] Spare her;
and kill me.

STREPHON.   Thats better.

THE NEWLY BORN.   Much better.

THE SHE-ANCIENT [*handling the Female Automaton in the same manner*] Which of you shall we kill?

THE FEMALE FIGURE. Kill us both. How could either of us live without the other?

ECRASIA. The woman is more sensible than the man. *The ancients release the Automata.*

THE MALE FIGURE [*sinking to the ground*] I am discouraged. Life is too heavy a burden.

THE FEMALE FIGURE [*collapsing*] I am dying. I am glad. I am afraid to live.

THE NEWLY BORN. I think it would be nice to give the poor things a little music.

ARJILLAX. Why?

THE NEWLY BORN. I dont know. But it would. *The Musicians play.*

THE FEMALE FIGURE. Ozymandias: do you hear that? [*She rises on her knees and looks raptly into space*]. Queen of queens! [*She dies*].

THE MALE FIGURE [*crawling feebly towards her until he reaches her hand*] I knew I was really a king of kings. [*To the others*] Illusions, farewell: we are going to our thrones. [*He dies*].

The music stops. There is dead silence for a moment.

THE NEWLY BORN. That was funny.

STREPHON. It was. Even the Ancients are smiling.

THE NEWLY BORN. Just a little.

THE SHE-ANCIENT [*quickly recovering her grave and peremptory manner*] Take these two abominations away to Pygmalion's laboratory, and destroy them with the rest of the laboratory refuse. [*Some of them move to obey*]. Take care: do not touch their flesh: it is noxious: lift them by their robes. Carry Pygmalion into the temple; and dispose of his remains in the usual way.

The three bodies are carried out as directed, Pygmalion into the temple by his bare arms and legs, and

the two Figures through the grove by their clothes.
Martellus superintends the removal of the Figures, Acis
that of Pygmalion.   Ecrasia, Arjillax, Strephon, and
the Newly Born sit down as before, but on contrary
benches; so that Strephon and the Newly Born now face
the grove, and Ecrasia and Arjillax the temple.   The
Ancients remain standing at the altar.

ECRASIA [*as she sits down*] Oh for a breeze from the hills!

STREPHON.   Or the wind from the sea at the turn of the tide!

THE NEWLY BORN.   I want some clean air.

THE HE-ANCIENT.   The air will be clean in a moment. This doll flesh that children make decomposes quickly at best; but when it is shaken by such passions as the creatures are capable of, it breaks up at once and becomes horribly tainted.

THE SHE-ANCIENT.   Let it be a lesson to you all to be content with lifeless toys, and not attempt to make living ones.   What would you think of us ancients if we made toys of you children?

THE NEWLY BORN [*coaxingly*] Why do you not make toys of us?   Then you would play with us; and that would be very nice.

THE SHE-ANCIENT.   It would not amuse us.   When you play with one another you play with your bodies, and that makes you supple and strong; but if we played with you we should play with your minds, and perhaps deform them.

STREPHON.   You are a ghastly lot, you ancients.   I shall kill myself when I am four years old.   What do you live for?

THE HE-ANCIENT.   You will find out when you grow up.   You will not kill yourself.

STREPHON. If you make me believe that, I shall kill myself now.

THE NEWLY BORN. Oh no, I want you. I love you.

STREPHON. I love someone else. And she has gone old, old. Lost to me for ever.

THE HE-ANCIENT. How old?

STREPHON. You saw her when you barged into us as we were dancing. She is four.

THE NEWLY BORN. How I should have hated her twenty minutes ago! But I have grown out of that now.

THE HE-ANCIENT. Good. That hatred is called jealousy, the worst of our childish complaints.

Martellus, dusting his hands and puffing, returns from the grove.

MARTELLUS. Ouf! [*He sits down next the Newly Born*] That job's finished.

ARJILLAX. Ancients: I should like to make a few studies of you. Not portraits, of course: I shall idealize you a little. I have come to the conclusion that you ancients are the most interesting subjects after all.

MARTELLUS. What! Have those two horrors, whose ashes I have just deposited with peculiar pleasure in poor Pygmalion's dustbin, not cured you of this silly image-making?

ARJILLAX. Why did you model them as young things, you fool? If Pygmalion had come to me, I should have made ancients of them for him. Not that I should have modelled them any better. I have always said that no one can beat you at your best as far as handwork is concerned. But this job required brains. That is where I should have come in.

MARTELLUS. Well, my brainy boy, you are welcome to try your hand. There are two of Pygmalion's pupils at the laboratory who helped him to manufacture the

bones and tissues and all the rest of it.   They can turn
out a couple of new automatons; and you can model
them as ancients if this venerable pair will sit for you.

ECRASIA [*decisively*] No.   No more automata.   They
are too disgusting.

ACIS [*returning from the temple*] Well, thats done.
Poor old Pyg!

ECRASIA.   Only fancy, Acis!   Arjillax wants to make
more of those abominable things, and to destroy even
their artistic character by making ancients of them.

THE NEWLY BORN.   You wont sit for them, will you?
Please dont.

THE HE-ANCIENT.   Children, listen.

ACIS [*striding down the steps to the bench and seating
himself next Ecrasia*] What!   Even the Ancient wants
to make a speech!   Give it mouth, O Sage.

STREPHON.   For heaven's sake dont tell us that the
earth was once inhabited by Ozymandiases and Cleo-
patras.   Life is hard enough for us as it is.

THE HE-ANCIENT.   Life is not meant to be easy, my
child; but take courage: it can be delightful.   What I
wanted to tell you is that ever since men existed, children
have played with dolls.

ECRASIA.   You keep using that word.   What are
dolls, pray?

THE SHE-ANCIENT.   What you call works of art.
Images.   We call them dolls.

ARJILLAX.   Just so.   You have no sense of art; and
you instinctively insult it.

THE HE-ANCIENT.   Children have been known to make
dolls out of rags, and to caress them with the deepest
fondness.

THE SHE-ANCIENT.   Eight centuries ago, when I was
a child, I made a rag doll.   The rag doll is the dearest
of all.

THE NEWLY BORN [*eagerly interested*] Oh! Have you got it still?

THE SHE-ANCIENT. I kept it a full week.

ECRASIA. Even in your childhood, then, you did not understand high art, and adored your own amateur crudities.

THE SHE-ANCIENT. How old are you?

ECRASIA. Eight months.

THE SHE-ANCIENT. When you have lived as long as I have—

ECRASIA [*interrupting rudely*] I shall worship rag dolls, perhaps. Thank heaven, I am still in my prime.

THE HE-ANCIENT. You are still capable of thanking, though you do not know what you thank. You are a thanking little animal, a blaming little animal, a—

ACIS. A gushing little animal.

ARJILLAX. And, as she thinks, an artistic little animal.

ECRASIA [*nettled*] I am an animated being with a reasonable soul and human flesh subsisting. If your Automata had been properly animated, Martellus, they would have been more successful.

THE SHE-ANCIENT. That is where you are wrong, my child. If those two loathsome things had been rag dolls, they would have been amusing and lovable. The Newly Born here would have played with them; and you would all have laughed and played with them too until you had torn them to pieces; and then you would have laughed more than ever.

THE NEWLY BORN. Of course we should. Isnt that funny?

THE HE-ANCIENT. When a thing is funny, search it for a hidden truth.

STREPHON. Yes; and take all the fun out of it.

THE SHE-ANCIENT. Do not be so embittered because

your sweetheart has outgrown her love for you. The Newly Born will make amends.

THE NEWLY BORN. Oh yes: I will be more than she could ever have been.

STREPHON. Psha! Jealous!

THE NEWLY BORN. Oh no. I have grown out of that. I love her now because she loved you, and because you love her.

THE HE-ANCIENT. That is the next stage. You are getting on very nicely, my child.

MARTELLUS. Come! what is the truth that was hidden in the rag doll?

THE HE-ANCIENT. Well, consider why you are not content with the rag doll, and must have something more closely resembling a real living creature. As you grow up you make images and paint pictures. Those of you who cannot do that make stories about imaginary dolls Or you dress yourselves up as dolls and act plays about them.

THE SHE-ANCIENT. And, to deceive yourself the more completely, you take them so very very seriously that Ecrasia here declares that the making of dolls is the holiest work of creation, and the words you put into the mouths of dolls the sacredest of scriptures and the noblest of utterances.

ECRASIA. Tush!

ARJILLAX. Tosh!

THE SHE-ANCIENT. Yet the more beautiful they become the further they retreat from you. You cannot caress them as you caress the rag doll. You cannot cry for them when they are broken or lost, or when you pretend they have been unkind to you, as you could when you played with rag dolls.

THE HE-ANCIENT. At last, like Pygmalion, you de-

mand from your dolls the final perfection of resemblance
to life. They must move and speak.

THE SHE-ANCIENT.   They must love and hate.

THE HE-ANCIENT.   They must think that they think.

THE SHE-ANCIENT.   They must have soft flesh and
warm blood.

THE HE-ANCIENT.   And then, when you have achieved
this as Pygmalion did; when the marble masterpiece is
dethroned by the automaton and the homo by the ho-
munculus; when the body and the brain, the reasonable
soul and human flesh subsisting, as Ecrasia says, stand
before you unmasked as mere machinery, and your impulses are shewn to be nothing but reflexes, you are
filled with horror and loathing, and would give worlds
to be young enough to play with your rag doll again,
since every step away from it has been a step away from
love and happiness. Is it not true?

THE SHE-ANCIENT.   Speak, Martellus: you who have
travelled the whole path.

MARTELLUS.   It is true. With fierce joy I turned a
temperature of a million degrees on those two things I
had modelled, and saw them vanish in an instant into
inoffensive dust.

THE SHE-ANCIENT.   Speak, Arjillax: you who have
advanced from imitating the lightly living child to the
intensely living ancient. Is it true, so far?

ARJILLAX.   It is partly true: I cannot pretend to be
satisfied now with modelling pretty children.

THE HE-ANCIENT.   And you, Ecrasia: you cling to
your highly artistic dolls as the noblest projections of
the Life Force, do you not?

ECRASIA.   Without art, the crudeness of reality
would make the world unbearable.

THE NEWLY BORN [*anticipating the She-Ancient, who
is evidently going to challenge her*] Now you are com-

ing to me, because I am the latest arrival.   But I dont
understand your art and your dolls at all.   I want to
caress my darling Strephon, not to play with dolls.

ACIS.   I am in my fourth year, and I have got on
very well without your dolls.   I had rather walk up a
mountain and down again than look at all the statues
Martellus and Arjillax ever made.   You prefer a statue
to an automaton, and a rag doll to a statue.   So do I;
but I prefer a man to a rag doll.   Give me friends, not
dolls.

THE HE-ANCIENT.   Yet I have seen you walking over
the mountains alone.   Have you not found your best
friend in yourself?

ACIS.   What are you driving at, old one?   What
does all this lead to?

THE HE-ANCIENT.   It leads, young man, to the truth
that you can create nothing but yourself.

ACIS [*musing*] I can create nothing but myself.
Ecrasia: you are clever.   Do you understand it?   I
dont.

ECRASIA.   It is as easy to understand as any other
ignorant error.   What artist is as great as his own
works?   He can create masterpieces; but he cannot improve the shape of his own nose.

ACIS.   There!   What have you to say to that, old
one?

THE HE-ANCIENT.   He can alter the shape of his own
soul.   He could alter the shape of his nose if the difference between a turned-up nose and a turned-down one
were worth the effort.   One does not face the throes of
creation for trifles.

ACIS.   What have you to say to that, Ecrasia?

ECRASIA.   I say that if the ancients had thoroughly
grasped the theory of fine art they would understand
that the difference between a beautiful nose and an ugly

one is of supreme importance: that it is indeed the only thing that matters.

THE SHE-ANCIENT.   That is, they would understand something they could not believe, and that you do not believe.

ACIS.   Just so, mam.   Art is not honest: that is why I never could stand much of it.   It is all make-believe. Ecrasia never really says things: she only rattles her teeth in her mouth.

ECRASIA.   Acis: you are crude.

ACIS.   You mean that I wont play the game of make-believe.   Well, I dont ask you to play it with me; so why should you expect me to play it with you?

ECRASIA.   You have no right to say that I am not sincere.   I have found a happiness in art that real life has never given me.   I am intensely in earnest about art.   There is a magic and mystery in art that you know nothing of.

THE SHE-ANCIENT.   Yes, child: art is the magic mirror you make to reflect your invisible dreams in visible pictures.   You use a glass mirror to see your face: you use works of art to see your soul.   But we who are older use neither glass mirrors nor works of art.   We have a direct sense of life.   When you gain that you will put aside your mirrors and statues, your toys and your dolls.

THE HE-ANCIENT.   Yet we too have our toys and our dolls.   That is the trouble of the ancients.

ARJILLAX.   What!   The ancients have troubles!   It is the first time I ever heard one of them confess it.

THE HE-ANCIENT.   Look at us.   Look at me.   This is my body, my blood, my brain; but it is not me.   I am the eternal life, the perpetual resurrection; but [*striking his body*] this structure, this organism, this make-shift, can be made by a boy in a laboratory, and is held back from dissolution only by my use of it.   Worse still, it can be broken by a slip of the foot, drowned by a cramp in the stomach, destroyed by a flash from the clouds.   Sooner or later, its destruction is certain.

THE SHE-ANCIENT.   Yes: this body is the last doll to be discarded.   When I was a child, Ecrasia, I, too, was an artist, like your sculptor friends there, striving to ᴄreate perfection in things outside myself.   I made statues: I painted pictures: I tried to worship them.

THE HE-ANCIENT.   I had no such skill; but I, like Acis, sought perfection in friends, in lovers, in nature, in things outside myself.   Alas! I could not create it: I could only imagine it.

THE SHE-ANCIENT.   I, like Arjillax, found out that my statues of bodily beauty were no longer even beautiful to me; and I pressed on and made statutes and pictures of men and women of genius, like those in the old fable of Michael Angelo.   Like Martellus, I smashed them when I saw that there was no life in them: that they were so dead that they would not even dissolve as a dead body does.

THE HE-ANCIENT.   And I, like Acis, ceased to walk over the mountains with my friends, and walked alone; for I found that I had creative power over myself but none over my friends.   And then I ceased to walk on the mountains; for I saw that the mountains were dead.

ACIS [*protesting vehemently*] No.   I grant you about the friends perhaps; but the mountains are still the mountains, each with its name, its individuality, its up-standing strength and majesty, its beauty—

ECRASIA.   What! Acis among the rhapsodists!

THE HE-ANCIENT.   Mere metaphor, my poor boy: the mountains are corpses.

ALL THE YOUNG [*repelled*] Oh!

THE HE-ANCIENT.   Yes.   In the hardpressed heart of

the earth, where the inconceivable heat of the sun still
glows, the stone lives in fierce atomic convulsion, as we
live in our slower way. When it is cast out to the sur-
face it dies like a deep-sea fish: what you see is only its
cold dead body. We have tapped that central heat as
prehistoric man tapped water springs; but nothing has
come up alive from those flaming depths: your land-
scapes, your mountains, are only the world's cast skins
and decaying teeth on which we live like microbes.

ECRASIA. Ancient: you blaspheme against Nature
and against Man.

THE SHE-ANCIENT. Child, child, how much enthusi-
asm will you have for man when you have endured eight
centuries of him, as I have, and seen him perish by an
empty mischance that is yet a certainty? When I discarded my dolls as he discarded his friends and his mountains, it was to myself I turned as to the final reality.
Here, and here alone, I could shape and create. When
my arm was weak and I willed it to be strong, I could
create a roll of muscle on it; and when I understood
that, I understood that I could without any greater miracle give myself ten arms and three heads.

THE HE-ANCIENT. I also came to understand such
miracles. For fifty years I sat contemplating this
power in myself and concentrating my will.

THE SHE-ANCIENT. So did I; and for five more years
I made myself into all sorts of fantastic monsters. I
walked upon a dozen legs: I worked with twenty hands
and a hundred fingers: I looked to the four quarters
of the compass with eight eyes out of four heads.
Children fled in amazement from me until I had to hide
myself from them; and the ancients, who had forgotten
how to laugh, smiled grimly when they passed.

THE HE-ANCIENT. We have all committed these follies. You will all commit them.

THE NEWLY BORN.   Oh, do grow a lot of arms and legs and heads for us.   It would be so funny.

THE HE-ANCIENT.   My child: I am just as well as I am.   I would not lift my finger now to have a thousand heads.

THE SHE-ANCIENT.   But what would I not give to have no head at all?

ALL THE YOUNG.   Whats that?   No head at all? Why?   How?

THE HE-ANCIENT.   Can you not understand?

ALL THE YOUNG [*shaking their heads*] No.

THE SHE-ANCIENT.   One day, when I was tired of learning to walk forward with some of my feet and backwards with others and sideways with the rest all at once, I sat on a rock with my four chins resting on four of my palms, and four of my elbows resting on four of my knees.   And suddenly it came into my mind that this monstrous machinery of heads and limbs was no more me than my statues had been me, and that it was only an automaton that I had enslaved.

MARTELLUS.   Enslaved?   What does that mean?

THE SHE-ANCIENT.   A thing that must do what you command it is a slave; and its commander is its master. These are words you will learn when your turn comes.

THE HE-ANCIENT.   You will also learn that when the master has come to do everything through the slave, the slave becomes his master, since he cannot live without him.

THE SHE-ANCIENT.   And so I perceived that I had made myself the slave of a slave.

THE HE-ANCIENT.   When we discovered that, we shed our superfluous heads and legs and arms until we had our old shapes again, and no longer startled the children.

THE SHE-ANCIENT.   But still I am the slave of this slave, my body.   How am I to be delivered from it?

THE HE-ANCIENT. That, children, is the trouble of the ancients. For whilst we are tied to this tyrannous body we are subject to its death, and our destiny is not achieved.

THE NEWLY BORN. What is your destiny?

THE HE-ANCIENT. To be immortal.

THE SHE-ANCIENT. The day will come when there will be no people, only thought.

THE HE-ANCIENT. And that will be life eternal.

ECRASIA. I trust I shall meet my fatal accident before that day dawns.

ARJILLAX. For once, Ecrasia, I agree with you. A world in which there were nothing plastic would be an utterly miserable one.

ECRASIA. No limbs, no contours, no exquisite lines and elegant shapes, no worship of beautiful bodies, no poetic embraces in which cultivated lovers pretend that their caressing hands are wandering over celestial hills and enchanted valleys, no—

ACIS [interrupting her disgustedly] What an inhuman mind you have, Ecrasia!

ECRASIA. Inhuman!

ACIS. Yes: inhuman. Why dont you fall in love with someone?

ECRASIA. I! I have been in love all my life. I burned with it even in the egg.

ACIS. Not a bit of it. You and Arjillax are just as hard as two stones.

ECRASIA. You did not always think so, Acis.

ACIS. Oh, I know. I offered you my love once, and asked for yours.

ECRASIA. And did I deny it to you, Acis?

ACIS. You didnt even know what love was.

ECRASIA. Oh! I adored you, you stupid oaf, until I found that you were a mere animal.

ACIS.   And I made no end of a fool of myself about
you until I discovered that you were a mere artist.   You
appreciated my contours!   I was plastic, as Arjillax
says.   I wasnt a man to you: I was a masterpiece ap-
pealing to your tastes and your senses.   Your tastes and
senses had overlaid the direct impulse of life in you.
And because I cared only for one life, and went straight
to it, and was bored by your calling my limbs fancy
names and mapping me into mountains and valleys and
all the rest of it, you called me an animal.   Well, I am
an animal, if you call a live man an animal.

ECRASIA.   You need not explain.   You refused to be
refined.   I did my best to lift your prehistoric impulses
on to the plain of beauty, of imagination, of romance,
of poetry, of art, of—

ACIS.   These things are all very well in their way and
in their proper places.   But they are not love.   They
are an unnatural adulteration of love.   Love is a simple
thing and a deep thing: it is an act of life and not an
illusion.   Art is an illusion.

ARJILLAX.   That is false.   The statue comes to life
always.   The statues of today are the men and women
of the next incubation.   I hold up the marble figure before the mother and say, "This is the model you must
copy."   We produce what we see.   Let no man dare to
create in art a thing that he would not have exist in life.

MARTELLUS.   Yes: I have been through all that.
But you yourself are making statues of ancients instead
of beautiful nymphs and swains.   And Ecrasia is right
about the ancients being inartistic.   They are damna-
bly inartistic.

ECRASIA [*triumphant*] Ah!   Our greatest artist vin-
dicates me.   Thanks, Martellus.

MARTELLUS.   The body always ends by being a bore.
Nothing remains beautiful and interesting except

thought, because the thought is the life.   Which is just what this old gentleman and this old lady seem to think too.

THE SHE-ANCIENT.   Quite so.

THE HE-ANCIENT.   Precisely.

THE NEWLY BORN [*to the He-Ancient*] But you cant be nothing.   What do you want to be?

THE HE-ANCIENT.   A vortex.

THE NEWLY BORN.   A what?

THE SHE-ANCIENT.   A vortex.   I began as a vortex: why should I not end as one?

ECRASIA.   Oh! That is what you old people are.   Vorticists.

ACIS.   But if life is thought, can you live without a head?

THE HE-ANCIENT.   Not now perhaps.   But prehistoric men thought they could not live without tails.   I can live without a tail.   Why should I not live without a head?

THE NEWLY BORN.   What is a tail?

THE HE-ANCIENT.   A habit of which your ancestors managed to cure themselves.

THE SHE-ANCIENT.   None of us now believe that all this machinery of flesh and blood is necessary It dies.

THE HE-ANCIENT.   It imprisons us on this petty planet and forbids us to range through the stars.

ACIS.   But even a vortex is a vortex in something. You cant have a whirlpool without water; and you cant have a vortex without gas, or molecules or atoms or ions or electrons or something, not nothing.

THE HE-ANCIENT.   No: the vortex is not the water nor the gas nor the atoms: it is a power over these things.

THE SHE-ANCIENT.   The body was the slave of the vortex; but the slave has become the master; and we

must free ourselves from that tyranny.   It is this stuff
[*indicating her body*], this flesh and blood and bone and
all the rest of it, that is intolerable.   Even prehistoric
man dreamed of what he called an astral body, and asked
who would deliver him from the body of this death.

ACIS [*evidently out of his depth*] I shouldnt think too
much about it if I were you.   You have to keep sane,
you know.

The two Ancients look at one another; shrug their
shoulders; and address themselves to their departure.

THE HE-ANCIENT.   We are staying too long with you,
children.   We must go.

All the young people rise rather eagerly.

ARJILLAX.   Dont mention it.

THE SHE-ANCIENT.   It is tiresome for us, too.   You
see, children, we have to put things very crudely to you
to make ourselves intelligible.

THE HE-ANCIENT.   And I am afraid we do not quite
succeed.

STREPHON.   Very kind of you to come at all and talk
to us, I'm sure.

ECRASIA.   Why do the other ancients never come and
give us a turn?

THE HE-ANCIENT.   It is so difficult for them.   They
have forgotten how to speak; how to read; even how to
think in your fashion.   We do not communicate with
one another in that way or apprehend the world as you
do.

THE HE-ANCIENT.   I find it more and more difficult to
keep up your language.   Another century or two and
it will be impossible.   I shall have to be relieved by a
younger shepherd.

ACIS.   Of course we are always delighted to see you;
but still, if it tries you very severely, we could manage
pretty well by ourselves, you know.

THE SHE-ANCIENT.   Tell me, Acis: do you ever think of yourself as having to live perhaps for thousands of years?

ACIS.   Oh, dont talk about it.   Why, I know very well that I have only four years of what any reasonable person would call living; and three and a half of them are already gone.

ECRASIA.   You must not mind our saying so; but really you cannot call being an ancient living.

THE NEWLY BORN [*almost in tears*] Oh, this dreadful shortness of our lives!   I cannot bear it.

STREPHON.   I made up my mind on that subject long ago.   When I am three years and fifty weeks old, I shall have my fatal accident.   And it will not be an accident.

THE HE--ANCIENT.   We are very tired of this subject. I must leave you.

THE NEWLY BORN.   What is being tired?

THE SHE-ANCIENT.   The penalty of attending to children.   Farewell.

The two Ancients go away severally, she into the grove, he up to the hills behind the temple.

ALL.   Ouf!   [*A great sigh of relief*].

ECRASIA.   Dreadful people!

STREPHON.   Bores!

MARTELLUS.   Yet one would like to follow them; to enter into their life; to grasp their thought; to comprehend the universe as they must.

ARJILLAX.   Getting old, Martellus?

MARTELLUS.   Well, I have finished with the dolls; and I am no longer jealous of you.   That looks like the end. Two hours sleep is enough for me.   I am afraid I am beginning to find you all rather silly.

STREPHON.   I know.   My girl went off this morning. She hadnt slept for weeks.   And she found mathematics more interesting than me.

MARTELLUS.   There is a prehistoric saying that has
come down to us from a famous woman teacher. She
said: "Leave women; and study mathematics." It is
the only remaining fragment of a lost scripture called
The Confessions of St. Augustin, the English Opium
Eater. That primitive savage must have been a great
woman, to say a thing that still lives after three hundred
centuries. I too will leave women and study mathematics, which I have neglected too long. Farewell,
children, my old playmates. I almost wish I could feel
sentimental about parting from you; but the cold truth
is that you bore me. Do not be angry with me: your
turn will come. [*He passes away gravely into the
grove.*]

ARJILLAX.   There goes a great spirit. What a
sculptor he was! And now, nothing! It is as if he
had cut off his hands.

THE NEWLY BORN.   Oh, will you all leave me as he has
left you?

ECRASIA.   Never. We have sworn it.

STREPHON.   What is the use of swearing? She swore.
He swore. You have sworn. They have sworn.

ECRASIA.   You speak like a grammar.

STREPHON.   That is how one ought to speak, isnt it?
We shall all be forsworn.

THE NEWLY BORN.   Do not talk like that. You are
saddening us; and you are chasing the light away. It
is growing dark.

ACIS.   Night is falling. The light will come back
to-morrow.

THE NEWLY BORN.   What is tomorrow?

ACIS.   The day that never comes. [*He turns towards
the temple.*]

All begin trooping into the temple.

THE NEWLY BORN [*holding Acis back*] That is no answer. What——

ARJILLAX. Silence. Little children should be seen and not heard.

THE NEWLY BORN [*putting out her tongue at him*]!

ECRASIA. Ungraceful. You must not do that.

THE NEWLY BORN. I will do what I like. But there is something the matter with me. I want to lie down. I cannot keep my eyes open.

ECRASIA. You are fallng asleep. You will wake up again.

THE NEWLY BORN [*drowsily*] What is sleep?

ACIS. Ask no questions; and you will be told no lies. [*He takes her by the ear, and leads her firmly towards the temple*].

THE NEWLY BORN. Ai! oi! ai! Dont. I want to be carried [*She reels into the arms of Acis, who carries her into the temple*].

ECRASIA. Come, Arjillax: you at least are still an artist. I adore you.

ARJILLAX. Do you? Unfortunately for you, I am not still a child. I have grown out of cuddling. I can only appreciate your figure. Does that satisfy you?

ECRASIA. At what distance?

ARJILLAX. Arm's length or more.

ECRASIA. Thank you: not for me. [*She turns away from him*].

ARJILLAX. Ha! ha! [*He strides off into the temple*].

ECRASIA [*calling to Strephon, who is on the threshold of the temple, going in*] Strephon.

STREPHON. No. My heart is broken. [*He goes into the temple*].

ECRASIA. Must I pass the night alone? [*She looks round, seeking another partner; but they have all gone*].

After all, I can imagine a lover nobler than any of you. [*She goes into the temple*].

It is now quite dark.   A vague radiance appears near the temple and shapes itself into the ghost of Adam.

A WOMAN'S VOICE [*in the grove*] Who is that?

ADAM.   The ghost of Adam, the first father of mankind.   Who are you?

THE VOICE.   The ghost of Eve, the first mother of mankind.

ADAM.   Come forth, wife; and shew yourself to me

EVE [*appearing near the grove*] Here I am, husband. You are very old.

A VOICE [*in the hills*] Ha! ha! ha!

ADAM.   Who laughs?   Who dares laugh at Adam?

EVE.   Who has the heart to laugh at Eve?

THE VOICE.   The ghost of Cain, the first child, and the first murderer.   [*He appears between them; and as he does so there is a prolonged hiss*].   Who dares hiss at Cain, the lord of death?

A VOICE.   The ghost of the serpent, that lived before Adam and before Eve, and taught them how to bring forth Cain.   [*She becomes visible, coiled in the tree*].

A VOICE.   There is one that came before the serpent.

THE SERPENT.   That is the voice of Lilith, in whom the father and mother were one.   Hail, Lilith!

Lilith becomes visible between Cain and Adam.

LILITH.   I suffered unspeakably; I tore myself asunder; I lost my life, to make of my one flesh these twain, man and woman.   And this is what has come of it. What do you make of it, Adam, my son?

ADAM.   I made the earth bring forth by my labor, and the woman bring forth by my love.   And this is what has come of it.   What do you make of it, Eve, my wife?

EVE.   I nourished the egg in my body and fed it with

my blood. And now they let it fall as the birds did, and
suffer not at all. What do you make of it, Cain, my
first-born?

CAIN. I invented killing and conquest and mastery
and the winnowing out of the weak by the strong. And
now the strong have slain one another; and the weak live
for ever; and their deeds do nothing for the doer more
than for another. What do you make of it, snake?

THE SERPENT. I am justified. For I chose wisdom
and the knowledge of good and evil; and now there is no
evil; and wisdom and good are one. It is enough. [*She
vanishes*].

CAIN. There is no place for me on earth any longer.
You cannot deny that mine was a splendid game while it
lasted. But now! Out, out, brief candle! [*He vanishes*].

EVE. The clever ones were always my favorites. The
diggers and the fighters have dug themselves in with the
worms. My clever ones have inherited the earth. All's
well. [*She fades away*].

ADAM. I can make nothing of it, neither head nor
tail. What is it all for? Why? Whither? Whence?
We were well enough in the garden. And now the fools
have killed all the animals; and they are dissatisfied
because they cannot be bothered with their bodies! Fool-
ishness, I call it. [*He disappears*].

LILITH. They have accepted the burden of eternal
life. They have taken the agony from birth; and their
life does not fail them even in the hour of their destruction. Their breasts are without milk: their bowels are
gone: the very shapes of them are only ornaments for
their children to admire and caress without understanding. Is this enough; or shall I labor again? Shall I
bring forth something that will sweep them away and
make an end of them as they have swept away the beasts

of the garden and make an end of the crawling things
and the flying things and of all them that refuse to live
for ever? I had patience with them for many ages: they
tried me very sorely. They did terrible things: they
embraced death, and said that eternal life was a fable.
I stood amazed at the malice and destructiveness of the
things I had made: Mars blushed as he looked down on
the shame of his sister planet: cruelty and hypocrisy became so hideous that the face of the earth was pitted
with the graves of little children among which living
skeletons crawled in search of horrible food. The pangs
of another birth were already upon me when one man
repented and lived three hundred years; and I waited to
see what would come of that. And so much came of it
that the horrors of that time seem now but an evil dream.
They have redeemed themselves from their vileness, and
turned away from their sins. Best of all, they are still
not satisfied: the impulse I gave them in that day when
I sundered myself in twain and launched Man and
Woman on the earth still urges them: after passing a
million goals they press on to the goal of redemption
from the flesh, to the vortex freed from matter, to the
whirlpool in pure intelligence that, when the world
began, was a whirlpool in pure force. And though all
that they have done seems but the first hour of the infinite
work of creation, yet I will not supersede them until
they have forded this last stream that lies between flesh
and spirit, and disentangled their life from the matter
that has always mocked it. I can wait: waiting and
patience mean nothing to the eternal. I gave the
woman the greatest of gifts: curiosity. By that her
seed has been saved from my wrath; for I also am curious; and I have waited always to see what they will do
tomorrow. Let them feed that appetite well for me. I
say, let them dread, of all things, stagnation; for from

the moment I, Lilith, lose hope and faith in them, they are doomed. In that hope and faith I have let them live for a moment: and in that moment I have spared them many times. But mightier creatures than they have killed hope and faith, and perished from the earth; and I may not spare them for ever. I am Lilith: I brought life into the whirlpool of force, and compelled my enemy, Matter, to obey a living soul. But in enslaving Life's enemy I made Life's master; for that is the end of all slavery; and now I shall see the slave set free and the enemy reconciled, the whirlpool become all life and no matter. And because these infants that call themselves ancients are reaching out towards that, I will have patience with them still; though I know well that when they attain it they shall become one with me and supersede me, and Lilith will be only a legend and a lay that has lost its meaning. Of Life only is there no end; and though of its million starry mansions many are empty and many still unbuilt, and though its vast domain is as yet unbearably desert, my seed shall one day fill it and master its matter to its uttermost confines. And for what may be beyond, the eyesight of Lilith is too short. It is enough that there is a beyond. [*She vanishes*].